Baseball Books

ALSO BY MIKE SHANNON
AND FROM MCFARLAND

---

*Coming Back to Baseball: The Cincinnati Astros
and the Joys of Over-30 Play* (2005)

*Everything Happens in Chillicothe:
A Summer in the Frontier League
with Max McLeary, the One-Eyed Umpire* (2004)

*The Day Satchel Paige and the Pittsburgh
Crawfords Came to Hertford, N.C.:
Baseball Stories and Poems* (1992)

*Diamond Classics: Essays on 100 of the Best Baseball
Books Ever Published* (1989, paperback 2005)

Baseball Books
A Collector's Guide

MIKE SHANNON

McFarland & Company, Inc., Publishers
Jefferson, North Carolina, and London

[Library of Congress Online Catalog]
Shannon, Mike.
    Baseball books : A collector's guide / Mike Shannon.
    p.   cm.
    Includes bibliographical references and index.

    ISBN-13: 978-0-7864-3139-7
    (softcover : 50# alkaline paper)

    1. Baseball — Collectibles — Handbooks, manuals, etc.
    2. Baseball — Collectors and collecting — Handbooks, manuals, etc.
    3. Book collecting — Handbooks, manuals, etc.
    GV875.2.S53   2008
    796.357 — dc22   2007030443

British Library cataloguing data are available

©2008 Mike Shannon. All rights reserved

No part of this book may be reproduced or transmitted in any form or by any means, electronic or mechanical, including photocopying or recording, or by any information storage and retrieval system, without permission in writing from the publisher.

Cover image: ©2007 Shutterstock

Manufactured in the United States of America

McFarland & Company, Inc., Publishers
  Box 611, Jefferson, North Carolina 28640
  www.mcfarlandpub.com

For Bobby Plapinger — friend,
Mets fan, honorable businessman,
smart ass ... a giant in his field

ACKNOWLEDGMENTS

My heartfelt thanks to all of the following, who made some contribution to this book, in one way or another: John Allen, Paul Bauer, Steve Cummings, Tom Eckel, Wayne Greene, Bill McGill, Dick Miller, Willis Monie, Becky & Brian Nielsen, and Mike Wickham. Special thanks must go to Mark Schraf, whose knowledge of baseball books is surpassed only by his generosity, unflagging amiability, and capacity for friendship.

As always, my deepest gratitude goes to my family, an All-Star lineup if there ever was one: John Hubert, Willie Mae, Sis, Susie, John, Tim, Meg, Casey, Mick, the Babe, Nolan Ryan, and, most of all, Derms.

Ad Majorem Dei Gloriam

TABLE OF CONTENTS

Acknowledgments	vi
Preface	1
1. A Short History of Baseball Books	5
2. Which Baseball Books to Collect	44
3. Where to Find Baseball Books	68
4. How to Care for Your Collection of Baseball Books	85
5. How Much to Pay for Baseball Books	93
Price Guide	103
Glossary	179
Appendix A: Baseball Book Awards	201
Appendix B: Interview with Willis Monie	205
Bibliography	211
Index	213

PREFACE

One of my many friends who are baseball book collectors once told me that his wife didn't get the collecting part. "Once you've read the books, why do you need to keep them all around?" she asked him. My friend and I nodded at each other and chuckled at his wife's lack of understanding of the mentality of the baseball book collector. I don't know if my friend actually gave his wife a cogent, detailed answer to her query, or if he simply ignored it and changed the subject. My guess is that he took the latter course, intuiting that if the matter needed to be explained, then it probably wouldn't be understood.

Implicit in the wife's question is both an acknowledgement of the utilitarian nature of books — the idea that books are useful for the knowledge they impart and for the information they contain — and an assumption that once the book has been mined for its contents it is in essence emptied and no longer needed. This assumption is false, of course, as good books bear multiple readings, out of a desire to repeat a wonderful reading experience but also because of the inevitability of human forgetfulness over time. But it also misses a perhaps even more important point: that books are more, far more, than their intellectual content. At least to book lovers they are. To bibliophiles the book is a work of art, a miracle of human ingenuity, and a tangible expression of the highest strivings of the human spirit. It is also impossible to divorce the physical book from the pleasure of reading. A book is more than a device of transmission, although the purveyors of sterile non-book formats do not seem to realize this. To state the obvious but unappreciated (at least by some), a book is an object that has a feel all its own. It is a pleasure to hold and to page through, our progress marked by every turn of the page and the end of the journey clearly in sight from the beginning. Books also have personalities, as they come in multifarious shapes and sizes, are constructed of different materials, and come packaged in a deliciously dizzying array of dust jackets and covers, every one unique in its combination of title, type faces, photographs, colors, and message. Books, in other words, have an aesthetic, as well as a utilitarian, value, and it is an appreciation for that aesthetic value which makes book collectors of readers.

Actually, baseball book collecting is not the only collecting activity which puzzles some people. Collecting anything at all seems pointless to some, since as we all know we can't take anything with us when we depart this world. But such a dismissal ignores the existence of the basic gathering/hoarding human instinct, and it also misses the point, which is to enjoy our stay while we are here. The starting point for baseball book collectors is the game itself, which we grow up loving more than sleep, lunch, and our families. As kids we find that reading about the game increases our love of it, and as adults we are relieved to find that reading becomes a substitute for playing it. Indeed, most of us read (and write) baseball better than we ever played it. The collecting habit for most baseball fans begins with baseball cards. It is only natural, once we grow up, to transfer that drive to baseball books, the true baseball cards of adults. The only drawback is that we now need bookcases, not shoe boxes, to house our collections. On the other hand, bookcases full of shelf-worthy volumes are a feast for the eyes, a variety-charged antidote to the mundane, and how empty looks a house without them, regardless of how stuffed it is with other furniture and the trappings of life. Once we are hooked on baseball books and we begin to grasp the enormity of the baseball book universe, we are appalled and excited and stimulated to begin the chase for the treasures we have heard about and the search for finds we haven't even had rumors of.

There is also the monetary aspect of baseball book collecting. Any good collection begins to accumulate real financial value, although to realize the gains the collection must be liquidated. Thus, we collectors believe this task is best left to our descendents or, in lieu of them, to a good and knowledgeable friend for the benefit of our baseball-book-value-ignorant descendents. The monetary value comes in third behind the other two values of a baseball book collection, but it is not unimportant, and if a baseball book collector is ever backed into a corner defending his obsession, he can always pull out this trump card.

The humble little book in your hands had its genesis in a desire to provide baseball book collectors with the same sort of handy pricing information that has been supplied in many different forums for many years now to baseball card collectors. Information on baseball book prices has always been sketchy and diffuse and reliably found only in the catalogs of a few used baseball book dealers. I thought it was high time to begin giving baseball books the same respect for their financial values as others give baseball cards. I also realized that there is more to baseball book collecting than the collector figuring out how much he should pay for any particular volume, and so the book addresses several other important matters. Presumably beginners in the field will benefit the most from this book, but I am hopeful that more advanced collectors will also glean ideas and reminders which will further the enjoyment and profitability he derives from his engagement in our mutual passion for books about the greatest game in the world.

My father never received a college education, but he has as fine an understanding of life as anyone I have ever met. It was he who told me that every stage in a man's life has its compensations. As I've gotten older, I've come to know the truth of this statement. As the physical energy and restlessness of youth begin to ebb, there is more time and patience for contemplation and reading. Nothing can replace the sandlot friends of our adolescence or the teammates we loved on countless Little League, American Legion, high school, and college baseball teams. And there is no substitute for the company of the friends we enjoy today. But a wonderful solace are all the prized baseball books on our shelves, and our ability to turn solitude into a blessing, the ultimate result of all our youthful baseball endeavors.

And what of my friend's wife today? Well, she apparently came to understand more about her husband and his benign obsession. Not only are they still married, but with her approval my friend has informed me that they are adding a baseball library room, complete with sliding ladders, to the back of their house. Ladies and gentlemen, raise your glasses, and join me in a toast to great baseball books and to the wonderful people who love them enough to collect them!

1

A Short History of Baseball Books

> *"Baseball is the writer's game. From the Elysian Fields of Hoboken to the green fields of the mind, the grand old game and the printed word were made for each other."*—John Thorn in The Armchair Book of Baseball

The origins of the baseball book are as difficult to pin down as those of the game itself, yet it should surprise no one that the advent of books about the game followed closely upon the heels of the "invention" and dissemination of baseball. Complicating the matter of determining when the first baseball book was published is the problem of defining exactly what constitutes a *book* about baseball. Judging by what is routinely included in their sales and auctions most dealers of early baseball printed material are not troubled by the problem, and they freely classify as books many 19th century (and some 18th century) publications which the average collector today would not recognize as such were the items in question of contemporary issuance. The key factor seems to be the rarity of any particular publication; and as long as they are sufficiently rare, and presumably capable of fetching a high price, many pamphlets, booklets, chapbooks, and even parts of books not completely devoted to the subject of baseball are treated as "baseball books" by the typical dealer. Of course, every collector is free to devise his own definition, to include whatever items he wishes to in his baseball book collection, and to ignore his definition whenever it pleases him; and I suspect that most collectors do in fact operate in just such a manner. Nevertheless, given the fact that the baseball book publishing industry as it exists today did not spontaneously appear but developed only after a long and gradual evolution, it does make sense to include even in a brief history such as this those publications which are generally recognized as important first steps along the baseball book evolutionary path.

Most collectors and dealers too are guided in this regard by the Bible of baseball books, Anton Grobani's *Guide to Baseball Literature* (1975), which is so well known by those immersed in our subject that it is referred to simply as "*Grobani*," a sort of eponymous substitution whereby the author's name stands in for the name of his book, as in "This biography of *Hot Foot Harry* is not in *Grobani*." And, although it may not be apparent at first glance, Grobani took a wide view of the subject (notice that he used the word "literature" not "books" in his title). He included not only books, "booklets," and books which are only partly devoted to baseball, but other non-book forms of literature, such as magazines, periodicals, reports, dissertations, scorebooks, schedules, yearbooks, newspapers, and at least one coloring book! Our problem becomes much less of a dilemma then if we follow the lead of Mr. Grobani and take a more rather than less inclusive approach.

We would do well to also be guided by the work of David Block, the author of the most carefully researched and documented history of the origins of baseball yet to be published, *Baseball Before We Knew It: A Search for the Roots of the Game* (2005). As many readers undoubtedly know, with *Baseball: A Comprehensive Bibliography* (1986) (two supplements were published in 1993 and 1998, and a second edition was published in 2006) and *Baseball by the Books: A History and Complete Bibliography of Baseball Fiction* (1990), Myron Smith, Jr. and Andy McCue both made outstanding bibliographic contributions which supplement Grobani's *Guide to Baseball Literature*, primarily by updating it. Perhaps not as well known yet is the fact that Block's bibliography of early printed sources that make reference to baseball and baseball-related games supplements *Grobani* by *predating* it! Block's bibliography, which begins in 1450 and extends to the start of the Civil War (1862), has a total of 179 entries. Many of the publications in the Block bibliography are children's chapbook primers of a few pages length. They are invariably extremely rare, and some are even unique. They discuss precursors of baseball, such as "stool ball," "trap ball," and "goal ball" ... often briefly at that ... and so they are not of much interest to the average collector of baseball books; who would have trouble affording such publications anyway. (For example, a possibly unique second edition copy of a little chapbook called *Children's Amusements* which was published in 1822 sold in a 2005 auction of baseball memorabilia for $13,000.) On the other hand, it is precisely the precious rarity and historical importance of such publications which interest advanced collectors and make Block's bibliography another indispensable tool for those desirous of building baseball book collections beyond the ordinary.

Allowing, as both Grobani and Block do, for the inclusion of booklets and chapbooks, the history of the baseball book then may be said to begin in London, England, in 1744 with the publication of *A Little Pretty Pocket-Book, Intended for the Instruction and Amusement of Little Master Tommy and Pretty Miss Polly*. Written and published by John Newberry, it is not only the first children's book intended primarily for entertainment, but also the first publication to use the word "Base-Ball." The heart of this 95-page book are the 32 poems (presented one to a page) describing youthful games and activities of the times; each illustrated by a crude woodcut and concluded by a rhymed moral. The poem and moral on the page entitled "Base Ball" read:

> The Ball once struck off,
> Away flies the Boy
> To the next destined Post,
> And then Home with Joy.
> Thus Seamen, for Lucre
> Fly over the Main,
> But, with Pleasure transported
> Return back again.

The woodcut accompanying the poem shows a trio of lads in tri-cornered hats playing the game. While none of the three are holding a bat, one holds a ball he is ready to throw, and there are three bases marked by posts.

A Little Pretty Pocket-Book is so rare that the only surviving examples of the English version are single copies of the 10th (1760), 11th (1763), and 12th (1767) editions. No copies of two pirated American versions (1762 and 1786) exist, and only a few copies of the first major American edition published in 1787 exist in libraries and private collections. Oddly enough,

Grobani did not include this seminal little work in his bibliography even though it had been recognized by numerous writers (such as Douglas Wallop in *Baseball: An Informal History*) whose works are themselves included in *Guide to Baseball Literature*.

A number of other fascinating, pre-Civil War publications omitted by Grobani but included by Block had a role in the development of the baseball book and are sought after by advanced collectors. They include:

- The aforementioned *Children's Amusements*, a 30-page chapbook originally published in 1820 which is important for its landmark woodcut illustration of one child pitching a ball to another one batting, called "Playing Ball":

- *The Boy's Own Book*, an English publication (1828) which contains (according to Block) "the first printed description in English of a bat-and-ball base-running game played on a diamond." As such, it was essential in helping Robert Henderson (author of *Ball, Bat and Bishop*) debunk the myth that Abner Doubleday had invented baseball in 1839:

- *Good Examples for Boys*, another 30-page chapbook that offers as one of its little morality tales the story (with woodcut illustration) of the boy who is commended by his father for freely confessing to breaking a mirror by batting a ball inside the house!

- *The Book of Sports*, a volume of 164 pages which Block calls "one of the crown jewels of early baseball books." Written by Robin Carver and published in Boston in 1834, it includes the first authentically American illustration of baseball (a woodcut of boys playing the game on the Boston Common), as well as the first association of the term "base" or "goal" with a diamond-shaped playing field:

- *The Boy's Book of Sport: A Description of the Exercises and Pastimes of Youth*, an 1835 24-page booklet which lists "base ball" first among "the most common" boys' games in America and introduces the terms "innings" and "diamond"; and

- *Owed 2 Base Ball in Three Cant-Oh's!*, a humorous narrative poem of 16 pages involving the starting nine of the Mercantile

Base Ball Club of Philadelphia and published in 1860, thus making it the first baseball poem issued as a discrete publication.

Two other 19th century juvenile books of note: *The American Boys Book* (1864) which was the first American book to include a color baseball plate, and *Sports and Pastimes of American Boys* (1884), edited by Henry Chadwick and treasured for its colorful multi-part chromolithographic cover, highlighted by a baseball scene at the center.

The earliest item included in *Guide to Baseball Literature* is the first entry in the "Early Club Constitutions" section: *Constitution of Olympic Ball Club of Philadelphia*, which was published in 1838, the year after the Olympic Club's Constitution was codified and five years after the Club was formed. Grobani did not consider the booklet to be a baseball publication since, according to him and others, the Olympic Club played not baseball but a forerunner of the game known as "town ball." Grobani accords the honor of being "the first baseball publication" to a different constitution, the *By-Laws and Rules of the Eagle Club*, a booklet published in 1852 by a New York team which was formed in 1840. Even if we were not to count any of the publications discussed above (such as *A Little Pretty Pocket-Book* or Robin Carver's *The Book of Sports*), the honor would be misplaced because the club constitution of a much more famous team, the New York Knickerbockers, preceded that of the Eagle Club. While Grobani recognized the importance of the Knickerbockers, pointing out that the Club adopted the first set of baseball rules on September 23, 1845; he overlooked the 1848 W. H. B. Smith Book and Fancy Job Printer first edition of the Knickerbocker *By-Laws and Rules* that Block cites and mistakenly presents the Wilbur & Hastings revised editions of 1858–60 as the original Knickerbocker *By-Laws and Rules*. A number of other amateur "clubs" published Constitutions and By-Laws during the 1850s and early '60s, but by far the most collectible ones are those published by the Knickerbockers.

By the late 1850s baseball was surging in popularity, and to satisfy the public's interest in the game Boston publisher Mayhew & Baker added baseball information to their booklet on cricket and released the new volume as *A Manual of Cricket and Base Ball* in 1858. Identified by Grobani as "the first baseball publication issued for public sale," the 25-page book devotes five pages to club rules, instructions on how to play the Massachusetts game, and a diagram of a baseball field. An ex-library copy in VG condition of this extremely significant and rare book sold at auction for $1,900 in 2005. Mayhew & Baker must have been satisfied with the sales of *A Manual of Cricket and Base Ball* because they published an expanded, all-baseball follow-up of the book the next two years under the title *Base Ball Players' Pocket Companion*. Because it features a wonderfully quaint portrayal of a fielder gold-stamped into the limp leather cover and because the text contains the rules for both the Massachusetts and the New York game — the latter of which soon became ascendent — *Base Ball Players' Pocket Companion* is treasured by collectors. Fewer than ten copies of the 1859 edition of the book exist; fewer than five of the 1860 edition. A third edition of the book (with a slightly different cover) was published in 1861 by a different Boston printer (Mudge & Son), and what may be the only copy of it known to exist was sold in 1993 at the Baltimore Book Company Auction for $4,600. Twelve years later the same copy was sold by Robert Edward Auctions for $8,500.

In 1866 the first general history of the game and one of the cornerstone volumes of baseball literature, *The Book of American Pastimes* by Charles A. Peverelly, was published. Although the book covers cricket, rowing, and yachting too, it devotes 180 of its 556 pages to the individual histories of the most prominent teams in the amateur National Association of Base Ball Players (formed in 1859), such as the Knickerbockers, Eckfords, Atlantics, Excelsiors, Gothams, and Mutuals and includes year-by-year statistics and scores of numerous important games. The groundbreaking nature of Peverelly's book is evident in the fact that the second general history of baseball was not published for another 22 years, until 1888 when Jacob Morse's *Sphere and Ash* appeared. A copy of the Peverelly book in Near-Fine condition sold in 2006 for $1,400.

Brooklynite Henry Chadwick, the "Father of Baseball," spent his entire adult life writing about baseball, bringing about innovations and needed rules changes, and trying to keep the game out of the clutches of gamblers. Chadwick covered baseball for more than 20 newspapers and magazines, originated and edited the first annual guide produced for public sale (*Beadle's Dime Baseball Player*, 1860–81), and authored far more baseball books during this period of infancy for the baseball book than anyone else. Any of Chadwick's books would make a distinguished addition to any baseball library, but his most sought-after title is *The Game of Baseball*, which just happens to be the first hardback book entirely devoted to baseball. Published in 1868, *The Game of Baseball* is a combination of rules, instructions on how to play the game, sketches of prominent players of the day, summaries of noteworthy contests, and history. As few as a dozen copies of the book are known to exist, and in 2005 a copy in VG-Fine condition sold for $7,000.

The first team history ever published appeared in 1874. Entitled *Record of the Boston Baseball Club, 1871–1874* (Rockwell and Churchill), the book was written by George Wright, the team's shortstop and the younger brother of Harry Wright. Both Wrights had been members of baseball's first professional team, the Cincinnati Red Stockings, but when the Cincinnati club reverted to amateur status after the 1870 season, the Wrights moved to Boston to help form that city's entry in the first professional league, the National Association of Professional Base Ball Players. Wright's book is about the Boston Red Stockings' first four seasons in the fledgling league and includes scores, averages, box scores, standings, and player sketches. As might be expected, the league had organizational, financial, and disciplinary problems, and it folded after the 1875 season; its demise brought on in part by the success of the Boston club which won the championship every year but the first. A saddle stitched, perhaps unique copy of this extremely rare book (with no cover) sold in 2006 for $1,500. Boston claims the honor of producing baseball literature's second team history as well: *A History of the Boston Baseball Club*, written by George V. Tuohey and published in 1897 by M. F. Quinn. The Tuohey book, which covers Boston's years in the National Association and the club's subsequent seasons in the National League through 1897, is not quite as rare as Wright's book, but it is a treasured baseball book nonetheless. In 1999 a copy of the Tuohey book sold in Sotheby's famous Barry Halper auction for $1,437. While some added value accrued to it because of its ex–Halper collection status, the rebound copy was missing its original board covers. Mike "King" Kelly's highly autobiographical collection of anecdotes and sketches of opposing players called *Play Ball* is a third book which certifies Boston's standing as a baseball power and literary inspiration of the period. Published in 1888, this highly sought-after little book was issued only as a paperback, and it is very difficult to find a copy of it with its fragile cover, featuring a drawing of the author's visage, intact.

At least nine other books, published before the turn of the century, bear mentioning. *Our Baseball Club and How It Won the Championship* by Noah Brooks, appeared in 1884 and is the first novel devoted exclusively to baseball. (An earlier novel by Brooks, *The Fairport Nine*, which was published in 1880, contains descriptions of a baseball game in its first and last chapters. In addition, William Everett authored a pair of adolescent novels with some baseball in them that pre-date *The Fairpost Nine*.) *Base Ball: How to Become a Player*, an instructional published in 1889, was written by one of the most important figures of 19th century baseball. Hall of Famer John Montgomery Ward was not only a star pitcher and shortstop for the New York Giants, but also an educated man whose degrees from Penn Sate and the Columbia School of Law elevated the image of the professional ballplayer and qualified Ward to lead the labor rebellion that resulted in the formation of the outlaw Players League in 1890. The brief history with which Ward opens his book was, according to the SABR Publications Director Mark Alvarez, "probably the best available at the time — a sensible and valuable look at the development of baseball flawed only by Ward's chauvinistic insistence that our game was a purely American sport, not descended from or related to English ball and bat games." *Baseball*, written by Newton Crane and published in 1891, and *Baseball* by Richard G. Knowles and Richard Morton (1896), both appeared in Britain. Containing rules, instructions, and history, both volumes review recent baseball play in England and tout the rising popularity of the game there. (A copy of Crane's book was offered on eBay in 2006, but the reasonable minimum bid of $900 was not met.) Published in 1896, *In Memoriam: Aaron Burt Champion* is a tribute to the president of the Cincinnati Red Stockings from 1867 through 1870, and the booklet could be considered the first baseball biography Described by Grobani as baseball's "first literary work," *The Krank: His Language and What It Means* is also the first baseball book of humor. Published in 1888 and written by wealthy eccentric Thomas Lawson, *The Krank* is a book about baseball fans, employing the term coined by Henry Chadwick. In poetry and prose the first half of the 64-page book tells the story of a typical krank's day at the ballpark in a derisive but good-natured manner, while the second half of the book is a glossary of terms related to this odd bird and his habits. *The Krank* is revered for its originality of subject and treatment and for its rarity (as few as three copies are known to exist), yet the most amazing thing of all about it is that its cover is made from the actual covers of baseballs! (Lawson also published a book on yachting which used ship sails as its covers.) Finally, outside of Henry Chadwick, the period's most important baseball book author was Harry C. Palmer, the syndicated columnist at *The Sporting Life* who went along on the baseball world tour of 1888–89 organized by Albert Goodwill Spalding. Palmer authored four books, three of which concern the world tour to some degree or other: *Baseball: The National Game of the Americans* (1888); *Athletic Sports in America, England and Australia*, the most popular of Palmer's book (1889); and *Sights Around the World with the Base Ball Boys* (1892). The fourth book, *Stories of the Base Ball Field*, was published in 1890 and featured small circular portraits of Cap Anson and Charles Comiskey on the cover. Grobani describes the book's contents as "a collection of dressing room yarns and humorous incidents in the lives of major league stars."

In recent years some baseball historians have taken the revisionist stance that Cap Anson was not that responsible for bringing about the implementation of the game's color line after all, yet this adjustment has hardly dampened collectors' enthusiasm for *A Ball Player's Career*. The book is the game's first autobiography, Anson was baseball's greatest hitter in the nineteenth century, and, as baseball book dealer Wayne Greene says, Anson "pulls no punches" in the book "referring to Clarence Duval (the singing and dancing mascot who went with the White Stockings on their 1888–89 world tour) as a 'chocolate-covered coon' and 'no-account nigger.'" To further recommend itself the book also has a wonderful green cover, embossed with a drawing of Captain Anson, and its plain, direct title is unimproveable.

With the publication of *A Ball Player's Career* in 1900, baseball literature made a promising beginning to the new century; and while the quantity of baseball books released during the century's first two decades remained low by today's standard, the quality of the books published was very high indeed. Between 1901 and 1919, the following early diamond classics all made their debuts: *Fun and Frolic with an Indian Ball Team* (1900) by Guy Green; the first publication of *Casey at the Bat* in book form (1901); *Baseball,*

1845–1871 (1902) by Seymour Church; *Ted Sullivan's Humorous Stories of the Ball Field* (1903) by Ted Sullivan; *The Garry: A Book of Humorous Cartoons: Pickings from the Diamond* (1904), about the flamboyant owner of the Cincinnati Reds, Garry Herrmann; *Sol White's Base Ball Guide* (1907), the first history of black/Negro League baseball; *Baseball in Cincinnati* (1907/08) by Harry Ellard; *A Brief History of Baseball* (1909) by Francis Richter, a booklet of records, statistics, and yearly summaries, later enlarged and reprinted in 1914 as *Richter's History and Records of Baseball, the American Nation's Chief Sport*; a pair of biographies about baseball player-turned preacher Billy Sunday (*The Spectacular Career of Rev. Billy Sunday, Famous Baseball Evangelist* by Theodore Frankenberg, 1913; and *The Real Billy Sunday* by Elijah Brown, 1914); a pair of 1914 books chronicling the exhibition world tour taken by the Chicago White Sox and New York Giants during the winter of 1913–14 (*World Tour, National and American League Baseball Teams* and *History of the World's Tour* by Ted Sullivan); the first great baseball novel, *You Know Me, Al* (1916) by the incomparable Ring Lardner; and the most ironically-timed baseball biography that could ever be published, G. W. Axelson's *Commy*, released in 1919, the year owner Charles Comiskey's White Sox became known forever more as the Black Sox.

The unquestionable literary highlight of this period was the three-year flowering of 1910–1912 which produced more than a dozen baseball book blooms. In 1910 the first attempt at a truly comprehensive baseball history, *The National Game* by Alfred H. Spink, was published. The book does a thorough enough job of describing the origins of the game, of summarizing the seasons from 1871 to 1910, and of recording all the championship games played from 1884 to 1910; but the lasting contribution of *The National Game* is to be found in its photos (nearly 200 of them) and in its biographical sketches of hundreds of players, owners, managers, umpires, and journalists of the era.

Spink's book was followed a year later by A. G. Spalding's *Baseball: America's National Game*, another general history and the most famous of all early baseball books. Himself a towering figure of baseball history, Spalding was the first pitcher to win 200 games, he served as president of the Chicago team in the original National League for ten years, and he organized the first around-the-globe baseball tour. Skeptics have accused Spalding of writing his book in order to promote the sporting goods busi-

1. A Short History of Baseball Books

ness which bore his name, but there is little reason not to give equal credence to: 1) the sincerity of his belief that baseball was an American invention, perfectly suited to the American character, and 2) his desire to fulfill the obligation laid on him by his old friend Henry Chadwick, who requested that Spalding author a history of the game and bequeathed to him his extensive baseball library to aid in the completion of the task. While the shortcomings of *Baseball: America's National Game* as history are undeniable, the book is still valuable for the insights it provides into the mind of one of the game's pioneers, and it is only the most jaded of readers who cannot enjoy the enthusiasm which Spalding evinced in passages such as the following:

> I claim that Base Ball owes its prestige as our National Game to the fact that as no other form of sport it is the exponent of American Courage, Confidence, Combativeness, American Dash, Discipline, Determination, American Energy, Eagerness, Enthusiasm, American Pluck, Persistence, Performance, American Spirit, Sagacity, Success, American Vim, Vigor, Vitality.
>
> Base Ball is the American Game *par excellence*, because its playing demands Brain and Brawn, and American manhood supplies these ingredients in quantity sufficient to spread over the entire continent.

The most profusely illustrated baseball book yet to be published, with a photo or illustration appearing on nearly every page, *The Book of Baseball* by William Patten and J. W. McSpadden also appeared in 1911. To accommodate the illustrations (including a photo of Shoeless Joe Jackson as a member of the 1910 New Orleans Pelicans), the publishers (the editors of *Colliers* magazine) employed an over-sized format, and at fifteen and a half inches, the book is probably the tallest baseball book ever published (with the possible exception of one or two bargain titles of recent vintage). The book's unusual size; the quaint picture cover of a batter waving a bat in front of a "standup" catcher that is based on a painting by Penfield; and the hodge-podge of a text which resembles in its disparate parts the make-up of a contemporary pre-season magazine all combine to make *The Book of Baseball* a unique publication of its era and an irresistible golden fleece of a baseball book to collectors.

The 1910–1912 star burst of baseball book excellence was rounded out by the appearance of: one instructional that turned on a baseball-as-war analogy (*The Battle of Baseball* by C. H. Claudy, 1912) and another more philosophical in nature (*Letters from a Baseball Fan to His Son* by S. Dewitt Clough, 1910), which is also quaintly bound with red ribbon; an anecdotal history of the minor leagues, *Humor Among the Minors* (1911) by Edward Ashhenback and Jack Ryder; a classic pair of recollections also full, as was the custom of the times, of playing advice, *Touching Second* (1910) by Johnny Evers and Hugh Fullerton and *Pitching in a Pinch* (1912) by Christy Mathewson; and five notable literary works: the first hard cover edition of *Casey at the Bat* (1912), a book of humor entitled *Around the World with the Baseball Bugs* (1910) by Jack Regan and Will E. Stahl, and three original volumes of baseball poetry; *Baseball Ballads* (1910) by Grantland Rice, *Right Off the Bat* (1911) by William Kirk, and *Baseballogy* (1912) by Edmund Vance Cooke. The rarity of such an explosion of brilliance, diversity, and originality in the early history of baseball books is evident in the fact that another such event would not occur until the 1960s.

Over the next two decades baseball fans were treated to a lot of good reading and provided with sufficient information in the form of numerous guides and annuals, team publications, the sports sections of the nation's numerous daily newspapers, and the two most important baseball periodicals of the 20th century, *Baseball Magazine* and *The Sporting News*. Unfortunately, the 1920s and 1930s were the doldrums for baseball books, with volumes of lasting significance being published on average perhaps once a year. The strength of the period is to be found in the autobiography/biography genre, represented by *My Thirty Years in Baseball* (1923) by John J. McGraw; *Playing the Game* (1925) by Bucky Harris; *Ty Cobb: Idol of Baseball Fandom* by Sverre O. Braathen; *Babe Ruth: Idol of American Boyhood* (1930) by Dan Daniel; the first autobiography by an umpire, Harry "Steamboat" Johnson's *Standing the Gaff* (1935); and *Baseball: The Fan's Game* (1939) by Mickey Cochrane. While hardly a novelty as numerous records books by various authors and publishers had been steadily released since the 1880s, *The Baseball Cyclopedia* (1922) by Ernest Lanigan was an important first attempt at a comprehensive records book, for which supplements were issued from 1923 through 1932. *Who's Who in Major League Baseball*, compiled by Harold "Speed" Johnson and containing a full page photo, sketch, and record of every player, first appeared in 1933 and became an immediate hit. Three more editions of the book (1935–37) were issued under Johnson's direction, and those from 1938 through 1955 under that of John Carmichael (all editions but the original, released only in hardback, were issued in both hardback and paperback). Another record book of note made its debut a year after Johnson's *Who's Who*, *Daguerreotypes of Great Stars of Baseball*, which became one of the most popular books ever published by *The Sporting News*. Containing biographical data and the complete minor and major league records of the players included, the book has gone through several editions, manifestations, and editors. Other than instructionals, such as Byrd Douglas' *Science of Baseball* (1922) and *The Billy Evans Course in Umpiring* (1926); a small collection of poems by various authors, edited by Edward Lyman and called *Baseball Fanthology* (1924); and oddities, such as Christy Walsh's informal history of baseball ghost-writing, *Adios to Ghosts* (1937), the remaining books of note released during this period were the first minor league histories: John B. Foster's seminal *History of the National Association of Professional Baseball Leagues* (1926); William Ruggles' *History of the Texas League* (1932); and Fred Lange's *History of Baseball in California and Pacific Coast Leagues* (1938).

It was in the 1940s when it can be said that publishers truly "got into the business" of publishing baseball books, and what marked this development was the inauguration in 1943 of the most important series of baseball books to be published to this day: the team history series of G. P. Putnams & Sons. Several of the 16 volumes in the Putnam team history series, called the "Pennant Series" by the publisher, were written by experts, such as Frank Graham and Warren Brown, who were associated with the teams whose histories they penned; although the genial and capable Fred Lieb performed like the Babe Ruth of the series, authoring the volumes on the Cardinals (1944), A's (1945), Tigers (1946), Red Sox (1947), Pirates (1948), and Orioles (1955) and co-authoring (with Stan Baumgartner) the volume on the Phillies (1953). In an ingenious marketing ploy Putnam advertised their entire line of baseball books, which they labeled "The Big League Baseball Library," on the insides of their dust jackets and even urged readers to join "the Putnam Plan for 'One Baseball-Book-a-Month'—either for yourself or as an inspiring gift for young Americans, both boys and more girls than you might guess!'" The series' momentum petered out as the final three volumes were released, with the result that today the highest prices are commanded by the Phillies and Orioles books and the Washington Senators history (1954) written by Shirley Povich. Although obviously dated, the Putnam series stands up well, the books remaining useful as histories of the periods they cover and not merely desirable as literary artifacts. While later printings and volumes without dust jackets are plentiful, first editions with dust jackets are not so easy to find.

Two other series, of juvenile biographies, by Julian Messner and A. S. Barnes further demonstrated the publishing industry's discovery of baseball as a serious topic of interest, as well as its commitment to producing quality books on the subject. Both the Messner series (36 volumes), begun in 1951, and the Barnes series (16 volumes), begun in 1950, were written by men prominent in the newspaper and magazine sportswriting profession of the day; men such as Gene Schoor, Milton J. Shapiro, Tom Meany, and Al Hirshberg. With few exceptions, the biographies in both series were written about subjects still living at the time of publication, and unlike the scholarly, thoroughly-researched biographies to come, they are heavily anecdotal and written in a breezy, "gee-whiz" style. Particularly important are the Barnes bios of Ewell Blackwell, Jim Konstanty, Andy Pafko, and Hank Sauer and the Messner bios of Jackie Jensen, Pee Wee Reese, Bob Allison, Norm Cash, and Willie Horton, as these are the only biographies that the players have received. Yet, all the books in both series are of keen interest because of the challenge in finding copies of them in collectible condition due to the fact that most copies of the books were consigned to the dreaded school library market.

Another sign that the baseball book industry was beginning to mature was the steady increase in the number of adult autobiographies and biographies that occurred in the 1940s and 1950s and beyond. Former New York Yankees first baseman Lou Gehrig was judged to be of such interest to the baseball reading public that four different biographies of him were released between 1940 and 1942, the best of the bunch being Paul Gallico's *Lou Gehrig: Pride of the Yankees* (1942) and Frank Graham's *Lou Gehrig: A Quiet Hero* (1942). Two more biographies of the King of the Genre appeared in 1948—*Babe Ruth* by Martin Weldon and *The Babe*

Ruth Story by the Babe and Bob Considine — and by the time the decade ended a number of other notable bios and autobios, evincing a decided preference by publishers for superstar calibre subjects, had appeared, including: *Clowning Through Baseball* (1941) by Al Schacht, *McGraw of the Giants* (1944) by Frank Graham, *Lucky to Be a Yankee* (1946) by Joe DiMaggio, *Strikeout Story* (1947) by Bob Feller, *Judge Landis and Twenty-Five Years of Baseball* (1947) by J. G. Taylor Spink, *Jackie Robinson: My Own Story* (1948) by Robinson and Wendell Smith, *The Dodgers and Me* (1948) by Leo Durocher, *Walter Johnson: King of the Pitchers* (1948) by Roger Treat, and *Player-Manager* (1949) by Lou Boudreau.

Baseball (1947) by Robert Smith and *One Hundred Years of Baseball* (1950) by Lee Allen are examples of the overall improvement that historians began to demonstrate in their work, but the groundbreaking historical work of the period was *Ball, Bat and Bishop* (1947) by Robert W. Henderson, the first author to base his baseball book on the research of secondary sources using accepted methods of scholarship. *Ball, Bat and Bishop* was not the final word on the origins of the game, but its irrefutable debunking of the Doubleday creation myth was a major accomplishment which paved the way for future scholarly approaches to baseball history.

The publication in 1951 of the *Official Encyclopedia of Baseball* edited by Hy Turkin and S. C. Thompson, was one of two landmark events in the history of baseball book publishing to occur in the '50s, as the book was the most complete and most thorough baseball records book ever published. It was updated four times before the first edition of the Macmillan *Baseball Encyclopedia* in 1969 rendered it obsolete. The other highlight of the 1950s was the initial stirrings of the artistic trend that would eventually see baseball recognized as the most literary of sports, as represented by the publication of the first great baseball anthology and that of several notable novels. Other than *The Sun Field* (1923) by famed New York sportswriter Heywood Broun and *The New Klondike: A Story of a Southern Baseball Training Camp* (1926) by Peggy Griffith, nothing much had been accomplished in the adult baseball novel since Ring Lardner. That began to change around the mid-century mark with the appearance of *It Happens Every Spring* (1949) by Valentine Davies, *The Sunlit Field* (1950) by Lucy Kennedy, *The Natural* (1952) by Bernard Malamud, *The Southpaw* (1953) by Mark Harris, and *The Year the Yankees Lost the Pennant*

(1954) by Douglas Wallop. As wonderful as they are, both Davis' book (the tale of a scientist who devises a formula that makes baseballs avoid wood) and Wallop's (the baseball version of the Faust story) are basically entertainments — both were made into successful movies, Wallop's after it was first transformed into the smash stage musical, *Damn Yankees*. *The Natural* was entertaining too, but it was also a work of unmistakable literary merit that aspired to deal with serious moral questions through the dramatization of the predicaments and choices of the main character, slugger Roy Hobbs of the fictional New York Knights. *The Natural* was Malamud's first novel, and as he gained stature over the years as one of America's leading men of letters, it became an important precedent for other "serious" writers of fiction who wanted to utilize the fecund mythic, comic, and dramatic possibilities of baseball without compromising their status. With *The Southpaw* Harris proved himself to be a first-rate humorist and a worthy successor of Lardner. As Lardner did with Jack Keefe, Harris demonstrated a mastery of the American vernacular and idiom with the speech uttered by his hero, pitcher Henry Wiggen; however, Wiggen displayed a humanity and depth of character not present in Keefe, and the Henry Wiggen series (*Bang the Drum Slowly*, 1956; *A Ticket for a Seamstitch*, 1957; and *It Looked Like Forever*, 1979) further broadened, sequel by sequel, the trail that succeeding baseball fiction writers could travel with impunity. Collecting widely different types of baseball writing by many of the art's most accomplished practitioners from a variety of eras in the game's history, and graciously illustrated with a fetching assortment of cartoons, photos, and art, Charles Einstein's *Fireside Book of Baseball* (1956) demonstrated a richness of baseball literature that had been unsuspected by the general public. The book was a revelation to many, and its surprising commercial success emboldened the publisher, Simon & Schuster, to sign up a sequel, *The Second Fireside Book of Baseball*, which appeared a mere two years later. That book was successful too, and there remained enough outstanding unanthologized material that Einstein was able to produce yet another volume, *The Third Fireside Book of Baseball*, in 1968. The fourth volume of the series appeared in 1987 (in a much less pleasing, paperback format than its predecessors ... much to the dismay of Einstein); but it had to share the spotlight with some of the other great baseball anthologies that had been published in the interim, such as *Baseball I Gave You All the Best*

1. A Short History of Baseball Books

Years of My Life (1977) edited by Kevin Kerrane and Richard Grossinger, *Fielder's Choice: An Anthology of Baseball Fiction* (1979) edited by Jerome Holtzman, *Pig Iron Baseball* edited by Jim Villani and Rose Sayre (1982), and *The Armchair Book of Baseball* (1985) edited by John Thorn.

While *The Fireside Books* confirmed the public's receptiveness to quality baseball literature, *My Greatest Day in Baseball* (1945) edited by John Carmichael and *Big-Time Baseball* (1950) by Harold H. Hart and Ralph Tolleris proved something close to the opposite: that tidy profits could also be made from pedestrian baseball books, as long as they were well marketed or had a sufficiently interesting hook. Both the Carmichael book, a collection of 47 first-person game narratives by the players and a number of different "as told to" authors, and *Big-Time Baseball*, a miscellany of history, records, anecdotes, and player sketches directed at an adolescent audience, went through numerous editions and remain common books despite their age.

With the transcontinental shift of the Giants and Dodgers from New York to the West Coast at the end of the 1950s, baseball experienced the greatest structural transformation in the history of the game. The relocation of the two legendary franchises not only necessitated air travel, but they also led to expansions and realignments and a host of associated changes, the effects of which are still being felt today. This move to "nationalize" the National Pastime was paralleled in the early 1960s by a second literary baseball boom; a boom which can be considered to have initiated the modern era of the baseball book.

Interestingly enough, this second boom was ushered in by a major league player, pitcher Jim Brosnan who was nicknamed "The Professor," and by Dr. Harold Seymour, an academic who was an actual professor of history at Finch College. The popularity of baseball autobiography had already been well established by this time; however, in the 1960s and 1970s autobiographies by players and other baseball luminaries with axes to grind (i.e., apologias) proliferated, and the following are among the most gripping personal baseball narratives ever published: *My Life in Baseball: The True Record* (1961) by Ty Cobb and Al Silverton; *Veeck As in Wreck* (1962) by Bill Veeck and Ed Linn; *From Ghetto to Glory* (1968) by Bob Gibson and Phil Pepe; *My Turn at Bat* (1969) by Ted Williams and John Underwood; *The Way It Is* (1971) by Curt Flood and Richard Carter; *I Never*

Had It Made (1972) by Jackie Robinson and Al Duckett; and *Nice Guys Finish Last* (1976) by Leo Durocher and Ed Linn. Brosnan's contribution to baseball literature was to take the immediacy and authenticity of autobiography a step further, and he did this by writing seasonal accounts that put the reader as close to the players and the game on the field as it is possible for the printed word to get him. *The Long Season* (1960) and *Pennant Race* (1962) were the first baseball books to be written by an active major league player without any assistance from a professional wordsmith, and the literary artfulness they displayed created a new career for Brosnan after he retired from the game. More importantly, the commercial success of the two books, along with that of *Baseball Is a Funny Game* (1960), a collection of humorous anecdotes by former player Joe Garagiola, made it clear that well done baseball books could now be *expected* to enhance the bottom line.

The publication of Seymour's *Baseball: The Early Years*, also in 1960, represented another critical development in the history of baseball books: the discovery of baseball by the nation's academic presses. Based on Seymour's doctoral dissertation at Cornell University, *Baseball: The Early Years* demonstrated more than enough scholarship and connection to the world of ideas to satisfy the requirements of Oxford University Press while it was also lively and interesting enough to appeal to a large segment of the baseball reading public. After *Baseball: The Golden Age* came out in 1971, the two-volumes (sold separately and as a boxed set) became generally accepted as the standard history of the baseball period (up to 1930) they cover. Other academic presses were quick to follow Oxford's lead, and even before Seymour could get his second volume out, David Q. Voigt and the University of Oklahoma Press gave Seymour competition with the publication in 1966 of what would be the first volume of a three-volume general history of the game, *American Baseball: From Gentleman's Sport to the Commissioner's System*. The University of Oklahoma Press released volume II of Voigt's history, *American Baseball: From the Commissioners to Continental Expansion*, in 1970; and The Pennsylvania State University Press published volume III, *American Baseball: From Postwar Expansion to the Electronic Age*, in 1983, while also re-issuing the first two volumes.

The quality of the baseballs books published by the nation's academic presses has continued to be exceptionally high, and there is no better indication of that than the impressive showing the university presses have made right from the beginning in the baseball book competitions. For instance, *Spitball Magazine*'s Casey Award was inaugurated in 1983, and Oxford University Press had a book nominated as a Finalist that year (*Baseball's Great Experiment* by Jules Tygiel) and the following year (*Ty Cobb* by Charles Alexander). Both books were revelatory works of scholarship; Tygiel demonstrating how the process of integrating baseball went far beyond the efforts of Jackie Robinson in 1947, and Alexander finding the key to Cobb's aberrant personality and drive in the forgotten story of the death of Cobb's father at the hands of Cobb's mother. Through 2005 the baseball books of 16 different university presses (besides Oxford) have received Finalist nominations for the Casey Award: The University of Alabama Press, Columbia University Press, University of Illinois Press, Indiana University Press, The University of Kentucky Press, The University of Massachusetts Press, University of Missouri Press, University of Nebraska Press, University of North Carolina Press, University of Pennsylvania Press, Penn State University Press, Princeton University Press, Southern Illinois University Press, Temple University Press, University Press of Virginia, and Wayne State University Press. Moreover, three university presses and their authors have won Casey Awards: Oxford and Harold Seymour garnered the 1990 Casey for the long-awaited third volume of the history they started in 1960, *Baseball: The People's Game*; Princeton and Bruce Kuklick took home the 1991 Casey for *To Everything a Season: Shibe Park and Urban Philadelphia, 1909–1977*; and the 2000 Casey went to Massachusetts and Reed Browning for *Cy Young: A Baseball Life*. Under the leadership of director Dan Ross, Nebraska became one of the most enthusiastic and prolific university publishers of high quality baseball books; and in 1998 Southern Illinois took the unprecedented step of formalizing their efforts into a publishing series called "Writing Baseball," a program conceived and edited by Richard Peterson.

In 1963 Eliot Asinof published *Eight Men Out*, a sensational reconstruction of the infamous deeds surrounding the 1919 World Series. The book renewed interest in Asinof's realistic baseball novel, *Man on Spikes* (1955), but more importantly brought baseball's darkest days back into the spotlight and became for decades the standard version of events involving the Black Sox and the gamblers they conspired with. An even more influential book, and with the exception of the first volume of Seymour's history, the *most* influential baseball book of the decade, was Lawrence Ritter's *The Glory of Their Times* (1966). A professor of economics at New York University, Ritter was galvanized, upon the death of Ty Cobb in 1961, into attempting to preserve for posterity the stories of an entire generation of prominent ballplayers from baseball's Golden Era before they all passed away. *The Glory of Their Times* is the result of his efforts, the first-person stories of 22 dead-ball era players, such as Fred Snodgrass, Sam Crawford, and Joe Wood. Universally praised for the brilliance, vividness, and candor of its dramatic narratives, the book re-invigorated the subjects who were delighted that the world was suddenly interested in their exploits again, and it enjoyed very brisk sales, to the benefit of the subjects, who were all given an equal share of the royalties by the generous Ritter. Naturally, the book also spawned a host of imitations; and oral history, as the process of tape-recording and then transcribing interviews is known, became one of the most popular genres of baseball literature. Ritter's friend Donald Honig became an expert oral historian and published a trio of baseball oral histories in the 1970s: *Baseball When the Grass was Real* (1975), *Baseball Between the Lines* (1976), and *The October Heroes* (1979). Several other authors have turned in well-done baseball oral histories — Jerome Holtzman's *No Cheering in the Press Box* (1973) and John Holway's *Voices from the Great Black Baseball Leagues* (1975) are two of the best examples — but other would-be Ritters have not understood the art involved in writing oral history and have produced forgettable, sometimes unreadable, volumes. The only great adult baseball novel to appear in the 1960s was *The Universal Baseball Association, Inc., J. Henry Waugh, Prop.* (1968) by Robert Coover. On the surface the story of a reclusive accountant obsessed with playing a table-top dice baseball game he has invented, the book functions on a deeper level as an allegory for the intervention of God in human affairs. A stunning work of genius, the book illustrated that any limitations thought to be put on the imagination by baseball were merely illusory.

    Highlighted by the Big Red Machine's dominance of the National League, the thrill-a-pitch 1975 World Series, and the soap opera-ish revival of the New York Yankees under the meddling micro-management of owner George Steinbrenner, baseball surged in popularity in the 1970s. Baseball books too were more popular than ever before, and the quality of the books issued during the decade can only be described as spectacular. It was a "Decade of Classics," full of superbly written books on a number of new or neglected baseball topics. For instance, *Only the Ball Was White* (1970) by Robert Peterson was the first comprehensive history of the Negro Leagues, and it became the basic roadmap followed by a succession of other great Negro League researchers and writers, such as John Holway, Donn Rogosin, James Riley, Phil Dixon, and Larry Lester. In 1975 Robert Obojski published *Bush League* and accomplished for the minors pretty much what Peterson had done for the Negro Leagues. And, while Robert Whiting's book on Japanese baseball, *The Chrysanthemum and the Bat: Baseball Samurai Style* (1977) was not a comprehensive history, its exploration of the ways the Japanese have adapted the American National Pastime to their own spartan culture and community-oriented society fascinated readers and gave them a new appreciation for the difficulties *gaijins* (i.e., foreigners or, for all practical purposes, Americans) have faced in their efforts to make the adjustments necessary to enjoy success playing for Japanese teams.

The key development of the decade, however, was the artistic leap forward brought about by non-fiction authors who wrote not merely as baseball savants but as prose stylists of the first rank. These authors gave baseball a literary legitimacy it had not previously been able to claim, and before long writers from all corners were so anxious to weigh in on the subject and to prove a personal connection to the game that their writing about baseball became a form of self- and professional validation. The book which initiated this movement and which still best represents it today is *The Boys of Summer*, Roger Kahn's poignant memoir of the Brooklyn Dodgers of the early 1950s. The 1971 book, which contrasted the older and younger lives of the players and made of the differences a story representative of all men, bridged the gap between sports and "real life" as no other baseball book had ever done. It was hailed as the baseball book which had to be read by everyone, including the elites and intellectuals who couldn't find their way into a ballpark with a *Fodor's* and a guide dog; and it was the baseball book which received great credit for being "not just about baseball"— the characteristic guaranteed to win succeeding baseball books the approval of anti-jock reviewers for years to come. While Kahn has never quite reached the pinnacle of *The Boys of Summer* again — an observation hardly meant as a criticism — he has produced a rich canon of baseball books, many (like *The Boys of Summer*) highly autobiographical and all elegantly-written. Casey Award winner *Good Enough to Dream* (1984) and *Memories of Summer: When Baseball Was an Art, and Writing about It a Game* (1997) are two of his best. Even if the *Boys of Summer* had been his only baseball book, Kahn's legacy would be assured as the book muted forever the snob's dismissal of baseball as suitable material for literary aspirations of the highest order.

While it did not achieve the sustained greatness of *The Boys of Summer*, Roger Angell's *The Summer Game*, published the following year in 1972, displayed another master craftsman at work and brought Angell's exquisite essays and inimical game reports to a much wider audience than that of *The New Yorker* magazine, where his short pieces first appeared. Another of baseball's greatest novels appeared in 1973, this time coming from a writer already recognized as a major American novelist. A comic masterpiece of the first order, *The Great American Novel* by Philip Roth satirized baseball, classic works of literature, and countless other ideas and institutions cherished by the American public. Too much of a mixture to satisfy those only comfortable in either the faculty lounge or the sports bar, the novel nevertheless again expanded the imaginative parameters of baseball fiction. In 1974 Robert Creamer published *Babe: The Legend Comes to Life*, a riveting, finely detailed, and clarifying biography which set a new standard for the genre. The book was universally praised and considered by many to be not only the best biography about Ruth or any other baseball player, but also the best biography of *any* sports figure ever published. *Babe* overshadowed three other contemporaneous biographies of The Bambino which were also timed to take advantage of the renewed interest in Ruth brought about by Hank Aaron's methodical assault on the career home run record: Robert Smith's *Babe Ruth's America* (1974), Kal Wagenheim's *Babe Ruth: His Life and Legend* (1974), and Marshall Smelser's *The Life that Ruth Built* (1975). Lovers of literature were stunned again in 1975 when Pat Jordan's *A False Spring*, another beautifully-written and moving baseball book, was published. The book is the autobiographical account of Jordan's utter failure as a hot shot minor league pitching prospect in the Braves' organization, yet the telling is done with such self-excoriating honesty and hard-earned moral clarity that the story produces not disdain but a sense of cathartic triumph. The final belletristic baseball book of the decade, Charles Einstein's *Willie's Time: A Memoir*, appeared in 1979. The "as told to" author of three previous Mays biographies (*Born to Play Ball*, 1955; *Willie Mays: Coast-to-Coast Giant*, 1963; and *Willie Mays: My Life In and Out of Baseball*, 1966), Einstein attempted in *Willie's Time* to convey Mays' greatness by illustrating the changes that occurred in the American cultural and political landscapes over the course of May's long career; and the success of Einstein's efforts was represented by the book becoming the first baseball book to ever be named as a Finalist for the Pulitzer Prize.

Some of the other fine baseball books published during the decade — "minor classics" we might call them as they were simply overshadowed by the Literary Grand Slams mentioned above — were: *The Man Who Invented Baseball* (1973) by Harold Peterson, *Destiny's Darlings: A World Champion Little League Team Twenty Years Later* (1974) by Martin Ralbovsky, *One for the Record: The Inside Story of Hank Aaron's Chase of the Home-Run Record* (1974) by George Plimpton, *Some Are Called Clowns: A Season with the Last of the Great Barnstorming Baseball Teams* (1974) by Bill Heward and Dimitri V. Gat, *The Ballparks* by Bill Shannon and George Kalinsky, *Dock Ellis in the Country of Baseball* (1976) by Donald Hall, *The Lords of Baseball* (1976) by Harold Parrott, *The Image of Their Greatness* (1979) by Lawrence Ritter and Donald Honig, and *The Ultimate Baseball Book* (1979) edited by Daniel Okrent and Harris Lewine. Adult baseball novels finally began to appear with more regularity than a World Series sweep, and some of the best of the period were: *Babe Ruth Caught in a Snowstorm* (1973) by John Alexander Graham, *The Bingo Long Traveling All-Stars and Motor Kings* (1973) by William Brashler, *All G.O.D.'s Children* (1975) by John Craig, *Pride of the Bimbos* (1975) by John Sayles, *The Seventh Babe* (1979) by Jerome Charyn, and *Long Gone* (1979) by Paul Hemphill.

Lastly, the seventies were further defined by the increasing sales power of baseball books, as indicated by their more frequent and longer-lasting appearances on lists of best sellers. In 1970 knuckleballing relief pitcher Jim Bouton published a rollicking, hilarious diary that did not shy away from portraying all aspects of the ballplayers' lives, including their drinking and sexual escapades. Commissioner Bowie Kuhn's attempt to squelch the controversial book only increased the demand for *Ball Four*, which landed on the *New York Times* Best-Seller List and stayed there for 17 weeks, breaking the previous record of 15 weeks held by *Veeck As in Wreck*. *The Boys of Summer* promptly set a new record of 24 weeks and enjoyed the honor of being the first baseball book to hit #1 on the List (for six weeks), but then it was surpassed as the decade closed in 1979 by Peter Golenbock and Sparky Lyle's *The Bronx Zoo* which enjoyed a 29-week stay on the List. The *Bronx Zoo* held the record until it was unseated in 1990 by George Will's *Men at Work*, the book which remains the champ at 35 weeks. According to Marty Appel, who published an article in *Sports Collectors Digest* about baseball books on the *New York Times* Best-Seller Lists, 45 different baseball books have made the List through 2005. There is a clear New York flavor to these books; some unremarkable books have made the List and many great books have not; but the trend is definitely positive for baseball books, as more than a third (17) of the 45 appearances by baseball books on the *Times'* List have come since 2000. As for Bouton and Golenbock, their appearances on the List in the 1970s heralded very distinguished careers as baseball book authors. Some cynics devalued Bouton's authorship of *Ball Four* and tried to assign the lion's share of the credit for the book's wit and insights to sportswriter Leonard Shecter, who did make a major contribution to the book by editing it down from 1,500 to 520 manuscript pages; but Bouton proved himself to be a fine writer with an original mind by authoring several other good baseball books, including, most recently, a self-published account of his quixotic attempts to preserve the doomed minor league ballpark in Pittsfield, Massachusetts: *Foul Ball: My Life and Hard Times Trying to Save an Old Ballpark* (2003). Golenbock has made three more appearances on the *Times* Best-Sellers List (the most by any author of baseball books) with autobiographical "co-authors" Billy Martin, Graig Nettles, and Johnny Damon; and he also made team oral history his special province, producing the following well-received volumes of that type: *Dynasty: The New York Yankees 1949-1964* (1975), *Bums: An Oral History of the Brooklyn Dodgers* (1984), *Fenway: An Unexpurgated History of the Boston Red Sox* (1992), *Wrigleyville: A Magical History Tour of the Chicago Cubs* (1996), *The Spirit of St. Louis: A History of the St. Louis Cardinals and Browns* (2000), and *Amazin': The Miraculous History of New York's Most Beloved Baseball Team* (2002).

1. A Short History of Baseball Books

Despite the impressive sales records of the baseball books which elbowed their way onto best sellers' lists, especially when compared to those of books on other sports, baseball books and baseball book authors were almost completely ignored by the sponsors of the nation's book awards. To remedy this gross injustice, *Spitball: The Literary Baseball Magazine* instituted the Casey Award in 1983 and deemed that the Casey be given to the author and publisher of the book judged to be "the best baseball book of the year." Seven books were honored as Finalists for the 1983 Casey (*Baseball's Great Experiment* by Jules Tygiel, *The Celebrant* by Eric Rolfe Greenberg, *Hoopla* by Harry Stein, *Invisible Men* by Donn Rogosin, *Insider's Baseball* ed. by L. Robert Davids, *Take Me Out to the Ballpark* by Lowell Reidenbaugh, and *Who's on 3rd? The Chicago White Sox Story* by Richard Lindberg), and the first Casey was won by Greenberg for his historical novel about New York Giants pitching immortal Christy Mathewson and his biggest fan. If there had been any doubt about baseball's ability to sustain such an award by annually producing enough worthy candidates, it was quickly dispelled; as limiting the number of Casey Award Finalists each year was a bigger problem for *Spitball Magazine* than identifying enough good books to make a spirited competition. *Spitball* eventually settled on 10 as the target to shoot for when attempting to limit the number of Finalists to a work load manageable for the judges. Additional baseball book awards were later created (e.g., The Seymour Medal in 1996 and the Dave Moore Award in 1999), so that by the year 2000 it could be said that honor-worthy baseball books, authors, and publishers were in a good position to get the recognition they deserved.

In addition to the creation of the Casey Award, one of the two other important developments of the 1980s was the increased interest among baseball fans in baseball statistics, records, player evaluations, and comparisons of players from different eras. This interest had been growing since 1971, when a group of 17 men gathered in Cooperstown, New York, to form the Society for American Baseball Research (SABR), an organization that would be devoted to researching baseball history. SABR members made a number of important discoveries, some of which led to corrections of the statistical records, and the organization began publishing its own journals and magazines (and eventually books too) to promulgate the research findings of the members. "The mathematical and statistical analysis of baseball records," the type of research many SABR members were involved in, came to be known as "sabermetrics," and even before the organization was founded some books based on sabermetrics had been published, such as *Kings of the Mound: A Pitchers' Rating Manual* (1944) by Ted Oliver and *Percentage Baseball* (1964) by Earnshaw Cook and Wendell R. Garner. In the 1980s, as SABR membership ballooned to more than 4,000, sabermetric-type books proliferated. Some of these books, the ones which relied completely on numbers, statistics, and mathematical formulae, had immense soporific power over the typical reader; but others, such as *The Hidden Game of Baseball: A Revolutionary Approach to Baseball and Its Revealing Statistics* (1984) by John Thorn and Pete Palmer and *The Diamond Appraised* by Craig R. Wright and Tom House (1989), were fascinating and highly educational, as they used sabermetrics to shed light on fundamental baseball questions (e.g., does clutch hitting really exist?) while never forgetting the author's obligations to the reader. In addition to its key role in fostering an environment receptive to books of a sabermetric nature, SABR provided a general boost to the baseball book publishing industry and to the baseball book collecting hobby by forging a network of researchers and historians that has been a great aid to authors, SABR members and non-members alike; by creating a market of avid baseball book buyers that could be easily targeted by smaller publishers; and by serving, with its many opportunities for members to publish articles in the Society's periodicals, as a training ground for authors.

The most famous and most influential sabermetrician is Bill James, a Kansan who from 1977 through 1981 self-published his statistical analysis studies in annual volumes called *The Baseball Abstract*. After an article in *Sports Illustrated* brought James to the attention of the commercial publishing world, Random House signed James and published *The Bill James Baseball Abstract* annually for the next seven years. A swarm of imitators caused sales of the highly successful Random House *Abstracts* to level off, and James, hardly a one-trick pony, went on to other projects. As the annual *Abstracts* were running out of steam, James published *The Bill James Historical Baseball Abstract*, a volume which applied the methods of the annual *Abstracts* to historical baseball figures. *The Historical Abstract*, which is also a delightful cornucopia of oddball facts, intriguing profiles, and startling opinions, won the 1986 Casey Award and was followed by a number of other James books, the best of which are *This Time Let's Not Eat the Bones* (1989), *The Politics of Glory: How Baseball's Hall of Fame Really Works* (1994), and *The Bill James Guide to Baseball Managers* (1997).

The invention of fantasy league baseball (or "rotissiere" league baseball as it was originally called after the New York City restaurant where inventor Dan Okrent first explained the game's rules to others) in 1980 boosted the popularity of James' *Baseball Abstracts* for the player evaluations the book contained; but it also led to a new kind of book, the annual fantasy league guides that were published in the late 1980s and early 1990s to provide fantasy leaguers with player evaluations, rankings, and drafting recommendations. These guides, such as the *Elias Baseball Analyst* and the *Baseball Prospectus*, were usually published as oversized paperbacks and were by their nature understood to be of ephemeral value. Some of the related books that were not strictly fantasy league guides, such as *The Scouting Report* series which presented extremely detailed information on individual players' strengths and weaknesses, are still somewhat interesting to read, but they typically generate no more excitement among baseball book collectors than the typical out-dated fantasy league guide. On the other hand, if enough of these types of books are delivered to the nation's landfills so as to make the surviving copies extremely rare, the books may some day become collectible, especially if it is the *Bill James Abstracts* which become the rarities.

The third important development of the 1980s was another influx of new publishers interested in publishing baseball books: niche publishers, such as Diamond Communications and Sports Publishing LLC; regional publishers, such as Algonquin Books of Chapel Hill; and non-university-affiliated publishers of scholarly reference and academic books, such as Meckler Books, Greenwood Press, Scarecrow Press, and McFarland and Co., Inc. These companies published many deserving baseball books that larger commercial houses were not interested in (presumably because of the books' limited national appeal), and their efforts were often rewarded with critical acclaim and profitable sales. For instance, Casey Awards were won by both the Scarecrow Press, for Marty Appel's *Slide, Kelly, Slide: The Wild Life and Times of Mike "King" Kelly, Baseball's First Superstar* (1996), and by Diamond Communications, for David Pietrusza's *Judge & Jury: The Life and Times of Judge Kenesaw Mountain Landis* (1998). The most important of these publishers, by far, has been McFarland. While McFarland has not yet won a Casey Award, McFarland titles have received nine Casey Award Finalist Nominations, the most of any publisher other than commercial giants Macmillan (11 Nominations) and Simon & Schuster (10); and the company's baseball books have received an impressive number of other recognitions, including Seymour Medals, won by Arthur D. Hittner for *Honus Wagner: The Life of Baseball's "Flying Dutchman"* (1997) and by Tom Melville for *Early Baseball and the Rise of the National League* (2002). Most importantly, McFarland has released more than 300 different baseball titles on an amazingly wide variety of topics through the end of 2006 and has become, with its average of 30 new releases each year, perhaps the single most important baseball book publisher of any size. Particularly significant are the McFarland biographies of neglected but deserving players, such as Frank Baker, Hal Chase, Bill Dahlen, Pete Gray, Waite Hoyt, Tony Lazzeri, Al Lopez, Sal Maglie, Armando Marsans, Pepper Martin, Thurman Munson, Jim O'Rourke, Pete Reiser, Louis Sockalexis, Cecil Travis, Rube Waddell, Paul and Lloyd Waner, Hack Wilson, and Harry Wright.

Of course, baseball continued to attract fine writers, and five of the most prominent to emerge in the 1980s were *Washington Post* reporter Tom Boswell (*How Life Imitates the World Series*, 1982; *Why Time Begins on Opening Day*, 1984; and *The Heart of the Order*, 1989); Bill Curran (*Mitts: A Celebration of the Art of Fielding*, 1985 and *Big Sticks: The Batting Revolution of the Twenties*, 1990); David Falkner (*Sadaharu Oh: A Zen Way of Baseball*, 1984; *The Short Season: The Hard Work and High Times of Baseball in the Spring*, 1986; and *Nine Sides of the Diamond: Baseball's Great Glove Men on the Fine Art of Defense*, 1990); *Boston Globe* baseball writer Dan Shaughnessy (*One Strike Away: The Story of the 1986 Red Sox*, 1987; and *The Curse of the Bambino*, 1990); and Lonnie Wheeler (*Bleachers: A Summer in Wrigley Field*, 1988; and *The Cincinnati Game*, 1988).

The appearance of two great, soaring novels early in the decade, *Shoeless Joe* (1982) by W. P. Kinsella and *The Celebrant* (1983) by Eric Rolfe Greenberg, heralded the maturing of adult baseball fiction, and the short list of outstanding baseball novels to follow would have to include: *The Iowa Baseball Confederacy* (1986) by W. P. Kinsella, *The Curious Case of Sidd Finch* (1987) by George Plimpton, *A Flatland Fable* (1987) by Joe

Coomer, *If I Never Get Back* (1989) by Darryl Brock, *Blue Ruin* (1991) by Brendan Boyd, *The Brothers K* (1992) by David James Duncan, *Brittle Innings* (1993) by Michael Bishop, *Veracruz Blues* (1996) by Mark Winegardner, *Play for a Kingdom* (1997) by Thomas Dyja, and *Havana Heat* (2000) by Darryl Brock. The two great "small press" literary baseball journals, *Spitball: The Literary Baseball Magazine* and *The Minneapolis Review of Baseball*, began publishing in 1981, and they helped create the atmosphere that made possible the publication of baseball short story collections by single authors, such as *Short Season and Other Stories* (1988) and *Basepaths* (1995) by Jerry Klinkowitz; *Hitting into the Wind* (1994) by Bill Meissner; and *The Thrill of the Grass* (1985), *The Further Adventures of Slugger McBatt* (1988), and *The Dixon Cornbelt League* (1995) by W. P. Kinsella. Genre fiction writers also discovered baseball, and baseball mystery novels in particular began to proliferate — the one notable baseball effort by a writer of horror was turned in by Stephen King whose *The Girl Who Loved Tom Gordon* appeared in 1999. R. D. Rosen's *Strike Three, You're Dead* won the 1985 Edgar Award for Best First Mystery Novel; *The Burglar Who Traded Ted Williams* (1994) by Lawrence Block and *Double Play* (2004) by Robert B. Parker are examples of baseball books written by well-known mystery writers; and Crabbe Evers, Alison Gordon, and Troy Soos all penned baseball mystery series. Soos began his series of baseball mysteries involving utility infielder Mickey Rawlings in 1994 with *Murder at Fenway Park* (at the time of this writing the Soos series had expanded to six titles, the latest being *Cincinnati Red Stalkings*, published in 2003). Even baseball literature's poor relative, baseball poetry, began to prosper, as reflected by collections such as *Hummers, Knucklers, and Slow Curves: Contemporary Baseball Poems* (1991) edited by Don Johnson; and volumes of baseball poetry by single poets, the best of which were *Center Field Grasses: Poems from Baseball* by Gene Fehler; *Touching All the Bases* (2000) and *Waiting for Godot's First Pitch* (2001) by Tim Peeler, and *Cooperstown Verses: Poems about Each Hall of Famer* (2001) by Mark Schraf. All of this literary attention focused on a mere game confounded some observers who reacted against what they saw as the misplaced search for the meaning of life in baseball as represented by the sentimentality of the "fathers playing catch with sons" motif; yet there were plenty of critics willing to take it all seriously, and some of the more important critical studies of baseball literature to appear were: *Seeking the Perfect Game: Baseball in American Literature* (1989) by Cordelia Candelaria, *Making the Team: The Cultural Work of Baseball Fiction* (1997) by Timothy Morris, and *Imagining Baseball: America's Pastime and Popular Culture* (2000) by David McGimpsey.

It is not possible to name here all the other fine baseball books released during the decade, but three in particular were so well done as to be unforgettable: Kevin Kerrane's treatise on scouting called *Dollar Sign on the Muscle* (1984), about which Luke Salisbury said: "Kerrane does for scouting what Melville did for whaling — no one need write another book on the subject"; Mike Sowell's gripping narrative of the Carl Mays–Ray Chapman saga, *The Pitch that Killed* (1989); and Mark Winegardner's poignant biography of the old baseball scout who loved baseball too much, *Prophet of the Sandlots* (1990). In addition, journeyman outfielder Jay Johnstone and flamboyant umpire Ron Luciano did not create great works of literature, but they did, with help from as-told-to authors Rick Talley and David Fisher, respectively, produce some of the funniest and best-selling baseball books of the 1980s. Fans liked *Temporary Insanity: The Uncensored Adventures of Baseball's Craziest Player* (1985) so much that Johnstone and Talley were able to publish two sequels (*Over the Edge: Baseball's Uncensored Exploits from Way Out in Left Field, 1987;* and *Some of My Best Friends Are Crazy,* 1990); while Luciano and Fisher were able to parlay the yuks elicited by *The Umpire Strikes Back* (1982) into three sequels: *Strike Two* (1984), *The Fall of the Roman Umpire* (1986), and *Remembrance of Swings Past* (1988).

Baseball books were on such a roll as the final decade of the 20th Century began that the publishing industry's journal of record, *Publishers Weekly,* finally began to take the genre seriously, publishing a lengthy roundup review of new baseball book released each spring. Part of this interest was doubtlessly due to the fact that respected journalists and intellectuals, such as David Halberstam (*Summer of '49,* 1989) and George Will (*Men at Work*; 1990) had "crossed over" and authored acclaimed and highly successful baseball books. However, the articles in *PW* were invariably more bearish than bullish about the future of baseball books, as if the magazine couldn't quite believe what was happening before its eyes. Jeff Neuman, director of sports books at Simon & Schuster, was particularly pessimistic. In the February 16, 1990, issue Neuman said: "The number of titles being released in the market is still booming, but the sales have leveled out. I very much think it's becoming flooded. When you're talking about more than 100 books being released and the average fan may want to buy one or two, it becomes really hard for a book to stand out." Two years later in the February 17, 1992, issue Neuman further opined that the supposed glut of baseball books had caused all the possible literary bases to already be not merely touched but flat worn out. "What is there left to write about in baseball?" he asked. "Every conceivable idea has been published."

Some of this angst may have been due to the game itself, which experienced significant labor and financial troubles during these years. Interest in books about the business side of baseball had been growing, evidenced by the publication of titles, such as *The Business of Major League Baseball* (1989) by Gerald W. Scully, *The Business of Baseball* (1990) by James E. Miller, and *Baseball and Billions: A Probing Look Inside the Business of Our National Pastime* (1992) by Andrew Zimbalist; and two books issued in the spring of 1993 practically rang the game's death knell: *Coming Apart at the Seams: How Baseball Owners, Players & Television Executives Have Led Our National Pastime to the Brink of Disaster* by Jack Sands and Peter Gammons and *Play Ball: The Life and Troubled Times of Major League Baseball* by John Feinstein. The latter two books, which did not resonate with fans, flopped and paled in comparison to the book which (a year later) hit the nail on the head, John Helyar's *Lords of the Realm: The Real History of Baseball*. Written by the co-author of the smash exposé of corporate America, *Barbarians at the Gate*, *Lords of the Realm* reassured readers that baseball would survive its current troubles by illustrating that they were nothing new. As the blurb on the dust jacket stated, the book was "a penetrating, take-no-prisoners look at the hundred-year history of what's become a billion-dollar machine, a cutthroat industry that, while supposedly capturing the soul of America, is and always has been dominated by such greed, back-stabbing, and double-dealing that it puts the insanity of the RJR Nabisco takeover to shame." Besides providing some much-needed perspective, the book was also exceedingly funny!

Fortunately, few people interested in baseball books shared Neuman's pessimism over the future of the industry; nor did they speculate, as *PW* did in subsequent years, that others sports (such as basketball) might be pulling even with baseball in the sports books wars, or agonize over the possibility that the days of the blockbuster sports biography were long gone. Mediocre and redundant baseball books were published to be sure, as they always had been, but the overall quality of the baseball books released in the '90s remained high, as the increased competition *mandated* that authors turn in good work. Equally important, the flooding of the market that the big commercial houses viewed as a sales problem did not concern readers who reveled in the wide selection of baseball books now available on a yearly basis. The increase in the number of small-to-medium sized publishers willing to accept levels of sales considered paltry by the bigger houses based mostly in New York allowed enterprising authors the chance to complete in-depth studies on a wider and wider range of baseball topics. The big boys themselves even began to widen their scope, and the following is a mere sampling of the excellent books produced during the decade by publishers both big and small on minor baseball topics, such as: art (*The Art of Baseball* by Shelly M. Dinhofer, 1990), uniforms (*Baseball Uniforms of the 20th Century* by Marc Okkonen, 1991), movies (*Baseball in the Movies*, Hal Erickson, 1992), women (*Women at Play: The Story of Women in Baseball* by Barbara Gregorich, 1993), black writers (*Black Writers/Black Baseball: An Anthology of Articles from Black Sportswriters Who Covered the Negro Leagues* by Jim Reisler, 1994), inventions (*Banana Bats and Dingdong Balls: A Century of Baseball Inventions* by Dan Gutman, 1995), scorekeeping (*The Joy of Keeping Score* by Paul Dickson, 1996), night baseball (*Lights On! The Wild Century-Long Saga of Night Baseball* by David Pietrusza, 1997), memorabilia (*Treasures of the Baseball Hall of Fame* by John Thorn, 1998), and Cuban baseball (*Smoke: The Romance and Lore of Cuban Baseball* by Mark Rucker and Peter Bjarkman, 1999).

A sure sign of an expanded and healthy market for baseball books was the continued increase in baseball reference and illustrated books; two of the most expensive kinds of books to produce. Baseball photography began to get its due in the 1970s, with the publication of photo-dominated books such as *This Great Game* (1971), *That Old Ball Game: Rare Photographs from Baseball's Glorious Past* by David R. Phillips (1975), *The Ballparks* by Shannon and Kalinsky (1975), *The Game and the Glory* edited by Joe Reichler (1976), and *A Baseball Century: The First 100 Years of the National League* (1976). After *The Ultimate Baseball Book* hit the shelves in 1979 it was a whole new ballgame for illustrated baseball books. Typical of the reception the book received was that tendered by the *West Coast Review of Books*, which raved: "It's too bad we only go to five stars; this one deserves six. It is the most magnificent book about baseball past and present that has ever been published." The record-setting sales of the book, which has gone through several editions, led to the further publication of illustrated baseball books on a regular basis and gave publishers the courage to trot out some huge illustrated baseball books with price tags to match: *Topps Baseball Cards* (1985) and its companion volume, *Classic Baseball Cards: The Golden Years 1886–1956* (1987), both of which retailed for $80; *Baseball: A Treasury of Art and Literature* (1993) which retailed for $75; and *Baseball: An Illustrated History* by Geoffrey C. Ward and Ken Burns (1994), which retailed for $60. Other photography books showcased the work of single practitioners, such as Walter Iooss Jr. (*Baseball*, 1984; and *Classic Baseball: The Photography of Walter Iooss Jr.*, 2003), John Weiss (*The Face of Baseball*, 1990), George Brace (*The Game that Was: The George Brace Baseball Photo Collection*, 1996), Ron C. Modra (*Reflections of the Game: Lives in Baseball*, 1998), Ozzie Sweet (*Mickey Mantle: The Yankee Years: The Classic Photography of Ozzie Sweet*, 1998; and *The Boys of Spring: Timeless Portraits from the Grapefruit League, 1947–2005*, 2005), and the incomparable Charles Conlon (*Baseball's Golden Age: The Photographs of Charles M. Conlon*, 1993). Scads of illustrated team histories appeared — Donald Honig was a one-man illustrated team history industry — and Bruce Chadwick authored a delightful series of team histories that were illustrated by David M. Spindell's photos of memorabilia-type items associated with each team; *The Boston Red Sox: Memories and Memorabilia of New England's Team* and *The Bronx Bombers: Memories and Memorabilia of the New York Yankees* were the first two volumes in the series to appear, both in 1992. Finally, authors and publishers began using photobiographies as the most complimentary way of telling a player's life story. Four different photo-bios of Ted Williams appeared (*Ted Williams: A Portrait in Words and Pictures* by Dick Johnson and Glenn Stout, 1991; *Ted Williams: The Seasons of the Kid* by Richard Ben Cramer, 1991; *Ted Williams: A Tribute* by Jim Prime and Bill Nowlin, 1997; and *Ted Williams: My Life in Pictures* by Ted Williams with David Pietrusza, 2001), but the best of the bunch were volumes devoted to Babe Ruth (*The Babe: A Life in Pictures* by Lawrence S. Ritter and Mark Rucker, 1988), Nolan Ryan (*Nolan Ryan: The Authorized Pictorial History* edited by D. Kent Pingel, 1991), Jackie Robinson (*Jackie Robinson: An Intimate Portrait* by Rachel Robinson with Lee Daniels, 1996), and Kirk Gibson (*Bottom of the Ninth*, by Kirk Gibson with Lynn Henning, 1997).

When the first edition of *The Baseball Encyclopedia* was released in 1969, it instantly became the King of Records Books. Every library had to have a copy, as well as every pub where sports fans gathered, and baseball bibliophiles routinely identified it as "the book I would take to a desert island if I were allowed to take only one baseball book with me." Producing a book that could challenge the unquestioned ascendancy of *The Baseball Encyclopedia* was thought to be the literary equivalent of running the suicide squeeze play ... with a blindfolded batter (!), but John Thorn and Pete Palmer pulled off the dare-devilish stunt in 1989 with the publication of the first edition of *Total Baseball*. Thorn went into the project operating under the assumption that the title of the Macmillan *Baseball Encyclopedia* was a misnomer, as indeed it was. *The Baseball Encyclopedia* was not an encyclopedia at all but, as Thorn put it, "a big fat records book." *Total Baseball* was not a true encyclopedia either, but it was an amazingly comprehensive compilation of factual information with close to 700 pages of essays and articles on a wide variety of topics, such as team histories, foreign-born players, mascots and superstitions, scandals and controversies, streaks and feats, Japanese baseball, college baseball, trades and free agency, concessions, and baseball betting. The book was also, like the Macmillan *Encyclopedia*, a big fat records book, but *Total Baseball* offered the additional appeal of new statistics that had been created by sabermetricians, such as Bill James' Runs Created and Tom Boswell's Total Average. This brash coup by Thorn and Palmer did not cause the extinction of its rival, but it did enthrone their champion side-by-side with the formerly solitary king.

Despite the massive amount of information contained in these two supreme baseball record books, and flying in the face of the skeptics bemoaning the surfeit of baseball books in general, baseball reference books became a pillar of the genre in the 1980s and beyond. Even before *Total Baseball*, *The Baseball Encyclopedia* had competition: *The Sports Encyclopedia: Baseball* edited originally by David S. Neft, Richard M. Cohen, and Bert Sugar and published by St. Martin's. Although the Neft and Cohen book, as it came to be called, did not cause near as big a splash as *Total Baseball*, many fans found it useful for its arrangement of material, especially the year-by-year complete team rosters of every team, and its paperback format made it financially attractive to the budget-minded. Like *The Baseball Encyclopedia* and *Total Baseball*, *The Sports Encyclopedia: Baseball*, first published in 1974, has gone through numerous editions, whereby all the records, statistics, and entries are updated. Each edition of *Total Baseball*, it should be noted, has also contained articles and essays on new topics not found in previous editions.

Several of the other reference books released during these years represented landmark events in the history of baseball books. First and foremost, Grobani's *Guide to Baseball Literature* which appeared in 1975 charted the baseball book landscape for the first time and uncovered numerous long-forgotten obscurities. Coming as it did from a respected publisher of reference books (Gale Research Company), the Grobani book also cast baseball books as a subject to be taken seriously, and it became an immediate boon to librarians, researchers, writers, collectors, and used and rare book dealers; especially those dealers specializing in baseball books, such as Bobby Plapinger, who circulated his initial baseball book catalog (actually more of a list than a catalog) in 1986. SABR members were justifiably proud when their organization published in a magazine-sized softcover format Philip J. Lowry's *Green Cathedrals* (1986), the first research-derived compilation of basic data (dates, locations, measurements, tenants, etc.) on all ballparks used by major league and Negro League teams. Lowry's seminal work was later re-published in hardcover by trade publisher Addison-Wesley (1992), and the subject received an additional boost when McFarland published Michael Benson's sweeping *Ballparks of North America: A Comprehensive Historical Reference to Baseball Grounds, Yards and Stadiums, 1845 to Present*. Marc Okkonen took on the fascinating subject of baseball uniforms, which had previously been virtually untouched, and in 1991 published his great illustrated chronicle *Baseball Uniforms of the 20th Century*. *Professional Baseball Franchises: From the Abbeville Athletics to the Zanesville Indians* (1993) by Peter Filichia; *SABR Presents the Home Run Record Encyclopedia: The Who, What, and Where of Every Home Run Hit Since 1876* (1996) edited by Bob McConnell and

David Vincent; and *Baseball by the Numbers: A Guide to the Uniform Numbers of Major League Teams* (1997) by Mark Stang and Linda Harkness were other groundbreaking references of immense utility to others that resulted from visionary and laborious research. These books attested, as no other type of book did, to the fans' insatiable thirst for baseball knowledge, and many other valuable baseball references have been published, including, but certainly not limited to: *Baseball: A Comprehensive Bibliography* (1986) by Myron J. Smith; *The Dickson Baseball Dictionary* (1989) by Paul Dickson; *Everything Baseball* (1989) by James Mote; *The Ballplayers* (1990) edited by Mike Shatzkin; *The Whole Baseball Catalog: The Ultimate Guide to the Baseball Marketplace* (1990) by John Thorn and Bob Carroll; *Baseball by the Books: A History and Complete Bibliography of Baseball Fiction* (1991) by Andy McCue; *The Baseball Chronology: The Complete History of the Most Important Events in the Game of Baseball* (1991) edited by James Charlton; *Baseball Nicknames* (1992) by John C. Skipper; *The Encyclopedia of Minor League Baseball* (1993) by Lloyd Johnson and Miles Wolff; *The Biographical Encyclopedia of the Negro Baseball Leagues* (1994) by James C. Riley; *The Baseball Timeline: The Day-by-Day History of Baseball, from Valley Forge to the Present Day* (1997) by Burt Solomon; *The Cultural Encyclopedia of Baseball* (1997) by Jonathan Fraser Light; *The Great Encyclopedia of 19th Century Major League Baseball* (1997) by David Nemec; *Japanese Baseball: A Statistical Handbook* (1999) by Daniel E. Johnson; *The Complete Book of Baseball's Negro Leagues: The Other Half of Baseball History* (2001) by John Holway; and *The Midsummer Classic: The Complete History of Baseball's All-Star Game* (2001) by David Vincent, Lyle Spatz, and David W. Smith. The deepest baseball fanship is always rooted in loyalty to a particular team (and/or player) and Mark Gallagher had the brainstorm of compiling an encyclopedic records book that would be devoted to his favorite team, the New York Yankees. *The Yankees Encyclopedia*, a 500-page tome first published in 1982 by Leisure Press, has gone through several revised and updated editions, and it inspired a series of similar volumes on other teams, most notably *The Phillies Encyclopedia* (1983) by Rich Westcott and Frank Bilovsky.

Finally, although the editors of some of the biggest houses, who always seem to be looking for a magic publishing formula based on the latest best-seller, did not grasp it, recent seasons have proven that there are as

1. A Short History of Baseball Books

many paths to publishing successful baseball books as there are pitches in a World Series. Greg Rhodes, for instance, could not find a publisher interested in doing books about his hometown, "small market" Cincinnati Reds, so he started his own company to do just that. Road West Publishing started in 1994 with *The First Boys of Summer: The 1869–1870 Cincinnati Red Stockings, Baseball's First Professional Team* and went on from there to publish five more outstanding Reds books: *Crosley Field: An Illustrated History of a Classic Ballpark* (1995); *Big Red Dynasty: How Bob Howsam and Sparky Anderson Built the Big Red Machine* (1997); *Reds in Black & White: 100 Years of Cincinnati Reds Images* (1999); *Redleg Journal: Year by Year and Day by Day with the Cincinnati Reds Since 1866* (2000); and *Opening Day: Celebrating Cincinnati's Baseball Holiday* (2004). These rigorously-researched, well-written volumes paid off for Rhodes both economically and professionally, as his reputation as the Reds' unofficial historian made him the obvious choice when the position of Director for the Reds' new Hall of Fame & Museum needed to be filled.

Arcadia Publishing also saw an opening in the lineup and hustled into the action. Specializing in illustrated histories of small towns and cities since its founding in 1993, Arcadia discovered that its 128-page/approximately 200-photo format is perfect for conveying lively presentations of numerous baseball stories. Its "Images of Baseball" series includes volumes on topics as diverse as *Grand Junction's Juco World Series* by Myles Schrag, *Notre Dame Baseball Greats: From Anson to Yaz* by Cappy Gagnon, and *Playing for Time: The Death Row All Stars* by Chris Enss (all published in 2004); but the staple of the Series are the histories of minor league baseball played in cities, such as Asheville, Bridgeport, Chillicothe (OH), Columbia (SC), Columbus (OH), Dallas, Eau Claire, Fort Worth, Greenville and Spartanburg, Indianapolis, Little Rock, Louisville, Mobile, New Orleans, Newark, Oklahoma City, Omaha, Portsmouth (VA), South Bend, and Wichita.

Uncounted new baseball titles, such as *Sut McCaslin: A Baseball Romance* by Steve Spoerl (2000), have also been made available all through the 1990s by on-demand publishers, an economical and less-stigmatized form of vanity publishing. On-demand publishers, such as iUniverse, Trafford Publishing, and Book Surge Publishing, typeset a book for a nominal fee (usually several hundred dollars), print three or four copies for the author, and after that print additional copies of the book one-at-a-time as they are ordered. Some baseball books printed by traditional vanity publishers were not without merit; and vanity-published books such as *Baseball's Great Tragedy* by Bob McGarigle (1972); *20 Years Too Soon* by Quincy Trouppe (1977); and *The Gabby Hartnett Story* by James M. Murphy (1983) are highly collectible books today because they are quite hard to find. Theoretically, books from on-demand publishers should never enjoy the kind of price increase associated with scarcity; but once an on-demand publisher goes out of business, all bets are off in regard to the prices of the baseball books the defunct on-demand publisher once published one copy at a time. In addition, readers may be surprised at the quality of some of the baseball books published via the on-demand process. For example, highly respected baseball thinker and commentator Rob Neyer wrote a book about the Boston Red Sox and then ran into an unresolvable conflict with the traditional publisher which had the book under contract. As a result, *Feeding the Green Monster* was released in 2001 by Time Warner Books' on-demand publishing arm, iPublish.

Finally, no one should fear that the hey day of baseball books is coming to an end any time soon. Recent years have shown that baseball will continue to supply talented authors with all the material they need to fashion books of lasting value. After a shelf full of hagiographies, we thought we knew Joe DiMaggio. With his intrusive, scathing, iconoclastic bombshell, *Joe DiMaggio: The Hero's Life* (2000), Richard Ben Cramer showed us there was another side to the great Yankee center fielder. *The Oldest Rookie: Big League Dreams from a Small-Town Guy* (2001) by Jim Morris and Joel Engel was the beautifully-told story of the billion-to-one shot coming in. It had "major motion picture" written all over it, and that million-to-one shot came in too. With all the attention that had been showered on Jackie Robinson and the other black players who followed immediately in his footsteps, what more was there to say about the integration of baseball? Plenty, as it turned out, which Howard Bryant showed us with *Shut Out: A Story of Race and Baseball in Boston* (2002). In a book as sweet and touching as Cramer's biography of DiMaggio was disgusting and disappointing, David Halberstam told the story of Ted Williams' buddies making one final road trip to see their dying comrade in *Teammates: A Portrait of a Friendship* (2003). We had no business expecting any further "big books" about such over-worked baseball immortals; but then Leigh Montville and Jonathan Eig produced superlative biographies, *Ted Williams: The Biography of an American Hero* (2004) and *Luckiest Man: The Life and Death of Lou Gehrig* (2005), respectively, that provided fresh perspectives on the subjects and instilled in us renewed appreciation for them. And then, what of Michael Lewis' 2003 blockbuster, *Moneyball: The Art of Winning an Unfair Game*, the engrossing, controversial, inflammatory inside look at Oakland A's general manager Billy Beane and his anti-traditional methods of scouting, player evaluation, and contender-building? It was praised for being not only "the single most influential baseball book ever" (*Slate*), but also for being what "may be the best book ever written on business" (*Weekly Standard*). Clearly, the satisfaction that can be derived from the best baseball books published each year is as sure a bet as this uncertain world offers, and the only thing better than the past is what awaits the baseball bibliophile in the future.

2

WHICH BASEBALL BOOKS TO COLLECT

"In literature, as in love, we are astonished at what is chosen by others"—Andre Maurois

The simple answer to the question posed in the title of this chapter is "One should collect whichever baseball books one wishes to collect." This is not at all a facetious reply, as there is nothing more appropriately personal than a person's hobby; however, in real ways the answer is also unsatisfactory, as it implies a vagueness and arbitrariness that is certain if permitted to rule over one's acquisition choices to result in a collection that is disorganized, less pleasurable to the owner than it might be, and worth less than the sum of its parts. A collection of baseball books, like a collection of almost anything as varied and numerous as baseball books, needs to have a focus, and the collector needs to have a collecting plan. A focused collection is a better collection; it will attain a stature a collection lacking focus will not have; and when it comes time to sell the collection — and this time always comes, if not for the collector himself, then for his heirs — the focused collection should bring a better return than its counterpart. For all these reasons, the collector should know why he is adding every book he adds to his collection.

In order to have this knowledge, the collector must first deal with the key question of this chapter: Is he going to be a Completist or a Specialist? (Some may prefer to use the term "Generalist" as a more proper antonym to Specialist, but I prefer to use Completist because I think it approximates more closely the way many collectors actually proceed.)

2. Which Baseball Books to Collect

In all but the rarest of cases, true completist collecting at this point in time is actually a fantasy, a situation in which the baseball book collector deludes himself, as he has neither the money nor the space to even come close to achieving his goal. Even for large institutional libraries, such as the Library of Congress, the New York Public Library, and the National Baseball Library in Cooperstown, which have enormous budgets and resources compared to those of most individuals, completist collecting is an ideal and an attitude, more than a literal goal with an expectation that it will be achieved.

And this is nothing to be depressed about. Even if one could be a true completist, it's not a capability to be desired because there are a lot of "bad" baseball books (books which are erroneous, poorly written, or graphically dull) and just as many redundant baseball books, as well as books on subjects of absolutely no interest, which do not add anything significant to one's collection. Such books are not worthy of inclusion in a well-thought out and carefully maintained collection because they take up valuable space and can deny a book that is worthy its proper place.

Nevertheless, the fact is that most collectors start out with a Completist attitude ... with the goal of adding to their collection every baseball book they see which they don't already own. Indeed, that's how most collections acquire such large quantities of baseball book flotsam and jetsam in the first place; however, at some point would-be Completists realize the futility and illogic of such a practice. They usually then become Completists with limits, which is to say that they become Specialists: collectors who try to acquire every book within or related to a defined area (or areas) of interest.

Such collectors usually make the shift from Completist to Specialist subconsciously or at least without thinking very hard about the switch in philosophy. Moreover, they usually shift into a "Best Books" or "Books Which Interest Me the Most" mode of collecting. The resulting collections are obviously not nearly as focused as more narrowly specialized collections, but they are more focused, realistically assembled, and manageable than those constructed from a purely Completist perspective.

So, for all but the rarest of collectors with very deep pockets as well as very, very long shelves, it's not really a question of *if* one should be a Specialist rather than a Completist, but of *how* one should specialize.

There are at least five basic ways to specialize in baseball book collecting: by author; genre; topic; publishing era; classics.

Obviously, these are not mutually exclusive categories, and there is always going to be some overlap, in the sense that in most cases the same book could easily fall within the parameters of the collections defined by more than one of these ways of specializing. And, it goes without saying, every collector is free to employ more than one of these methods.

Collecting by author is the specialty likely to produce the smallest collection, but one way around this disadvantage — I say "disadvantage" because it's human nature to want more of a good thing, not less — is to collect more than one author, perhaps as many as a dozen or so. Specializing in several authors multiplies ones pleasures, as well as the challenges; and the latter are not always as inconsequential as one may think. Depending on the author, some of his books may be tough to find, especially in pristine condition; however, specializing in an author allows one to take the time to properly investigate his career and canon and become fully aware of his total output. Although this is a book about books, I would be remiss if I did not point out that author collectors often widen the scope of their collection to include more personal literary items associated with the author, such as manuscripts, diaries, and letters, as well as everything published by their author, including newspaper and magazine articles, book reviews, essays, short stories, pamphlets, excerpts in anthologies, and other types of ephemera. Going into this kind of depth ups the ante considerably and actually even puts dedicated baseball author collectors in the position of being able to assemble bibliographies of their authors. Author collecting also frees up money that can be used to acquire expensive books that collectors with broader interests and the same budget have to forego, a huge advantage and satisfaction.

A second way to specialize one's baseball book collection is to collect books by genre. With this method, one collects *types* of baseball books regardless of the book's author or topic or even, perhaps, its quality. The two most popular genres focused on by baseball book collectors are fiction and record/statistics books. Genre collectors are guided so steadfastly by the criterion of type that they sometimes add books to their collection which they have no intention of ever reading. This is especially true for the collectors of genres with the largest number of books, such as adult baseball fiction, and doubly true for the collectors of juvenile baseball fiction. Other genres with significant appeal for baseball book collectors are general histories, biographies, oral histories, instructionals, photography books, and poetry.

Specializing by topic is something that almost every collector of baseball books does to some extent, and it is usually not very difficult to discern a collector's particular baseball interest(s) by examining the books in his collection. One way to specialize by topic is to collect books about a certain team, and the typical collector at least keeps an eye out for books about his favorite team. Furthermore, many baseball fans who are not baseball book collectors per se make books about their favorite team part of their overall team collections. As with author collecting, specializing by topic should allow the collector more opportunities to go after the scarcer and costlier books, which when added to his collection begin to distinguish it from collections pervaded by common titles. Several topics have been popular with both collectors and publishers (who respond to collectors' buying decisions) for a number of years, such as ballparks, Latin baseball, and the Negro Leagues. While these topics may remain popular, it is likely that other topics may also begin to gather momentum. The following is a list of common baseball book collecting topics, and the asterisks following some of them indicate what are in my opinion the ones with the greatest chance of becoming "hot topics" in the near future.

- Adult Fiction
- All-Star Games/World Series
- Amateur Baseball
- Kids Baseball/Little League*
- Ballparks
- Biographies
- Broadcasters
- Business/Labor Issues
- Canadian Baseball*
- College Baseball*
- Eras (e.g., the 1920s)
- Geography (i.e., books related to a particular region, state, locality, hometown)

- The Hall of Fame & Hall of Fame Players
- Independent Professional Baseball*
- International Baseball*
- Japanese Baseball*
- Juvenile Fiction
- Latin Baseball
- Managers
- Memorabilia & Baseball Cards
- Minor Leagues
- Nineteenth Century*
- Negro Leagues
- Olympic Baseball*
- Oral Histories
- Owners & Executives
- Poetry
- Photography
- Picture Books* (i.e., illustrated children's books)
- Positions (e.g., books about catchers & catching)
- Scandals
- Special Achievements (e.g., 300-win pitchers; players who hit record-breaking home runs)
- Teams (i.e., particular teams, such as the New York Yankees)
- Women in baseball

    A fourth way to specialize a collection of baseball books is to collect by a particular era. This is not the same as collecting by topic, whereby one looks for books *about* a certain era. What is meant in this case is collecting books (about any and every baseball topic) *from* a certain era; in other words, the books that were published during a particular period of time. Naturally, this method of collecting is likely to be used by someone particularly interested in the era during which the books collected were published, and it is likely as well that such a collector also collects books about the era. The point of collecting books from, not merely about, an era though is that the books have a historical value as artifacts of their time period which can connect a collector to that time in a way contemporary books cannot. The farther back an era and its books go, the more powerful the connection between the collector and the books as artifacts, and so it is not surprising that many collectors who use this approach focus on baseball books published in the 19th century. Of course, there are other important and intriguing eras, such as the 1920s and the 1950s, which attract their share of collectors.

Finally, there is the most common approach of all, which is to collect the "Classics." In regard to literature in general, an honest definition of classic might be "those books which most everybody recognizes as famous and important but which nobody reads anymore." Such a definition won't do in regard to the concept of classic baseball books, which we presume the collector always desires to read (at least once), but an equally simple one may suffice; namely, that by "classic" baseball books we mean nothing more than "the best books." Obviously, best books, which is as subjective a term as "pretty girl," would not advance our knowledge very far either if there were not some more concrete ways of telling just which baseball books deserve to be considered the best. Fortunately, there are at least four things which can help us identify baseball classics: the lists and recommendations of authorities or experts; the recipients of baseball book awards; reviews of baseball books by qualified reviewers; and the consideration of reprinting as an indication of quality.

Let us examine each of these four means of identifying classic baseball books and let us begin with the lists and recommendations of authorities.

The first significant attempt to identify great baseball books was made by George R. Kaplan in a witty article that appeared in the Winter 1984 edition of *The Minneapolis Review of Baseball*. Although Kaplan entitled the article "The Absolutely Indispensible Irreducible 25-Book Baseball Library," he actually recommends 68 books; the numerical difference being merely another example of Kaplan's flippant, sarcastic writing style. The sarcasm of the piece aside, Kaplan's picks are "Indisputedly Inauguarbly Perceptive" with the possible exception of a few seldom heralded titles, such as *Sports Illusion, Sports Reality* by Leonard Koppett, *Government and the Sports Business* edited by Roger G. Noll, and *Steinbrenner* by Dick Schaap.

The first widely-circulated attempt to identify great baseball books appeared in 1985 in *The Bill James Historical Baseball Abstract*, a penetrating mountain of historical research and statistical analysis. There is no single list of books in *TBJHBA*; rather the recommendations are seeded throughout the first section of the book ("The Game," which takes a decade-by-decade approach to baseball history) in a "Decade in a Box" feature (e.g., "The 1930s in a Box"). Each "Decade in a Box" is a series of "small questions with short answers," which detail superlatives ("Most Aggressive Baserunner") and pieces of off-beat information ("Drinking Men"). "Best Baseball Books" is one of the categories found in every "Decade in a Box."

For the most part, the book recommendations in *The Bill James Historical Baseball Abstract* are made not by Bill James, but by his buddy Jim Carothers, who at the time was (and may still be today) a teacher of English literature at the University of Kansas. In most instances, Carothers' picks for each decade are merely listed under the "Best Baseball Books" heading in each "Decade in a Box"; however, beginning with the 1940s he adds brief commentary about his picks later in each chapter. It is in these commentary sections that James adds his own comments and picks, such as *Judge Landis and Twenty-Five Years of Baseball* and *Nice Guys Finish Last*. For "The 1920s in a Box" Carothers' response to "Best Baseball Books" is "None." Later in the chapter James offers the following explanation: "Jim Carothers, asked to name the best baseball books of each decade, responds, 'If I were writing the history of baseball literature, there would be few, if any, selections from the twenties and thirties, many more from the sixties and seventies.'" At the end of the last chapter in Section 1: The Game, "The 1970s," Carothers contributes four additional lists: 1) important American novels with baseball allusions, 2) "Good Recent Baseball Books," 3) baseball fiction that has been turned into movies, and 4) "Some Good Baseball Books Nobody Talks About."

Overall, Carothers' picks show good judgment, despite his claiming (without offering any support for the claim) that two of his selections, *Ball Four* and *The Boys of Summer*, are "Overrated." James, by the way, states that he does not endorse Carothers' opinion of the two books.

In 1987 "The Essential Baseball Library" was published in the second volume of *The SABR Review of Books*. This list was an expansion of a phone survey, done the year before and undertaken to answer the question "What Baseball Books Do You Return to Most Often?" The eleven participants in the phone survey whose responses were published in the first volume of *The SABR Review of Books* were: Roger Angell, Marty Appel, Joe Garagiola, Bill James, Leonard Koppett, Tony Kubek, Dan Okrent, Pete Palmer, Larry Ritter, Allan Roth, and Dan Schlossberg. To come up with "The Essential Baseball Library" editor Paul Adomites conducted and synthesized the responses of a written survey, which invited 50 select SABR members to submit lists of their favorite fifty baseball books. The twenty-three members (including Adomites himself) who decided to participate in the survey were: Dick Beverage, Alan Blumkin, Bill Borst, Jack Carlson, Jon Daniels, Jay Feldman, Cappy Gagnon, Mark Gallagher, Bob Hoie, Lloyd Johnson, Tom Jozwik, Jack Kavanagh, Phil Lowry, Vern Luse, John Pardon, Frank Phelps, Larry Ritter, Louis Rubin, Leverett T. Smith, Adie Suehsdorf, Jules Tygiel, and David Voigt. In the end, while more than 200 books were mentioned by the respondents, 57 titles made the final cut (to be listed, a work had to be nominated by more than three participants). Although Adomites did not ask the participants to pick books by category, he published "The Essential Baseball Library" with the books divided into the following groups: Statistics, History, Team Histories, In Their Own League (sort of a miscellaneous category), Fiction (*Shoeless Joe* and *The Natural* are the only two books in this category), The Minors, Biography/Autobiography, Anthologies and Collections, Negro Leagues, and Ballparks. "The Essential Baseball Library" actually contains more than 57 books, as several multi-volume titles (such as David Voigt's *American Baseball*) and the "Putnam team histories" are counted as single entities. In a number of instances, Adomites includes the comments that accompanied the selections of the participants, as well as his own comments on the results of the survey. "Not surprisingly," he says, "the two works mentioned most often were *The Macmillan Baseball Encyclopedia* and Lawrence Ritter's *The Glory of Their Times*."

In September of 1987 *Sports Illustrated* published a long article about the sports books business by Jack McCallum called "Jock Lit." Towards the end of the article, McCallum presents two lists ("Fifteen Books that Everybody Says Should be in Your Sports Library" and "Ten Others that You Shouldn't Miss Either"), which include the following baseball titles: *The Long Season, Ball Four, The Boys of Summer, Veeck as in Wreck, The Summer Game, Babe, The Glory of Their Times, Bang the Drum Slowly, A*

False Spring, Eight Men Out, The Armchair Book of Baseball, Out of My League, and *The Celebrant.*

Two years after the publication of "The Essential Baseball Library" my own *Diamond Classics: Essays on 100 of the Best Baseball Books Ever Published* appeared. As far as I know, it was the first and it remains the only book-length attempt to identify, summarize, and evaluate great baseball books. Published in hardcover by McFarland, *Diamond Classics* was originally supposed to include essays on up to 200 books; however, as the time spent on the project (three years) and the number of pages (455) in the book lengthened, publisher Robert Franklin and I agreed that we would cut the thing off at around 100 essays. There are actually 102 essays in the book, a detail no reviewer has ever taken note of.

I made no attempt to rank the books included in *Diamond Classics,* and so the essays, which run from three to more than six pages in length, are arranged alphabetically by title. For each title in the book I included a complete bibliographic description (including subsequent editions of the title) and a list of other baseball books written by the author. For most titles I also included one or two excerpts from reviews of the books, a feature we called the "Critical Reception." For some books I included digressive but interesting information in "Comments"; and we used black & white photos of 23 of the books' dust jackets to illustrate the book.

In the introduction to the book I identified three criteria I used in determining which books to include in *Diamond Classics*: 1) the book's relative availability, 2) the book's level of interest to the average reader, and 3) the book's contribution to the field of baseball literature. Readers interested in an explanation of these criteria should consult the introduction of *Diamond Classics*; suffice it to say here that I acknowledged "the personal nature of the selections—notwithstanding the absolutely indisputable stature of many of the titles." Since all but two of the books included in *Diamond Classics* were published after 1950, I also thought it fair to say that my work was a book about "modern baseball literature."

With the advent of the new and improved *Spitball* in 1993, I began a serial continuation of *Diamond Classics* in the pages of the literary baseball magazine I co-founded in 1981. As a large number of outstanding baseball books have been published since 1989, an update of the book is definitely overdue.

2. Which Baseball Books to Collect

In the same year that *Diamond Classics* was published, Paul Adomites presented in the first edition of *Total Baseball* (edited by John Thorn and Pete Palmer) the most extensive list of recommended baseball books ever published. To assemble his annotated list which he calls "The Ultimate Baseball Library," Adomites attempted to identify "the best books in each of the areas of baseball writing" without regard to a book's availability or its monetary value. "The Ultimate Baseball Library" includes 444 titles distributed into 18 categories: Statistics; General History; Team Histories; Fiction/Humor/Drama/Verse; The Minors; Biography — Collective; Biography — Players; Biography — Managers; Biography — Executives; Anthologies and Collections, Anecdotes and Reminiscences; Negro Leagues; Ballparks; Guides/Record Books/Annuals/Dictionaries; Umpires and Umpiring; Instructionals; Pictorials; World Series and All-Star Games; and Miscellaneous. Given Adomites' pre-selection adoption of categories and his decision to make the entire baseball book universe eligible for inclusion, the expansiveness of his list is hardly surprising. Nor is it surprising, given the fact that Adomites acknowledges the help of many friends in the Society for American Baseball Research (particularly that of Frank Phelps and other members of the SABR Bibliography Committee), that the list contains what some collectors would consider to be an over abundance of the type of records and statistics books which are of interest mainly to those involved in research. Despite these quibbles, "The Ultimate Baseball Library" is an outstanding and seminal list that can be of great value to any collector.

Baseball fiction lovers may feel, with some justification, that the novel is not properly represented in most of the lists and works under discussion here. The clear exception to this oversight is "Baseball's Dozen best Adult Novels," which editor Peter C. Bjarkman included in *Baseball & The Game of Life*: a collection of 15 baseball short stories (some new, some reprinted) originally published in 1990 by Birch Brook Press. Bjarkman supplemented this initial list with another one called "Fifty Recommended Baseball Novels," and it is difficult to think of any serious omissions of worthy candidates published up to that time from the two lists combined. In a nod of recognition towards another often-overlooked genre of baseball books, Bjarkman also included in *Baseball & The Game of Life* a list of 15 "Baseball Literature Anthologies."

The Whole Baseball Catalogue (John Thorn and Bob Carroll, eds.) was also published in 1990, and it too contained annotated lists of baseball book recommendations, compiled and written by Lloyd Johnson. In a chapter called "Going by the Book," which also contains advice on how to become a published baseball book author, Johnson presents three lists. In the first list he attempts to demonstrate that one could build "a well-balanced, informative, entertaining baseball library for $250." This shoe-string budget library consists of 16 volumes (14 of them in paperback form) which Johnson calculates would cost $237.70. Realizing that this "Poor Fan's Guide to Baseball Books" would satisfy none but the cheapest of cheapo collectors, he moves on to his other two, more substantial lists, one for non-fiction and one for fiction. The non-fiction list contains an additional 61 books (which he divides into Statistics and Records, History, Biography, Anthologies and Collections, and Miscellaneous), not counting the Putnam histories and annuals such as *The Bill James Baseball Abstracts* and *The Sporting News Guides* and *Registers*. The fiction list contains 21 novels and short story collections by Zane Grey (*The Red Headed Outfield and Other Baseball Stories*) and Charles E. Van Loan (*Score by Innings*). Johnson's comments on the books are regularly pithy and occasionally wry.

In *Memories of Summer: When Baseball Was an Art, and Writing about It a Game* (published in 1997), Roger Kahn says that he doesn't enjoy reviewing books (the few reviews he's done "have been more trouble than they were worth"). Nor does he relish evaluating baseball books, a process he likens to composing a term paper, "which was, for me at least, a wretched form of writing."

Nevertheless, the great Kahn concludes *Memories of Summer*, a remarkably vivid and memorable account of his involvement in the baseball newspaper writing business in the 1950s, with an annotated list of his favorite baseball books, which he calls "The Golden Dozen." Two notes of interest about his list: 1) Kahn ranks his selections ... *Nice Guys Finish Last* and *Bang the Drum Slowly* tie for first place; and 2) places #9 and #10 in his list are taken by "any collection of pieces by John Lardner or Red Smith." By the way, the books by these two authors which Kahn mentions are not devoted exclusively to baseball (*It Beats Working* and *Strong Cigars and Lovely Women* by Lardner and *Out of the Red* and *Strawberries in the Wintertime* by Smith).

2. Which Baseball Books to Collect

Towards the end of 1999 a coffee-table style history of American sports in the twentieth century called *ESPN SportsCentury* appeared. The book was a companion to a television series of the same name, and the strategy of both the book and the television series was to trace the evolution of American sports by identifying and profiling the 100 greatest athletes of the century. The ten-chapter book takes a decade-by-decade approach, with each chapter consisting of: 1) a major profile of the athlete deemed to best represent the decade; 2) shorter profiles of other athletes prominent in the decade; and 3) a "Playbook" section, a hodge-podge of information about things such as classic games and events, champions in major sports, coaches, "Influences," and "Debuts and Exits." The "Time Capsule" part of the "Playbook" section is devoted to cultural matters, such as movies, "Fashion" (i.e., uniforms), politics, television, and "Reading List." Although editor Michael MacCambridge mentions many contributors in the "Acknowledgements," he does not say who, if anyone, helped him decide which baseball books were worth mentioning in the "Reading List" parts of each chapter. It should be pointed out that, in keeping with the historical/evolutionary thrust of the book, there is no attempt to compile anything even close to a comprehensive list of best baseball books in ESPN SportsCentury. What the book's "Reading List" does is mention books (both baseball and otherwise), writing, and publication events (such as the inauguration of various important sports periodicals) which are representative of the best things of their kind that were produced in each decade. Baseball books get the most notice in the chapter on the 1970s, which is described as "arguably, the true golden era for sports journalism." In the "Reading List" for this decade seven baseball books are mentioned: *Ball Four*, *The Boys of Summer*, *The Summer Game*, *Babe*, *Only the Ball Was White*, *The Bingo Long Traveling All-Stars and Motor Kings*, and *Nice Guys Finish Last*.

In 2002 *The National Baseball Hall of Fame and Museum Desk Reference* by Lawrence Lorimer appeared, and one of the most interesting parts of the 608-page tome is Lorimer's list of recommended baseball books. After a one-page introduction in which he is careful to state that "This list is necessarily selective," Lorimer presents his annotated choices, grouped into eight categories: Statistics and Reference; History; Players and Insiders; How to Play, How to Watch; Reflections and Reporting; Anthologies,

Humor, Miscellaneous; Fiction; and Children's and Young-Adult Fiction. Inside each category, the selections are arranged alphabetically by author's last name. In the Children's and Young-Adult Fiction section, Lorimer includes the series of YA baseball novels written by Clair Bee and John R. Tunis, specifically mentioning only *Strike Three* (by Bee) and *The Kid from Tompkinsville* (by Tunis). Although decidedly contemporary and somewhat sketchy, Lorimer's is a solid list.

Finally, in their issue for December 16, 2002, the editors of *Sports Illustrated* presented their picks for "The Top 100 Sports Books of All Time." While a boxing book (*The Sweet Science* by A. J. Liebling) claimed the number one spot in this annotated list, baseball definitely took top overall honors, as 30 of the 100 selected titles were baseball books. The most surprising thing about the list is the appreciation shown by the *SI* editors for baseball fiction, as nearly a third of the baseball books they named as their favorites are novels. The following are the 30 baseball books which made the *SI* "Top 100" list, with the book's ranking in parentheses: *The Boys of Summer* (2), *Ball Four* (3), *You Know Me, Al* (5), *Bang the Drum Slowly* (14), *The Summer Game* (18), *The Long Season* (19), *The Natural* (24), *Babe* (27), *Joe DiMaggio: The Hero's Life* (31), *Veeck as in Wreck* (33), *A False Spring* (37), *The Unforgettable Season* (41), *The Celebrant* (42), *The Bill James Historical Baseball Abstract* (44), *Shoeless Joe* (47), *Eight Men Out* (49), *Baseball's Great Experiment* (50), *Dollar Sign on the Muscle* (52), *The Bronx Zoo* (53), *The Baseball Encyclcopedia* (55), *The Glory of Their Times* (57), *The Complete Armchair Book of Baseball* (58), *Lords of the Realm* (60), *The Universal Baseball Association* (61), *Only the Ball Was White* (74), *The Great American Novel* (78), *Can't Anybody Here Play This Game?* (84), *The Science of Hitting* (86), *No Cheering in the Pressbox* (93), and *The Bingo Long Traveling All-Stars and Motor Kings* (98).

None of these lists are the final answer for any collector in and of themselves. There are other lists and bibliographies of value too, such as Mark Rucker's run-down of illustrated baseball books in the Premiere Issue of *The SABR Review of Books (1986);* the reccomendations in "The Way I See It: Short Reactions to Important Baseball Book Topics," which appeared in the Summer 1989 issue of *Spitball: The Literary Baseball Magazine*; Larry Gerlach's 1994 survey of baseball histories in *The Journal of Sport History*; and Barry Sloate's survey of rare and historical baseball books published in the September 1995 issue of *The Vintage & Classic Baseball Collector*. However, I strongly recommend a familiarity with the lists discussed here and a knowledge of their points of agreement.

Baseball book collectors seeking to identify the classics can also profit from studying which books have won the major baseball book awards, of which there are three: the Casey Award, the Seymour Medal, and the Dave Moore Award (Complete lists of the winners of these three baseball book awards appear in Appendix A).

The first award made specifically to honor baseball books (as well as the publishers of baseball books) was the Casey Award. Sponsored by *Spitball: The Literary Baseball Magazine* (first published in 1980), the first Casey was awarded in January of 1984 at the inaugural Casey Awards Banquet. Seven books were named as finalists for the first Casey (*Baseball's Great Experiment, The Celebrant, Hoopla, Invisible Men, Insider's Baseball, Take Me Out to the Ballpark,* and *Who's on 3rd? The Chicago White Sox Story*), and *The Celebrant* by Eric Rolfe Greenberg was chosen as the winner.

All types of baseball books are eligible for Casey Award nomination, and the nominated finalists are not divided into categories. There is only one Casey winner each year although "non-winning" finalists receive Nomination Awards. The editors of *Spitball* determine which books become nominated finalists for the Award, and the Casey is judged each year by a newly-seated panel of three judges who are independent of the magazine. (At this point, no judge has served more than once.) Judges are invited to serve based on their knowledge of and interest in baseball literature, and they are not paid. The judges are asked to determine which of the nominated finalists makes the greatest contribution to baseball literature, with "literature" being defined in the broadest sense. They are also instructed to use five criteria in assessing each nominated book: literary quality, analytical quality, informational content, originality, and artistic appeal. The judges do not meet or hold telephone conversations in order to come to a consensus. Rather, they vote independently of each other, filling out a ballot which ranks the nominated books from "best" to "least best" and returning the ballot to the editors of *Spitball*, who then tabulate the results of the three ballots in order to determine which book and author is the Casey winner. The actual Casey Award is a bronze plaque, embossed with the original Napoleon Lajoie-holding-a-quill pen logo of *Spitball Magazine*, which is itself mounted to a wooden plaque. Through 2005 there have been 23 Casey's awarded, and 220 books have been nominated for the Award.

The Seymour Medal, sponsored by the Society for American Baseball Research, is an award which honors the best book of baseball history or biography published during the preceding calendar year. Named after Dr. and Mrs. Harold Seymour, the award was the brain child of Thomas R. Heitz, the former Librarian of the National Baseball Library, and Lloyd Johnson, the former President of SABR. According to the award guidelines "To be considered for the medal, a work must be the product of original research or analysis. The winning book should significantly advance our knowledge of baseball and should be characterized by understanding, factual accuracy, profound insights and distinguished writing." Only one Seymour Medal per year is allowed to be awarded, and no medal is to be awarded "If, in the judgment of the awards committee, a worthy candidate cannot be found."

The Seymour Medal competition is judged by a committee of three SABR members who are appointed by the President and who serve three-year terms, which are staggered so that one person rotates off the committee each year. SABR solicits from publishers submissions of baseball books which may qualify for the award; any SABR member may make his own recommendations; and any member of the judging committee may add a book to the list of finalists to be judged. If a medal is to be awarded, the judging committee must select at least three books as finalists. At least six weeks before the medal is to be presented, the judges make their final selection by conferring among themselves, in person or via a conference call set up by the SABR office. The Seymour Medal is made of bronze, features the faces of Dr. and Mrs. Seymour in profile on its obverse, and is presented every spring at the annual Seymour Medal Conference held at Cleveland State University. The first Seymour Medal, for books published in 1996, was won by David Zang for *Fleet Walker's Divided Heart* (University of Nebraska Press).

The Dave Moore Award, sponsored by *Elysian Fields Quarterly*, was inaugurated in 1999 and is named after a Minneapolis television personality who was also a big supporter of the baseball magazine based in St.

Paul, Minnesota. According to the guidelines, the Dave Moore Award is to be presented to "the author of the most important work of literature on baseball from the previous year." More specifically, the guidelines state that "The 'most important' baseball book shall be one that uses baseball as a means to express our sense of who we are as a culture, as a society, and as individual human beings. Books eligible for this award are likely to come from the following categories of writing: A particularly brilliant use of original historical research; A significant look at an important figure or aspect of the game; A unique, memorable work of fiction. Because Dave Moore was not afraid of supporting unpopular causes, and willing to embrace the underdog, particular consideration will be given to emerging authors, especially those published by the small press."

Six finalists for the Award are chosen each year by a selection committee, and a jury panel of five makes the final decision. The Dave Moore Award is presented in February during the annual Ball Park Tours/EFQ Hot Stove League banquet in St. Paul, and the winner receives a commemorative plaque and a $100 honorarium. The winner of the first Dave Moore Award, for books published in 1999, was Roberto Gonzalez Echevarria for *The Pride of Havana: A History of Cuban Baseball* (Oxford University Press).

Book reviews are a third important source of opinions about baseball books ... or at least they can be when they are done well and under the right conditions. Such a qualification implies that all book reviews and book reviewers are not created equal. This is indeed the case, and to be able to easily tell the difference between the good and the bad it helps to actually have a philosophy of book reviewing. I have one, which I have formed after three decades of reading and writing reviews of baseball books, and I am happy to share it with you here.

The #1 rule of book reviewing is that the reviewer must actually review the book! Again, it may sound as if I'm being facetious, but Rule #1 is broken all the time, and usually in one of three ways. First, the "reviewer" doesn't bother to read the book — after all, reading books in their entirety is time consuming — but he still feels qualified to comment on it. Don't believe this happens? Then read carefully some brief "reviews" and ask yourself if the author of the piece could not have based his comments merely on a look at the table of contents, a quick thumb through the book, and perhaps the opinions of others who had read the book. The brevity of a review is not in itself an indictment, but lacking clear evidence of a strong familiarity with the content, argument, and details of a book, such a cursory "review" is not really a review; it is a mention.

The second type of bogus review is the one which is based on either the book's dust jacket blurb or the comments in the publisher's publicity release. Since the dust jacket is available to all while the publicity release is available only to those who have access to book review copies, it is more likely for the lazy or incompetent reviewer to borrow from the latter than the former in an attempt to hide his borrowings. In either case, and even when the lazy/incompetent reviewer has read the book, such "reviews" are next to useless.

Finally, while not fraudulent, the third type of non-review can be the most annoying of all, and it's what I call the "Show Off Review." In this case the reviewer has almost certainly read the book under discussion; the problem is that he doesn't tell us much about the book. Instead, he tells us everything he knows about the subject of the book (maddeningly, what he puts forward as his knowledge may have come from the book, but he doesn't say if it has or not) or ... he tells us how he would have written the book if it had been up to him to do so. And then he concludes what is invariably a lengthy piece of writing by adding, almost as an afterthought, something along the order of "Oh, yeah; so-and-so has written a book about this subject, and it's not bad, I guess."

Assuming a reviewer abides by Rule #1 and actually attempts to review the book under discussion, what constitutes a good review? What should a good review do, in other words? Several things, namely: it should define the book, as to its type or genre, if this is not obvious by the title; it should state the book's main idea, theme, or approach as soon as possible; it should summarize as much of the book as is needed for the reader to gain a basic understanding of the book; it should indicate how the book is different from similar, previously published works; it should point out serious flaws and deficiencies; and it should provide an overall evaluation of the book that is fair and unambiguous. As for dazzling displays of wit and writing ability, if the reviewer can provide these in addition to the essentials of a good review mentioned above, so much the better; but such displays are not a substitute for the essentials themselves.

Obviously, in order for someone to be able to review baseball books in the manner described above, he must be literate, but also knowledgeable about baseball and baseball books. In other words, he must be a qualified reviewer. Unfortunately, unqualified people sometimes review baseball books, especially in the pages of the nation's daily newspapers. Some editors still have "It's the Toy Dept." mentality about sportswriting and sports books, and so when it comes time to review a baseball book, the thought process is, "Hey, let's give it to Joe or to Sue. They've been to baseball games before." A dead give-away that the reviewer is unqualified is his gushing enthusiasm for a pedestrian book on an overdone subject, say the 300th history of the New York Mets, as one of the greatest baseball books ever published. Such a reviewer is an amateur — even if he is getting paid!

A few more points worth discussing. First, the reviewer should always be identified. If a review of a baseball book is done by a well known and highly respected writer or historian such as John Thorn or David Q. Voigt, there can be no doubt that the reviewer is qualified. We may not agree with everything such a reviewer says, but we have to respect his opinion. In the case of a not-so-well-known reviewer, the publication can list some of his credentials (such as his own authorship or membership in SABR, The North American Society for Sport History, or other professional or educational associations) as an indication of his qualifications. And as long as a name is attached to the reviews, even if the reviewer is at first a total stranger, he will begin to accumulate a track record with us, as we learn either to trust or not to trust his opinions, just as we do with those of particular movie reviewers.

Second, responsible reviewers should keep the nit-picking to a minimum and should never denounce a generally good book for small mistakes, even several of them. If a writer is sloppy and uninformed and produces a book which is error-ridden, that's a different story, and censure is warranted. As it is for dishonesty. But there is some wisdom in the old saying that "If a book had to be perfect before it could be published, no book would ever be published." And I agree with the spirit (if not the literal meaning) of Cervantes' comment on the subject: "There is no book so bad but there is something good in it." I'm not saying we should ever ignore a book's faults, but I do find it preferable whenever possible to emphasize the positive, rather than the negative. While I prefer the positive reviewer, there is nothing wrong with the reviewer who tends to be critical, and even highly critical, as long as he is also fair. And we certainly want to know when a book is, perhaps not terrible, but merely redundant or pedestrian. On the other hand, reviews born out of jealousy, vindictiveness, or prejudice are totally unacceptable, and a reviewer who demonstrates that he is capable of succumbing to such motivations should not be trusted in the future.

These musings on the proper role of criticism in book reviewing bring us to a final point: the fact that you, the reader, must be your own final judge. Book reviews should only be a guide, another tool for you to use in deciding not only whether or not to read a certain baseball book, but also whether or not to add it to your collection. Sometimes a competent and fair review is enough to convince us that we can probably do without adding the baseball book under discussion to our collection. But sometimes, especially when the book under consideration is highly controversial, the reviews are so extreme (with some of them being extremely critical) that there is nothing for the reader to do besides read the book for himself. Take a recent book, for example, Richard Ben Cramer's iconoclastic *Joe DiMaggio: The Hero's Life*. This book was panned in several quarters and received especially virulent vituperation from New York Yankee fans and older baseball fans who had never questioned the validity of the mythic image DiMaggio had carefully crafted for himself over decades, an image of spotless character, sophistication, and heroic superiority. This image had been extolled in DiMaggio biography after DiMaggio biography, but Cramer told the other side of the story, and many people not only didn't like it, they absolutely hated it. Is every word of the book true? Who knows. Is there some exaggeration? Probably. Does the author put his spin, his interpretation on some events and conversations recorded in the book? Of course. Does he delve into areas of the subject's life others dared not even acknowledge existed? Most definitely! But this doesn't mean that the book is malicious or unworthy of our attention. My own feeling is that the book, though perhaps not without its faults, does provide balance on the subject that had been completely missing before, and there is no doubt that the book is a fascinating, totally engrossing read. More to the point, the highly negative reviews such a controversial book receives should only convince you of the need to read the book for yourself.

2. Which Baseball Books to Collect

Although there is no telling where a review of a baseball book may turn up, there are four main sources of baseball book reviews. First, there is the baseball and sports press. *Spitball* and *Elysian Fields Quarterly* (formerly the *Minneapolis Review of Baseball*) have taken the reviewing of baseball books seriously since their inceptions in 1983, and I venture to say that no other publications in the world are more important to the subject than these two. William J. McGill and Mark Schraf (in *Spitball*) and Stephen Lehman, Chuck Chalberg, and Tom Goldstein (in *EFQ*), among others, have proven themselves to be perceptive and reliable reviewers of baseball books in the pages of baseball's two literary magazines. *Sports Weekly* (formerly *Baseball Weekly*) and *Baseball America* both publish special issues every spring that feature extensive announcements of forthcoming baseball books, and book reviews are routinely included in these issues (David Plaut is the driving force behind *Sports Weekly's* effort and an outstanding reviewer as well). General sports magazines such as *Sports Illustrated* and *The Sporting News* (reviews by Steven P. Gietschier are recommended) occasionally review baseball books, as do some publications devoted to specific teams, such as *Yankees Magazine* and *Cubs Vineline*. *Sports Collectors Digest*, a tabloid-sized sports card and memorabilia hobby publication, has for a periodical of its type an unusually enlightened attitude towards the importance of baseball literature. Thus, in the pages of *SCD*, editor T. S. O'Connell and columnist Richard D. Miller review current baseball books, while columnist Marty Appel focuses on older books and their authors. And, finally, there are publications devoted to the review of baseball books which though defunct are worth seeking out. In the latter 1980s and early 1990s, several baseball book newsletters were briefly published. Bill Borst's *The American Baseball Review*, which lasted four issues, contained interviews and book news in addition to reviews and ironically bore the slogan "An idea right for the times." A similar and equally short-lived newsletter was Ron Mayer's *All About Baseball Books*, which in its inaugural issue contained excellent advice about where to find "old, out-of-print and rare baseball books." Although it was not devoted exclusively to baseball, Barry Mandell reviewed numerous baseball books in his newsletter, *The SportsBook File*, which lasted almost two years. There is a good chance that because of their ephemerality and charm these little publications will one day become collector's items in their own right. Of all the publications devoted exclusively to baseball books the most important are *The SABR Review of Books* (which lasted five issues) and *The Cooperstown Review* (two issues), both of them conceived and edited by Paul Adomites. The issues of both journals are filled with thoughtful and penetrating reviews and essays on baseball books of the day and on older ones, as well. The demise of these publications was truly a shame, and the inability of *The SABR Review of Books* to survive, despite its connection to the Society, somewhat surprising.

A second helpful source of baseball book reviews are the journals of the publishing and library trades; particularly, the *New York Times Book Review* and *Library Journal*. *Publishers Weekly* (*PW*) also reviews baseball books frequently, but their reviews are unsigned and thus suspect in terms of the reviewer's qualifications. The general press is a third source of baseball book reviews, and this category covers everything from the nation's daily newspapers to financial publications such as the *Wall Street Journal* to consumer magazines as varied as *Playboy* and *People*.

Finally, the world of academe provides a great deal of commentary on baseball books, some of which takes the form of book reviews. A number of scholarly journals devoted to the study of various aspects of sports review baseball books from time to time; of even greater interest are two scholarly journals devoted to the study of sports literature which regularly review baseball books: *Aethlon: The Journal of Sport Literature* (formerly called *Arete*) which is published by East Tennessee State University and *Nine: A Journal of Baseball History and Social Policy Perspectives* which is published by the University of Nebraska Press. Both journals are outstanding and intelligible to the layman, as are their baseball book reviews. Worth mentioning also are the numerous critical studies, in both essay and book form, which pin baseball (and sports in general) to the table and dissect it in order to discover its meaning or relationship to society. While such critical works are not reviews per se and although the jargon used in them can sometimes be daunting, baseball books (particularly baseball novels) are at their core; and so, much can be learned from them about the baseball books they discuss. Some of the more important critical studies which examine baseball books are: *The American Dream and the National Game* by Leverett T. Smith, Jr. (Popular Press, 1975); *Dreaming of Heroes: American Sports Fiction, 1868–1980* by Michael V. Oriad

(Nelson-Hall, 1982); *Laurel and Thorn: The Athlete in American Literature* by Robert J. Higgs (University Press of Kentucky, 1981); *Making the Team: The Cultural Work of Baseball Fiction* by Timothy Morris (University of Illinois Press, 1997); *Seeking the Perfect Game: Baseball in American Literature* by Cordelia Candelaria (Greenwood Press, 1989); *The Sporting Myth and the American Experience: Studies in Contemporary Fiction* by Wiley Lee Umphlett (Bucknell University Press, 1975); and *Sport and the Spirit of Play in Contemporary American Fiction* by Christian K. Messenger (Columbia University Press, 1990). (All of these works include bibliographies which the interested collector can use to find additional critical studies involving baseball books.)

A fourth and final indication of a book's quality is its reprinting — not the original edition going into multiple printings which can also be a sign of quality — but its being brought back to new life after having gone out of print. Reprinting by definition establishes a publisher's faith in the value of a book, as well as the publisher's belief in a renewed (and possibly long-standing) market for the book, and so collectors should take seriously the "stamp of approval" that reprinting confers. For a serious collector, this means of course adding not the paperback reprint of the book to his collection, but a hardback copy from the first printing of the first edition of the book. Penguin led the way in this area by reprinting, as part of The Penguin Sports Library, a number of modern baseball classics, such as *The Long Season*, Jimmy Breslin's *Can't Anybody Here Play This Game?*, *Babe*, *How Life Imitates the World Series*, *Why Time Begins on Opening Day*, and David Falkner's *The Short Season*. Reprinted baseball books have also become an important part of the line of several other publishers, including the University of Nebraska Press (*The Celebrant* and *Babe Ruth's Own Book of Baseball*); Southern Illinois University Press (Eliot Asinof's *Man on Spikes* and Lee Gutkind's *The Best Seat in Baseball, But You Have to Stand!*); SABR (*Base Ball: How to Become a Player* by John Montgomery Ward and F. C. Lane's *Batting*); Ivan R. Dee (*Long Gone* by Paul Hemphill and *El Beisbol* by John Krich); and Brassey's (*Baseball: The Writers' Game* and *Weaver on Strategy* by Earl Weaver with Terry Pluto). Especially noteworthy are the efforts of Camden House, Inc. of Columbia, South Carolina, which in 1983 and 1984 reprinted three of the rarest and most important of baseball books: *The Game of Base Ball: How to*

Learn It, How to Play It, and How to Teach It (1868) by Henry Chadwick; *Sol White's Official Base Ball Guide* (1907); and *Sphere and Ash: History of Base Ball* (1888) by Jacob Morse. These three treasures were printed in hardback on acid-free paper and in a limited edition, presumably of 500 copies each (while each states that it is a limited edition, only the third volume, *Sphere and Ash*, indicates the exact number of copies in its limited edition). The originals are so rare — the publisher says in the Introduction about the *Sol White* book that "We were able to trace only a single copy in public hands"— that these reprints have become quite valuable in their own right.

Before leaving the subject of this chapter, a few words must be said about the trio of great baseball bibliographies: Anton Grobani's *Guide to Baseball Literature* (Gale Research Company, 1975); Myron J. Smith, Jr.'s *Baseball: A Comprehensive Bibliography* (McFarland, 1986; 2d ed, McFarland, 2006); and Andy McCue's *Baseball by the Books: A History and Complete Bibliography of Baseball Fiction* (Wm. C. Brown Publishers, 1991). All three books are stupendous works of scholarship and — even though they don't make recommendations — indispensible resources for collectors. The three books are so well-known and oft-cited that collectors usually refer to them by the authors' last names. The out-of-print *Grobani* is so revered that it has itself become an expensive book to acquire.

Smith's massive compilation (updated in 1993) contains more than 22,00 entries, the majority of which are magazine articles. In sections A through F the entries are grouped under the headings "Reference Works"; "General Works, History, and Special Studies"; "Professional Leagues and Teams"; "Youth League, College, and Amateur/Semi-Pro Baseball"; "Baseball Rules and Techniques"; and "Collective Bibliography"; while the largest section the book, Section G (entries 9796 through 21251), is devoted to "Individual Biography" with the entries on big league players, managers, coaches, umpires, executives, and media personnel arranged alphabetically by the last name of the biographee (from Hank Aaron to Richie Zisk). While *Smith* is the more useful overall, many baseball book collectors prefer *Grobani* because it focuses largely on books, is easier to use, and contains some entries not found in *Smith*. (*Smith* has author and subject indices, while *Grobani* has only a title index; however, the Bibliography Committee of SABR has compiled an author index for *Grobani*.) As for McCue, this annotated compilation is amazingly thorough, a pleasure to peruse, and the "Boy Scout Handbook" of baseball fiction collectors.

In conclusion, keep in mind that the information presented in this chapter is meant to help you decide what kind of baseball book collection you want. This information may be used as tools to help you acquire the books needed for that collection, but only you can decide what kind of baseball book collection will provide the satisfaction you seek.

3

WHERE TO FIND BASEBALL BOOKS

"Where do old, used books go? The answer is simple: books end up just about everywhere."—Ian C. Ellis in Book Finds: How to Find, Buy, and Sell Used and Rare Books

As the first comprehensive and heavily-illustrated volume on its subject, *The Ballparks* by Bill Shannon and George Kalinsky is one of the most sought-after of modern baseball books. Years after I had become a serious collector of baseball books, I remembered having seen a stack of the book on the bargain table of a Waldenbooks at the local mall and regretted deeply not having had the sense to purchase at least one copy of the book. Several years after that a friend called to say that his elderly father was leaving his apartment for an assisted living facility. The father no longer had any use for a freezer in perfectly good working order, and the freezer was ours for simply removing it from the apartment and taking it home. And, oh yes ... there were two baseball books for me that the father no longer wanted. They would be left for me inside the freezer, which had already been unplugged and defrosted of course.

Our friend couldn't remember the titles of the books, so I naturally assumed that they were nothing special. Still, I appreciated his thoughtfulness. When the day came to pick up the freezer, I'd almost forgotten about the books, but I remembered them before we started moving the big trunk-shaped appliance. I opened the lid of the freezer, and there suspended in the wire basket normally used to stock frozen fish sticks lay the books: a well-read copy of *The Bronx Zoo* and, as you've probably already guessed, a near perfect copy of *The Ballparks*, dust jacket intact. Ever since that day, my memory of lifting the lid of that freezer (which didn't work worth a darn) is what I imagine it feels like to open a treasure chest.

For the record, that's my baseball book hunting "You Never Know" story. You may have one of your own. As unusual as mine is, it does make the point rather nicely of this chapter: that you can and probably will at some point find baseball books you want in the strangest, most unlikely of places. Of course, we can't rely on such sources. There are more consistent sources, all of which can be fruitful to one degree or another. You may not have the time or inclination to try all of the sources to be discussed here, but you ought to at least consider them and take advantage of them when it costs you little in terms of time and convenience.

Garage Sales

Moving from (roughly) the least to most productive sources of used baseball books, let us begin with garage sales, aka "yard" sales and, in the northeast, "tag" sales. Unless you are an inveterate haunter of such sales to begin with, it will be a waste of time to visit a string of garage sales listed in the classified ad section of the Saturday morning newspaper in the hope of finding any baseball books at all, much less books you want and need to add to your collection. The thing to do is to focus on the ads which specifically mention books and, even better, baseball and/or sports books and baseball cards, collectibles, or memorabilia. Most baseball collectors are going to have at least a few baseball books in their collections, and if the sale is an "everything goes" liquidation—because of the death of the collector, a loss of interest by the collector, or a financial crisis, such as the need to pay for a child's college education—those books are going to be included in the sale. Still, the odds of finding baseball books this way are slim, and it would be advisable, if possible, to call ahead and ask if there will be baseball books included in the sale. (Phone numbers are sometimes included in garage sale ads; and you can use the phone canvasser's secret weapon, the Criss-Cross Directory, to find those numbers not included, unless they are unlisted.) Estate sales, whereby entire contents of a household go up for sale or bid (usually because of the death of the last member of the household), can also yield occasional opportunities. Most estate sales are advertised in Sunday newspaper editions and usually in considerable detail. Even if baseball or sports books are not mentioned in the list of items up for sale or bid, it might pay to check out the sale if baseball or sports "collectibles" or "memorabilia" are mentioned.

Antique Malls

Antique stores can be a surprisingly profitable place to find good used baseball books. The antiques business has undergone a major change in the last couple of decades that actually makes shopping antique stores much easier than before. To combat the ever-increasing costs of overhead in maintaining individual shops, antiques dealers now routinely band together to conduct their separate businesses under one roof, in giant antiques bazaars, usually called "antique malls." Now, instead of driving all over town or all over the county, the shopper can make one trip and examine the wares of scores of dealers in one spot.

The objection that one is not likely to get a good deal in such an environment, even if one should find desirable baseball books for sale, is answerable by the argument that one should not overestimate the knowledge of all antiques dealers just because they are engaged in the business of selling antiques. The antiques field is vast, and trends and hot segments of the market are constantly changing. No one can be an expert in every aspect of such a fluid endeavor, and so it is not surprising that the average antiques dealer spends his time and available brain cells trying to stay current on the values of more widely collected treasures such as Art Deco furniture and early American folk art rather than books about baseball.

It may be true that any antiques dealer worth his *Kovel's* price guide would, upon stumbling across an obviously old and rare baseball volume, attempt to do the research necessary to determine the book's value. Yet there are lazy and careless dealers just as there are such people in every other field. More to the point, baseball books which are not old but are still valuable have an excellent chance of slipping past most antiques dealers. Case in point, again from my own experience: Only five or six years ago I was thrilled to find a near mint hardback copy of *The Cincinnati*

Game (by Lonnie Wheeler and John Baskin) for sale at an antiques mall in Cincinnati. Although it was collaboratively published by the authors and a subsidy/vanity publisher, the book is one of the most innovative, fascinating, and graphically-arresting team histories ever published. It was also slighted by a print run in hardback of only 3,000 quickly-sold copies. I readily paid the antiques mall $12 for the dealer's copy of the book, which I had no trouble immediately re-selling for $100. So, again, YNK (you never know). You may find that some antiques dealers greatly overprice baseball books, just as they overprice baseball cards. Such dealers work from the assumption that since some baseball cards are worth a lot of money, all baseball cards are worth a lot of money. For dealers who live in such a fantasy world, it is a logical progression to believe that there is great value in each and every baseball item of any type, age, and condition, including all baseball books. The irony here is that while you won't get any bargains from such a dealer on lower end books, you may still get a bargain if he has a baseball book that is truly very valuable, since his prices reflect a general, pretty uniform inflation of value and not a valuation based on knowledge and sound judgement.

Thrift Stores

Not to be overlooked are the emporiums of used junk, furniture, and clothing generically known as "thrift stores." While Goodwill and St. Vincent De Paul thrift stores can be found in almost every medium-to-large sized city, countless other independent and locally-based thrift stores operating under countless different names also dot the American urban landscape. Most of these stores do have a book section, and it is true that most of the time, the majority of the books being offered for sale are junk: ex-library books, cheaply made Book Club editions, out-of-date medical texts and encyclopedia volumes, useless school texts, and vapid novels by obscure authors. Yet, there are exceptions, and occasionally you will find a thrift store that actually manages to attract donations of good books. This lesson was brought home to me one day when, as I was browsing the book shelves of a Goodwill store in Cincinnati, I ran into a woman I recognized: the owner of a used bookshop I patronized frequently. As I watched her work, she selected several volumes for purchase, including a guide to the table-top game Scrabble. After paying 35¢ for the guide, she undoubtedly inserted it into her store's inventory at a price of $10 or so — not a bad return for a few minutes of searching.

One important thing to remember: when there are multiple thrift stores in a town or city, each tends to acquire its inventory from the area in which it is located. And not all thrift stores are located in depressed areas of town. Ideally, you should check all the thrift stores you have time to check, but if there are shops in the nicer parts of town, you should always make a special effort to check them first. The prices will most likely be a little higher in the shops in the nicer part of town, but they should still be low enough to be real bargains and, most importantly, the chances of finding desirable baseball books will be much higher there.

"Want to Buy" Ads

Collectors can create a place to buy baseball books by running "Want to buy" ads. Such a source can be invaluable because it is in a sense reserved for the person running the ad. To be most effective the ads should be general in nature and should state that you are interested in purchasing baseball books, period. If you say that you are looking for rare books or first editions only or specific titles, you run the risk of defeating your purpose by leading potential respondents into thinking they don't have any books you would be interested in. What you want is a chance to decide for yourself if a respondent has books worth your purchasing. Keeping the ads general in nature will result in more responses from people who have nothing you want, but that is the price you need to be willing to pay to put the odds in your favor. You can also question the respondent about his holdings (presumably over the phone) once initial contact is made, screen out obviously dry wells, and decline to purchase the books being offered; however, you need to be a skillful interviewer and a good listener to make certain that you aren't too hastily declining to look at the respondents' books.

If you doubt the effectiveness of "Want to buy" ads, consider that Bobby Plapinger, the world's leading used baseball book dealer, consistently runs them in numerous publications. While Plapinger runs his ads in national publications, you might start by running ads in your local newspaper, whether it be a daily or weekly. Such ads would be cheaper than those in national publications, you would not be in competition with a professional like Plapinger, and you would also have the advantage of being able to inspect the books in person.

One thing to be prepared for if you do run "Want to buy" ads is the desire of the respondent for you to buy the whole collection, not just a few of his books. Even when you actually want only a few of the books, you probably should consider buying the entire collection. That's because when the respondent asks you to make him an offer on the whole collection, he wants to get rid of the books and will usually part with them all for not much more than you would be willing to pay only for the few you actually want. So why buy books you don't want? Because you give the respondent a few more dollars while taking away what to him has become unwanted clutter, which makes him happy; and you get some books you don't want which you can convert into books you do want by selling or trading the former. It's a win-win solution.

Library Book Sales

This may come as a surprise to some collectors, but library book sales can also be an important source of books for most any baseball book collection. It is true that many of the books offered in the typical library book sale are ex-library copies, but this drawback is not the whole story. First of all, ex-library books can still be read, after all, and such copies can suffice as substitutes until the time they can be replaced in the collection by their betters. In addition, if the book is rare enough, even an ex-library copy can have considerable value. A prominent Cincinnati used book shop, for instance, has in stock one copy of Albert G. Spalding's *America's National Game* (published in 1911), an ex-library copy that, with all its imperfections and missing plates, carries a price tag of $75. It would be a very picky collector who would not be thrilled to pick up such a book for 25–50¢ or $1, common price tags of ex-library books at library book sales.

Secondly, and this is the main point for those quick to write off library book sales ... all the books offered at library book sales are not ex-library books. Often, many of the books in the library sale have never been owned by the library but were donated to the library by the public: by non-book loving surviving spouses, by empty-nesters moving into smaller quarters, by philanthropical "Friends of the Library" types, and by people looking for tax deductions. The library simply collects the donated books, puts them in the sale, and pockets the proceeds to use in any number of ways ... perhaps to buy other books but perhaps to help pay the utility bill. Presumably somebody at the library examines all donations to evaluate the "keep-ability" of the books, but many desirable books will not be kept by the library for any number of different reasons: incompetent evaluators, a shortage of shelf space, the library's lack of interest in a particular book's subject, the book being a duplicate of a title already owned by the library, the library's desire to offer some quality selections in the sale to offset the junk, etc. In most cases, baseball is not going to be a high priority subject, and good baseball books donated to the library will likely make it into the sale.

Sometimes libraries offer preview sessions by paid admittance to their book sales before the sales are opened to the general public without charge. Presumably, a preview session with an admission charge is an acknowledgement by the sponsoring library that the sale will include collectible books. The admission charge for the typical preview session is about the cost of a fast food meal; and while there are no guarantees, it is probably a good idea to attend the preview session since you can be certain that the local used book dealers will be there getting first dibs on the best books ahead of the casual book buyers.

New Book Stores

While it is unlikely that you will ever find a rare or even an older collectible baseball book for sale in a new book store for the simple fact that such stores do not normally sell used books, the Barnes & Nobles and Borders of the world can nevertheless be profitably shopped by the savvy collector for their remaindered baseball books, which are books six months to a couple of years old. While many remaindered books are pedestrian efforts, remember that good books are remaindered everyday too. Sometimes a publisher simply prints too many copies of a book—although publishers try to make publishing as much of a science as possible, print runs are still often a guessing game. Other times a book does not fare well and gets remaindered because the public initially fails to recognize it for the good book that it is. In any case, bargain book shelves over time offer the collector many solid baseball books which he can pick up for about a quarter (or less) of the typical retail price. (Of the chain super stores, Barnes & Noble consistently offers the best selection of remaindered baseball books.) In addition, you should never be afraid to buy new books. Yes, it would be better to get a copy of a great new baseball book at a bargain price, but keep in mind that by the time an outstanding book that has been a success finds its way to the discount table, the first edition copies of it are usually long gone. To assure yourself of getting a first edition copy of any book at its original price, the safest thing to do is to buy it when it first comes out. If you pass on a new book you want when it debuts in the hope of first edition copies being remaindered, you may have to pay several times the original price later to obtain it. (There is also the probability that a remainder mark will deface the book if it is later remaindered.)

One word of caution about the books to be found in the bargain book sections of new book superstores. Make sure you know the difference between remaindered books from regular trade publishers and the offerings from bargain book publishers. The former are books that sold for the typical retail price when they were first published, while the latter are books that were meant, from the beginning, to sell for an apparently discounted price. When you buy a "bargain book" (rather than a remaindered book), you are actually paying full price. And while there can be exceptions, bargain books are usually not going to appreciate much in value.

Used Book Stores

With used book stores we arrive at the first of the three most fruitful sources of collectible baseball books. Of the three, used book stores are the most obvious, the most accessible (there will always be some people who are not "connected" to the Internet, while anyone can walk into a book store) and, ironically, also the one most in decline. The reason for this decline is the advent and increasing prominence of the buying and selling of used baseball books on the Internet. Maintaining a retail store is an expensive proposition, and selling over the Internet has become a highly popular alternative for many used book sellers because it eliminates much (although not all) of the normal costs associated with operating a bricks and mortar store.

The Internet has become such a huge part of the used book world primarily because of its superior convenience and the monumental number of its offerings; the fact that the seller can reach untold numbers of potential customers from all parts of the world (not just all parts of the country), while the buyer can likewise instantaneously shop thousands of bookseller inventories from around the globe without ever leaving home.

This exponentially effective pairing of buyers and sellers is a powerful attraction indeed, but it is not the whole story, as the convenience and inventory advantages of the Internet are offset by two not insignificant drawbacks often down played by champions of the Internet.

One, few if any booksellers with large store-sized inventories are able to get all of that inventory into the Internet market place at any one time. In other words, if a bookseller puts his books which interest you on-line, fine. But he may have for sale books you want at prices you are willing to pay which he simply does not have listed on-line. Drawback number two is that Internet book shopping works best when you are looking for a specific title and not nearly as well when you would like to browse. And browsing is the essence of the used book store experience: the pleasure of shopping when what might be discovered is unknown beforehand. There is nothing quite like the thrill of finding on a store shelf a wanted volume you did not even know existed. These happy discoveries can be more frequent than you might expect, since we are talking not just about obscure books published decades ago. There are so many new baseball books published every year that some titles are bound to escape the notice of the average collector, and browsing in used book stores is what best enables collectors to find copies of such books. Of course, it is possible to browse on the Internet, but it is also more difficult to do than in a used book store and not nearly as much fun. There is also no substitute for being able to examine books in person. Being able to examine a copy of a book you are already familiar with prevents the hassles entailed in having to return a copy of it purchased on-line which arrives in condition less than advertised. And, in the case of a book you were not previously familiar with, the decision to buy or not to buy is much easier made when you can pick up the book and look at it (and even read a few pages if desired) than when you have to rely on a bibliographic description of it, or even worse, nothing more than its title.

Although they are dwindling in numbers, used book stores do still exist, and most cities of any size at all still support several stores, if not dozens of them. Guidebooks such as the ones written by David S. and Susan Siegel (*The Used Book Lover's Guide to the Midwest*; one in a series of such books by the authors) are invaluable in helping collectors locate used book stores, especially those off the beaten, urban path; in addition, store owners in a common geographic area often band together themselves to provide brochures that guide customers to each other's shops.

Headquartered in Dallas, Texas, with more than 80 stores in 18 states, Half Price Books is a growing national chain of used book stores which is quickly filling the gap created by the wide-spread closing of individually-owned and operated used book stores. Although Half Price Books is mainly an outlet for publishers' overstock — which means that their stock tends to be somewhat homogenous from store to store — they do actively buy books from the public — which means that each store will have some titles that are not likely to be found at their other stores. This concept is especially important to remember for residents of larger cities, which may support two or more Half Price Books stores. It may pay off to regularly shop all the Half Price Books in your area, rather than assume that the stock in all of the stores is the same as the one you visit first. As the name indicates, the company generally prices its books at one half of the original cover price, but the company does make exceptions; by often putting books on sale and by charging more than half-price for harder-to-find titles and for books which command higher prices for some reason (first edition fiction by collectible authors, for example). Despite the fact that most baseball books in a Half Price Books store at any time will be paperbacks and uncollectible common titles, one can occasionally find a collectible baseball book there, which will be priced low enough to make a regular search of the shelves worthwhile. But be warned: do not sell, or allow your heirs to sell, your baseball book collection to the company. Half Price Books offers only "pennies on the dollar" for the books they buy, and if your books are sold to them you (or your heirs) will surely be short-changed.

Used book stores will survive only if collectors patronize them. To that end as well as that of building your baseball book collection, remember that book store owners, like collectors, have their own interests and that the inventories in their shops often reflect those interests. It is only natural for store owners who are sports fans themselves to make an effort to keep sports titles on their shelves. But even store owners who don't know the difference between Earned Run Average and the Equal Rights Amendment will try to build a baseball section in his store if he knows the demand for one is there. Thus, you should always make your interest in baseball books known to a store owner (especially when you do not find books you want in the store) in order to give him an incentive to make or keep baseball one of the areas on which he focuses his buying.

Herewith a few more pointers for effective used book store shopping:

- Always ask if the store has baseball books not on the shelves. A recently-acquired stack or box of baseball books that have not even been inventoried yet may be sitting in a back room, and the shop will probably allow you to look at them if you make your interest in them known.
- Take your time and browse carefully. Since you've gone to the trouble of making the trip to the store, don't rush the process, or you may overlook baseball books right under your nose. Consider, for instance, my experience during a recent visit to a shop in Maryland. A handmade sign affixed to the top shelf of the sports section said that baseball books were to be found below on the top two shelves. The top two shelves were mostly populated with baseball books, but as I looked closer I discovered that baseball books were scattered throughout the shelving section and its adjoining section, on a total of twelve long, densely-packed shelves. The books were crammed so tightly together that I then missed some baseball titles of interest during my first perusal of the twelve shelves

and discovered them only after a slower, second examination.
- Don't forget to check the other places in the store, other than the sports section, where baseball books may be found: the children's section, the local interest section, the sales table, the shelf or display case for signed copies and collectible first editions (usually fiction), and the rare book room, section, or display cases. If the shop does have a truly rare baseball book, you may not be prepared at the moment to spend what it would take to purchase the book. Nevertheless, knowing of the book's existence there is the first step in the process of acquiring it, whether you decide to try to work out some kind of trade or trade/purchase or simply save up for a purchase. There is always the chance too that you may find a baseball book that is recognized as rare yet which is still priced so attractively that you simply cannot pass it up.

Used Baseball Book Dealers

Despite the dominance of the Internet and their relatively few numbers, book dealers who regularly issue paper catalogs of used baseball books remain a vital source for serious collectors. The catalogs of such dealers are wonderfully useful because they combine the convenience of the Internet and the browse-ability of a used book store. True, we are talking about the inventories of single dealers, but in the case of the four leading catalog issuers, R. Plapinger, Wayne Greene, John Allen, and Mike Wickham, their inventories are very extensive. For instance, Plapinger's catalog for Fall/Winter 2004–2005, #36, is 54 pages long and runs to 782 annotated entries, not counting an additional 600+ unannotated entries for sale books, cheap paperbacks, and uncorrected proofs; while Greene's catalog for winter 2004–2005, #29, contains 1,092 annotated entries, all pertaining to books except for approximately 30 which describe non-book items, such as photos, brochures, phonograph records, and postage stamps. These catalogs run the gamut from the most common, inexpensive books to the most rare and expensive volumes; and, thus, everyone but the most advanced of collectors will always find in these catalogs some titles he wishes to add to his collection. It is also worth noting that most of these dealers have baseball books not listed in their catalogs; and, if you are seeking a specific title not listed in a dealer's catalog, it is worth asking him if he perhaps has a copy which he did not (for whatever reason) choose to list in the current catalog. It also goes without saying that these dealers will conduct book searches for you (almost always at no charge); which means that they will try to find a copy of a book you are looking for and then, with your approval, buy it and re-sell it to you at a price that includes a reasonable profit for themselves.

The best used baseball book catalogs, particularly those of Plapinger and Greene, also offer an educational benefit, as they function as valuable bibliographic documents. The Plapinger and Greene catalogs are routinely full of precise, detailed bibliographic data as to publisher, date of publication, the issuance of dust jackets, the presence of photos, etc.; as well as evaluations, recommendations, and opinions (of the catalogers and of others cited by the catalogers). The value of having these catalogs, in hand, and of being able to lay them aside and pick them up later with the information preserved (as opposed to information on the Internet which is likely to be ephemeral), cannot be over-estimated.

In order to maintain inventories sufficient enough to justify the issuance of their used baseball book catalogs, the dealers who issue them must continually replenish their stocks by buying new books. Because the catalog issuers gain reputations for being serious buyers, sellers (including book dealers who do not specialize in baseball books) often turn to them first; and that is one of the main reasons that these used baseball book dealers always have some of the hardest-to-find and rarest baseball books to offer.

Some of the paper catalog issuers are beginning to make selections of their inventories available on-line through one or the other of the used book search engines, and at some point in the future Internet selling may make the issuance of paper catalogs completely obsolete. However, as long as the paper catalogs are issued, they should be consistently acquired and read carefully by all serious collectors of baseball books.

The following is a list of used baseball book dealers who issue printed catalogs:

- John Allen
  P.O. Box 2453
  Duxbury, MA 02331

Phone: (781) 934-5495 (7-9 PM Eastern Time)
E-mail: bbook77@aol.com
Charge for catalog: a large SASE; next catalog sent free to customers who order books.

- Spider Cleaver Baseball Books
  (Mike Shannon)
  5560 Fox Road
  Cincinnati, OH 45239
  Phone: (513) 385-2268
  E-mail: spitball5@hotmail.com
  Charge for catalog: SASE with two first class stamps
- Wayne Greene
  P.O. Box 479
  Cathedral Station
  New York, NY 10025
  Phone: (212) 961-0351
  Fax: (212) 961-0351
  E-mail: greensparks@worldnet.att.net
  Charge for catalog: $3; next catalog sent free to customers who order books.
- ZK Sports Books
  (Mark Schraf)
  205 Horseshoe Road
  Morgantown, WV 26508
  Phone: (304) 594-0213
  E-mail: spitball@comcast.net
  Charge for catalog: none
- Mike's Baseball Books
  (Mike Wickham)
  P. O. Box 211483
  Chula Vista, CA 91921
  Phone: (619) 482-3953 Days; (619) 267-4828 Evenings
  E-mail: melbawick@aol.com
  Charge for catalog: none
- R. Plapinger
  P.O. Box 1062

Ashland, OR 97520
Phone: (541) 488–1220
E-mail: baseballbooks@opendoor.com.
Charge for catalog: $4; next catalog sent free to customers who order books.

The Internet

Finally, there is the Internet, which has become for many collectors the first choice of sources for used baseball books. While Internet buyers of new baseball books turn first to the Amazon and Barnes and Noble websites, both companies also offer used books on their websites through their own networks of used book dealers. For the most part, the used baseball books offered on Amazon and Barnes and Noble are used copies of newly-published and common titles. While the two giants of the book selling industry often list older and rare baseball books on their web pages, their dealers seldom actually have copies of such books for sale in their inventories.

To find copies of older and rare baseball books for sale, collectors turn instead to some of the major Internet listing services or "search engines" that offer the inventories of book dealers from around the country and the world who specialize in older used and rare books. Two of the more popular of these types of listing services are *abebooks* and *alibris*. Both are excellent sources, but collectors usually prefer shopping on one or the other of these two services due to habit or differences in the companies' policies or in the design, layout, or functioning of the companies' websites; however, keep in mind that while some book dealers patronize both services, most dealers pick one or the other as their listing service of choice.

Thus, when you are looking for a specific title, I would advise you to check both *abebooks* and *alibris* (as well as several other listing services). Because of an amazing conglomerated search engine called Bookfinder.com, you can do this without going to each of several listing services one at a time. According to its website, Bookfinder "partners with the major listing services and bookstores online, aggregating the inventories of well over 70,000 booksellers on our site." Bookfinder has over forty partners listed on its web page (including all the search engines already mentioned here), and you can bring up the website of any of those listing services or bookstores (such as Powell's located in Seattle, Washington) by simply clicking on its name in the listing on Bookfinders' home page. Or ... and this is the real beauty of Bookfinder ... you can use the "Search" function on Bookfinder's home page (searching by title or author), and search the inventories of ALL of Bookfinder's more than forty partners all at once! In other words, you can use one giant search engine (Bookfinder) to search multiple search engines. Truly, shopping has never been easier. If there is a drawback to using Bookfinder, it is that Bookfinder often produces duplicate listings due to the fact that some booksellers list the same book with two or more different listing services. Such duplication creates the impression that more copies of a particular book are available for sale than is the case, but by paying attention to the names of the sellers listed you can learn to quickly identify multiple listings of the same copy of a book and thus ascertain the true number of different copies of a title available.

An alternate Internet site where baseball books can be acquired is the gargantuan online auction house known as eBay perhaps the fastest growing online source for used baseball books. EBay is popular with sellers because the cost of doing business there is so comparatively low. Sellers pay eBay a small fee (sometimes as little as 20¢) to list a book (or a lot of books) and then a small percentage of the sales price when (and if) the book sells. Thus, the risk is near zero for sellers. Buyers of baseball books like eBay because there is a tremendous opportunity for bargains on the site. Since the vast majority of transactions on eBay are auctions, buyers (or "bidders" as they are properly called) can sometimes win a book for a song, the starting bid price (usually a very minimum amount) or a price not much higher than the starting bid price. The biggest drawback to buying baseball books on eBay is that many of the sellers are amateurs when it comes to books, and they often provide incomplete and inaccurate descriptions of the books they are auctioning. Many eBay book sellers are amateurs who do not understand the importance of condition and first edition status. Nor do they appreciate the negative effect that ex library condition has on a book. If an eBay seller does not specifically state that the book he is offering is a first edition, you can almost be certain that it is not ... and in far too many instances the book is an ex library copy as well. A second drawback are the exorbitant shipping fees charged by some sellers, who try to use the shipping fee to provide themselves a guaranteed profit. These drawbacks are offset by the buyer's ability to ask the seller questions (e.g., "Is this book an ex library copy?"), by the buyer protections eBay has in place (primarily but not limited to a "Feedback" system by which buyers and sellers are able to rate each other in terms of honesty, fairness, and reliability), and by the user-friendly features of the eBay site: primarily, the "Watch This Item" feature which enables the buyer to keep track of how the bidding on an item of interest to him is going, and the multiple ways one can search for items (such as "Most Recently Listed").

Overall, the Internet has had a tremendous effect on the baseball book market. One prominent baseball book dealer has compressed that effect into a pithy saying which he now repeats like a mantra: "There are no rare books anymore." While the saying is an exaggeration, it does bring attention to the main effect of so many baseball books being available for sale to anyone who is online: a decrease in the prices of common books and an increase in the prices of the rarer books. Because the wide-spread use of the Internet as a market place is a relatively new phenomenon, this effect may be temporary or it may be permanent. Only time will tell. The one thing that is certain is that it is now easier, if not quite as much fun as it used to be when the thrill of the hunt was more personal and more challenging, to build the baseball book collection you want.

4

HOW TO CARE FOR YOUR COLLECTION OF BASEBALL BOOKS

Books are the best things, well used; abused, among the worst. — Ralph Waldo Emerson

Experts on the subject of the care and preservation of books may pass this chapter by with a clear conscience. It behooves all others to stay and spend the few moments required to read the chapter and consider its advice carefully on the chance that they may learn something useful or be reminded of something important they have forgotten.

I am going to focus here on simple, common sense advice for the care of one's baseball books, much of which will take the form of "Do's and Don'ts." Moreover, the advice presented here is assumed to apply to books which are in good shape to start with. Repairs are beyond the scope of this chapter (as well as the level of my expertise); however, there are how-to books on the subject and those with a do-it-yourself spirit can profitably consult *The Booklover's Repair Manual: First Aid for Home Libraries* (Knopf, 2000) by Estelle Ellis with Wilton Wiggins and Douglas Lee. The book originally comes with a book repair kit of more than 20 tools and pieces of material needed for book repairs, and it offers clear directions and copious illustrations. Even if you want to have a go at making your own repairs though, my advice is to leave the repair of rare and very valuable baseball books to the professionals and to do your own repairs only on inexpensive books ... unless and until you became an expert yourself and are confident that you can make the repairs without making the damage to the books worse.

    The first thing one should be aware of in regard to the care of books is the environment in which the books are kept. Books have many enemies, including insects, children, pets, smoke, heat, sunlight, moisture, and water. Consequently, where in the house one keeps one's books can make a huge difference in the condition in which they are maintained. Some experts caution against keeping books in either the attic or the basement, but neither need be a problem as long as the space is clean, dry, well-ventilated, and temperature controlled; the latter meaning that the space should be kept cool (65° is considered the optimum temperature). Most basements are naturally cool but also subject to flooding, backed-up sewers, and burst water pipes. Most dangerous of all, basements can also subject books to excessive humidity, the major cause of mold and mildew. Baseball book collector and dealer Mark Schraf estimates that more books have been ruined by mold and mildew than by any other single problem, and he heartily recommends the use of a de-humidifier for any collector who keeps his book collection in the basement. If you do place a dehumidifier in your basement, I guarantee that you will be amazed at how much water the machine removes from the air in your home and at how quickly it does so. Although attics don't usually present these problems, they are subject to water damage from roof leaks; in addition, they can often be difficult to cool, and heat can cause as much damage as moisture or water (leaving a hardback book in the car on a hot day which results in a "swollen book" with bowed covers illustrates the harmful effects of heat). These cautions notwithstanding, basements and attics are sometimes the only options open to collectors (aside from moving to larger quarters or adding on to one's house), and either can work well as long as one corrects existing problems and guards against potential ones. I keep my baseball book collection in my basement, and I have a good friend who keeps his in his attic, and neither of us have had any problems endemic to these two parts of the typical house. However, if you have a choice, it is definitely the best course of action to keep your book collection in some part of the house other than the attic or the basement.

    Regardless of where in the house he keeps his books, the prudent collector will also be careful to guard against the deleterious effect of sunlight, which is the fading of a book's dust jacket, pages, and cloth covers. If the books cannot be kept away from windows which let in the rays of the sun, then blinds must be installed and kept lowered during the day.

Smoke too is very harmful to books, whether it be the smoke from cigarettes, cigars, or fireplaces. Ironically, many people keep books around working fireplaces because they have bought into the image of "cozying up to the fire with a good book" as the height of domestic pleasure. If you must read in front of a burning fireplace, make it be a cheap paperback version of the book, not a collectible version; and if you must stock the shelves surrounding the fireplace with books to achieve an aristocratic ambience, then use "dummies," books of little value, to achieve the same effect. Your collectible books, like your children, should be spared the effects of second-hand smoke.

Collectors should also be careful about where they take their books. More than a few people enjoy reading in the bath tub, but splashes from running water are almost certain to hit the book. Worse, a slip through the hands can mean total disaster. Collectible books should also never be taken aboard small boats or to the beach, for obvious reasons. Some experts even caution against reading collectible books outside altogether in case one is called inside, leaves the book outside on a table, and forgets that it is there until a rain storm has passed through. Perhaps the best way to avoid these situations is to make sure that one has a comfortable and inviting reading spot in close proximity to where the books are kept.

Once collectible books are housed in a room in which the proper environment for the books can be maintained, the books must be shelved, and shelved properly; not stacked up on the floor (and possibly used as end tables) or kept in boxes (if books must be stored in boxes, stand them upright on end and do not lay them flat) or worse. The bookshelf may seem to be a simple and obvious invention that came into being exactly as we know it today, but in fact the bookshelf has a complicated and evolutionary history that is detailed in Henry Petroski's fascinating study, *The Book on the Bookshelf* (Knopf, 1999). Suffice it to say here that one's choice in bookcases and shelving being largely a matter of taste and budget is fine, as long as the bookcases or shelving units serve their purpose, which is to protect the books while housing them and making them accessible to their owner. Some collectors may feel that wood is the only suitable material for bookcases, but there is nothing wrong with metal, and in fact most public and academic libraries use metal shelving. Regardless of the material in use, all surfaces which come into contact with the books must be smooth, and that is one reason the low budget method of supporting stacks of loose wooden shelves with pairs of ultra-rough, concrete cinder blocks, a method employed in many of America's college dormitory rooms, is not recommended. Another reason to avoid such shelving systems is that they do a poor job of keeping books free of dust, another enemy of books. The best way to ward off dust is to keep one's books in cabinets behind glass doors. Such cabinets also provide the best all-around protection. Short of this ideal, the next-best solution is to use only bookcases which have solid backs and sides. While fold-up bookcases put together with spindles may be cheap and easy to transport or store, they expose the books they house to dust on all sides, not to mention the fact that they are less sturdy than better constructed bookcases with solid sides and a solid back.

In terms of imposing some order on one's collection, there are many different ways to shelve one's books, and those ways need not concern us here; however, the physical aspects of shelving are a subject which we should touch upon. Regardless of whether one shelves by author or subject or one of the many other possibilities, size is a factor which should be taken into consideration when it comes to the shelving of baseball books, as baseball literature has its share of tall and odd-shaped books and then some. The problem is that when tall books are mixed in with their shorter counterparts, the covers of the tall books begin to splay over time. To prevent this, tall books should be shelved together so that their covers press against each other the length of the shelf. When the bookcase or shelving unit has adjustable shelves, shelving tall books together on their own shelves instead of mixing them in with shorter books on every shelf offers the additional advantage of creating room for an extra shelf or two. Naturally, a shelf of tall books weighs considerably more than a shelf of shorter books, and the weight of the former can bow wooden shelves. Thus, in the case of adjustable shelving it makes sense to assign tall books to the bottom shelf, which is usually reinforced by the base of the entire unit.

As one's collection grows, there is a tendency to shelve too tightly, to cram ever more volumes into the same space. Cramming increases the likelihood that the collector will do damage to his books when taking them off the shelf, by pulling the book down by its head, which can lossen or break the top of the spine. If books on a shelf are allowed a little breathing room, one may remove a volume properly, by gripping it by its spine or sides. The solution for cramming is a decrease in the number of books to be shelved or, preferably, the acquisition of additional shelving. On the other hand, shelving too loosely can cause books to lean over, a situation which left unattended results in loosened and twisted covers. Leaning can be easily rectified with the use of book ends or the use of a dummy volume, slipped into the space created by the removal of the wanted volume. The latter is the preferred method because it obviates the necessity of moving over as much as half a shelf of books to close the gap. In addition, books should not be shelved on their spines or fore-edges, nor should they be laid flat in a stack for any length of time. While the latter may seem to be a harmless practice, it is in fact a very damaging one, as the combined weight of the stack bears down on the binding of the book on the bottom of the pile.

The remaining advice I have to offer concerns the handling of individual books, one at a time, and can be formulated into a series of do's and don't's. First, the don't's:

- Don't write in your books. If you must write in the book, use pencil and press lightly, but never write in ink.
- Don't lay an open book face-down to save your place. While saving your place, you are destroying the book's binding.
- Don't lay an open book face-down on a copying machine. Take notes instead. Lots of them if necessary. However, if there is absolutely no way around making photo copies, do not under any circumstances close the lid and press down on the book, as some machines advise you to do.
- Don't fold down the corner of a page to save your place.
- Don't use anything for a book mark other than a slip of acid-free paper. Especially, do not use anything bulky, organic (like flowers), or metal as book marks. All such things will do damage to the book.
- Don't use the dust jacket as a book mark. Doing so will stretch the dust jacket out of shape.

- Don't eat or drink around your books. This is a difficult rule for many book lovers to follow, especially for those (like myself) who like to combine the pleasures of eating and drinking with that of reading; but your books have enough natural enemies without adding food stains and drink spills to the list.
- Don't leave books where pets, especially dogs, can reach them. Dogs love to chew on books, especially older ones which were assembled with hide glue, an animal product.

Finally, a few do's:

- Do dust your books, bookcases, and book shelves regularly.
- Do keep a log of books you have loaned. And, if you loan books at all frequently, consider putting bookplates into your books to help ensure that they are returned.
- Do protect your better books and their dust jackets by encasing them in the plastic covers made by the Brodart or Mylar companies.
- Do handle your books gently and respectfully. Even if it is read numerous times, a well-made hardback book will remain in Mint or Fine condition indefinitely if it is treated properly. Why wouldn't any collector give his books the care needed to ensure that they provide him with the maximum pleasure possible for as long as he is able to enjoy them.

Before closing this chapter, I must say a few words about weeding. The topic could just as easily have been discussed in Chapter 2 ("Which Baseball Books to Collect") in regard to the discussion about the difference between Completist and Specialist collectors, but I have chosen to save it for this chapter in order to emphasize weeding as a function of the proper care of a baseball book collection.

Quite simply, weeding is the permanent removal of books from a collection. As foreign as the idea is to most individual collectors, weeding is an accepted concept and rather commonplace activity in the world of institutional and public libraries. That doesn't mean that weeding is never controversial. Consider, for example, the weeding that occurred during the summer of 2001 at the Sulzer Regional Library, the third largest public library in Chicago. Although most everyone concerned agreed that an extensive weeding was long overdue at Sulzer, some concerned citizens were upset that the weeding was done mostly by outside experts instead of the local librarians who were presumed to be more familiar with the library's collection and clientele; that more advance notice of the weeding was not given to both the public and the Sulzer staff; and that perfectly good books were alledgedly discarded in addition to those suffering from broken spines, torn covers, and other damage. The extent of the weeding was also in dispute. The critics estimated that some 35,000 volumes were culled, while the official number released by the library administration was about 18,000. Whatever the actual number of books removed, the controversial weeding by the experts was an additional one, as internal weedings conducted by the Sulzer staff are conducted on an annual basis, just as similar weedings are done at every library in the Chicago Public Library system. In 2000, for instance, Sulzer removed 15,700 volumes in order to make room for 17,000 new books it added to the collection.

And this is the point for collectors of baseball books. At some point, every collector begins to run out of shelving space, and the necessity of weeding becomes apparent. Some collectors are able to deal with the necessity of weeding in a very sensible and dispassionate way. For instance, the late Lawrence Ritter, who maintained an apartment in New York City, once told me that his baseball book collection had reached its full capacity. "If I want to add a book, I have to get rid of one," he said.

Fortunately, most collectors are not in as dire a position as Ritter, but the truth, which many collectors do not wish to face, is that almost every collection of considerable size can benefit from a judicious weeding. Candidates for the weeding process generally fall into one of the following categories:

- duplicate books
- damaged books not worth repairing
- books on topics the collector has lost interest in
- books on topics the collector was never interested in
- paperback books which are identical to their hardback predecessors (as long as the hardback volume is in the collection)
- redundant books: books which add little if anything to our knowledge of over-done topics

- "bad books": books which are superficial, poorly written, marred by excessive error, or just plain dull.

The need for weeding can come at different times for different collectors and can depend on several varying factors, such as the size of one's living quarters, one's disposable income, one's goals and philosphy as a collector, the amount of time one has to devote to organizing and caring for his collection, and — perhaps most important of all — the level of tolerance one's spouse has for his baseball bibliomania. Nevertheless, certain circumstances are sure signs that a weeding is coming due: when you begin to stack books on the floor; when you find books laid horizontally on top of shelved books; when you begin to picture bookcases in parts of the house that have always been considered off-limits for your collection; and when you can write a book faster than you can find a book in your collection. For those who are reluctant to consider a weeding, even when it is obvious that one should be done, it may help to think of the process as a means of upgrading one's collection. Serious baseball card collectors, working on completing sets of high-priced cards, are constantly involved in the upgrading process. They keep lesser condition cards in their collection only until they can find replacements in better condition. While the weeding of a baseball book collection will not involve many one-on-one substitutions of a better condition copy of a book for a lesser condition copy of the same book, the weeding will obtain a similar result: a better collection. For once the weeded books have been donated, sold, or traded, the collector should be better able to provide the care the books remaining in the collection deserve. In addition, the weeding will have created shelving space for new acquisitions, all presumably more deserving of the space than the books they are replacing.

Finally, if a weeding is too difficult for a collector to handle emotionally, he can always enlist the help of a collecting friend who will not have the same emotional attachment to the books as the collector. Sometimes all it takes to let go is the question asked incredulously, "Why are you keeping *this* book around?"

5

How Much to Pay for Baseball Books

Many a collector has found that what he regrets is not his extravagances, but his economies.—*P. H. Muir in* Book Collecting As a Hobby: In a Series of Letters to Everyman

When we consider the question that is the focus of this chapter, it becomes apparent that there are theoretically three prices for every baseball book: 1) a price that is low, 2) a price that is high, and 3) a price that is just right. Whenever possible, collectors desire to pay the #1 price while they attempt to studiously avoid paying the #2 price; but in order to do either they must first know what the #3 price is. And therein lies both the dilemma faced by collectors and the need for a book such as this.

Before proceeding any further, I want to point out that establishing the prices in a baseball book guide will be more of an art than a science and especially so in comparison to the baseball card price guides with which most baseball collecting fans are familiar. This is because baseball card price guide compilers have two main advantages over anyone producing a price guide for baseball books. One, whatever the number of collectors of baseball books, there are undoubtedly many times more collectors of baseball cards ... which means that the market for baseball cards is vastly larger than the market for baseball books. Specific baseball cards are bought and sold (on the secondary market) many more times than are specific baseball books, and a price established upon numerous transactions involving an item is more reliable than a price established upon only a few transactions.

Two, the baseball card market is also much more transparent than the baseball book market. Information used to establish the prices in baseball card price guides has typically been supplied by hundreds of card shop owners, show dealers, and auctioneers, whose knowledge is based on thousands of transactions. In comparison, there are only a handful of baseball book dealers who do enough business to warrant the title; there are no shows (to my knowledge) devoted primarily to baseball books; and information on baseball books sold at auction is sporadic and sometimes difficult to ascertain (when multiple baseball books are auctioned as a single lot, it is impossible to know how much was paid for each book). True, the Internet has made the asking prices of thousands of baseball books by hundreds of sellers available for anyone to see, but there is no one keeping track of and publishing the actual sales records of these books. And so, the reporting system that aids in the compilation of baseball card price guides simply does not exist for baseball books. However, after years of collecting and buying used baseball books, of studying the catalogs of prominent baseball book dealers, of following auction results, and of selling baseball books myself, I am able to formulate a pricing rule of thumb that should be helpful for collectors and which will serve as the basis of the price guide at the end of this book.

Namely, that a used collectible baseball book will be worth roughly the average price of a current new hardback book in a bull market and somewhat less in a bear market.

This point can be best understood perhaps by making a comparison between books and automobiles. As every experienced car owner knows, because of depreciation the typical new car immediately loses significant value as soon as it is driven off the dealer's lot. And ... the car continues to lose value every year until its value depreciates to a negligible level. But this general rule does not affect all cars equally, nor does it apply at all to all cars. That is, some cars (such as Honda Civics and Ford Mustangs) depreciate at a much slower pace than the average car; while autos considered to be classics can wind up, decades after their introduction, to be worth many multiples of their original selling price and far more than the average new car.

An analogous but somewhat "price stabilized" situation exists for used baseball books. Meaning ... that while many used baseball books depre-

5. How Much to Pay for Baseball Books

ciate (like most autos) to a fraction of their original values, many other used baseball books have no trouble retaining close to 50%, not of their original values, but of the current value of new books. In addition, as stated previously, the more collectible used baseball books often command prices equal to those of new books; with prices for the scarcer books climbing several, perhaps many, times past the current prices for new books. Keep in mind that this "value" rule of thumb — that the average collectible used baseball book is worth, continually, about half the price (or more) of the average new hardback — is just that: a simplified, typified statement meant to indicate an average for thousands of items, hundreds of which will deviate slightly one way or the other. It is offered as a guide, not as a law cast in bronze, and the collector is enjoined to use it as such.

Although the general subject was covered in Chapter 2, it is also appropriate to remind you here, while discussing "How Much to Pay," that we are discussing the subject of this chapter mostly in regard to "collectible" books. And there are four things which make a baseball book collectible ... make it, in other words, a book which, in order to obtain, one would be willing to pay a price equal to or greater than half the cover price of its typical current new counterparts:

1) the book must be a first edition (An exception must be made for the later printings or editions of rare books, which are normally still desirable and valuable. Note also that Book Club editions, while never true first editions, sometimes fool collectors and even book dealers occasionally. *First Editions* edited by Edward N. Zempel and Linda A. Verkler is a great aid in learning to identify true firsts, and collectors are enjoined to become familiar with its contents);

2) the book must be the hardback version, unless it was issued originally as a paperback. ("Paperback originals," as such books are called, are true first editions and should be considered as collectible as hardback first edition copies. In the vast number of paperback original cases, the paperback is the only version of the book to ever be published. In rare instances, a paperback original has been followed by a hardback release of the same title; thus reversing the normal order of publication. Another exception to this rule would

be made for the scarce or rare paperback version of a scarce or rare book issued first in hardback, while a third exception would be made for a paperback which is substantially and meaningfully different from its hardback counterpart);

3) the dust jacket, if one was issued, must be present and in relatively acceptable condition; and

4) the book must be in demand.

While the first three of these criteria are rather cut and dried, the fourth is anything but; yet why one book is in demand and another is not is the crux of the matter. One would assume that the "best" books (however one arrives at a definition of "best") are always highly collectible books, and usually they are. But if such books are over produced—*Stolen Season* by David Lamb is a good example of an outstanding but readily-available book—used copies of them will be unlikely to command high prices. Conversely, a poorly done book or a book not very lively by today's standards can be prized by collectors for nothing more than its subject matter or historical importance. Similarly, scarcity and rarity are often characteristics of collectible books, yet not always. Some very tough-to-find baseball books are not very valuable simply because there are few collectors interested in them. "Demand" is usually produced then by some unmathematical combination of quality, subject matter, and rarity; and the best guide to determining it (outside of a price guide such as this) is one's own experience, judgement, and (apart from all considerations of pecuniary value) taste. (In other words, you should never hesitate to add a low-value book to your collection if you want the book for any reason.)

Again, although rarity does not guarantee value, rarity is always an important characteristic which potentially imbues a book with value. The problem is that rarity, like beauty, is an exceedingly difficult to define, if not indefinable, term. At least no one, to my knowledge, has defined rarity in reference to books. Defining "rarity" should principally be a matter of quantification; of determining, that is, the maximum number of copies of a book that could be extant before the book would have to be considered something less than rare. Certainly, determining just how many copies of a book remain extant would usually be a difficult thing to do, but without a commonly accepted definition to start with, it is inevitable

5. How Much to Pay for Baseball Books

that the term "rare" is going to mean different things to different people. For instance, veteran used and rare book dealer Willis Monie who maintains an extensive and fairly-priced selection of baseball books in his shop in Cooperstown, New York, prefers a Unique — Rare — Scarce — Common continuum. He believes that most dealers define a rare book as one for which there are 10 or fewer copies for sale at any time. However, Monie himself declines to associate a number with rarity, preferring to use the description "any book that is very tough to find and for which there is constant demand." If we had a clear definition of what constitutes a rare book, then we could work backwards and establish additional categories into which less rare books would fall. Lacking a universally accepted basis for such a continuum, I would nevertheless suggest that we put into use for our own collecting purposes the following continuum: Unique — Rare — Scarce — Uncommon — Common. Of course, the ideal situation would be for everyone to agree on what these categories mean and for it to be known with certainty into which category every book falls; yet even without such agreement and certainty, the collector can benefit from using the concept of the continuum to help him effectively gauge the true values of the baseball books he seeks. Also, please note that I am referring to the books which would fall into the Unique through Uncommon categories when using the term "collectible" books. This is not to say that you shouldn't have common books in your baseball book collection; every collection has them, the average collection contains many of them, and many common baseball books make quite valuable contributions to any collection. Just don't pay a "collectible book price" to obtain a common baseball book.

As a refinement of the answer to the question of how much to pay for collectible books specifically, I would advise paying "as little as possible but as much as necessary." To explain: while you can afford to wait on bargain-basement prices for common books because copies of those books will always be available for sale, a different rule applies to uncommon books you have been trying to add to your collection for some time. With such a book it is better to pay more than you want to in order to acquire the book, than to pass it over and run the risk of: a) not seeing it up for sale again for quite some time, or b) having to pay substantially more for it later if it does come up for sale again.

The important financial rule at work in the situation described in "b" is one which applies to all types of collectibles: namely, that the greatest rate of appreciation in value over time occurs for the best items. Common items may increase in value, but they will not come close to the rate of appreciation enjoyed by their rarer counterparts, simply because advanced collectors are always willing to pay a premium (and often a large premium) for the rare item in top condition.

Now this obviously does not mean that you should pay any price for a book (unless you are wealthy and money is no object) because it is possible to overpay for a book, even a rare one. And overpaying for a rare book is certainly going to cost you more, at least initially, than overpaying for a more common book. Nevertheless, you should bear in mind at all times the fact that it is the rarer books that will define your collection, do the lion's share of the work in establishing the value of your collection, and as you become a more sophisticated and advanced collector, provide you with the most satisfaction. It is worth paying a premium price to acquire the books that accomplish those benefits. *How much* more you should be willing to pay is a personal matter you will have to decide for yourself in varying circumstances; but the point, which is implied in this chapter's opening epigram, is that most collectors take the greatest pleasure in possessing and appreciating the best and often rarest items in their collections ... not the cheaper items acquired for next to nothing (notwithstanding the satisfaction many of us enjoy when contemplating good books acquired at bargain prices). Also keep in mind that the widest spread of prices (from one sale of a particular title to the next sale of that same title) will occur with the rarest books since such books are bought and sold with far less frequency than their more common counterparts. This situation makes it difficult to know if a rare book (and especially a unique book) is overpriced or underpriced for that matter, and the only remedy to the problem is to become as knowledgeable about the books one is interested in as possible and as informed about the current market and market trends as possible. In other words, the prices for the rare books listed in the following price guide are the most accurate that were available when this book was being writen; however, the past sales that these prices are based on will not prevent owners of the same titles from asking for higher prices.

Since condition is such an important factor in determining the value of any book, it is appropriate to discuss the subject in this chapter. The used and rare book industry recognizes six basic grades of condition: Mint, Fine, Very Good, Good, Fair, and Poor. Recognizable by all baseball card collectors, Mint, which designates a book in absolutely perfect condition, is a fairly new grade, but it seems to be becoming more acceptable every day. Fine means almost new but lacking the crispness of new and allows for the book having been read. Very Good refers to a book with only a few and minor blemishes or marks of wear. While the presence of a bookplate is permissible, writing in ink is not. More numerous small defects to the book, including the owner's name written in ink, would result in Good condition; while Fair condition would be the result of some serious flaws, such as water damage, slightly loose or bent covers, torn (but not missing) pages, underlining, and soiled or faded pages or covers. Poor condition refers to a book suffering from very serious problems, such as missing pages, removed illustrations, warping, badly marked or missing end papers, insect damage, a broken spine, or a very loose cover. The defects which can result in the lesser conditions are numerous, and every serious collector should familiarize himself with the terminology used to describe them. The following is a list of defects that can be found defined in the glossary on the website of the online used book seller *alibris*: bumped, chipped, cocked, cracked, crimped, faded, foxed, frayed, gnawed, gouged, price clipped, rubbed, scuffed, shaken, shelf worn, sprung, sunned, underlined, warped, worming, and yellowed.

As important as it is and as much as dealers and collectors try to impose objective control over it, condition will always remain something of a subjective matter and one which lends itself to important shades of difference. That is why dealers often combine grades (such as VG-G) and use pluses (+) and minuses (-) to indicate a more precise condition. Collectors will always try to obtain the best copy possible of a desired book, but the thing to keep in mind is that for most collectors the condition which is generally acceptable is VG, which *alibris* defines as "shows some signs of wear and is no longer fresh. Attractive." As such, VG is the condition assumed for all the prices listed in the price guide.

It is also extremely important to understand the effect that exceptional condition and dust jacket issues can have on the prices of baseball books. When the condition of the book and/or the dust jacket is better than VG, the book will command a correspondingly higher price, with the following rule prevailing: the rarer the book in outstanding condition, the higher the rise in price. In addition, the presence of a dust jacket when the dust jacket is rarely found can raise the price of a book dramatically. For instance, *Commy* by G. W. Alexson is a $30 book without a dust jacket, but a copy of the book with the DJ would be worth approximately $300, or ten times as much. Conversely, a dust jacket in less than VG condition should lower the price somewhat, while the absence of a dust jacket altogether can lower the price by 50% or more.

We must also say a few words here about volatility, the sudden and sometimes quite extreme increase or decrease in a book's price. Lots of things may happen to make a baseball book hot, but most often demand for a title increases suddenly because collectors and dealers realize that a book is scarcer than it was previously known to be. For example, *The Cincinnati Game* by Lonnie Wheeler and John Baskin did not become a particularly expensive book until it was learned that only 3,000 copies of the hardback were ever printed. Once the word got around, the price of the book rose sharply almost overnight.

On the other hand, the relatively small number of buyers, particularly for rare and extremely high-priced books, can serve as a book's own built-in depression mechanism which causes demand for the book at an extremely high price to be satisfied quickly, with a corresponding drop in price for other copies still on the market. Also, "Finds" (a find is the discovery of a previously unknown cache of an uncommon or scarce book) are always possible, and any find almost certainly leads to a drop in price for the book.

Finally, we should consider two other, oddball factors which affect baseball book prices. First, there is geography. While most baseball books will not be affected by geography, those that have a strong connection to a certain place may be affected. The effect is usually twofold: if the book with a strong connection to a particular city or area is a common one, then prices for the book in that city or area should be even lower than in other parts of the country because the book has already been so widely available there. Conversely, if the book with a strong geographical connection is a rarer book, then the price for that book in the city or area it has a connection to will be higher than elsewhere because the demand for the book will be greater in the city or area it has a connection to. The geographical factor is the reason baseball book dealers traveling to sports memorabilia shows load up with books connected to the city hosting the show and attempt to get premium prices for those books at the show.

The second oddball factor affecting prices is signatures or autographs. Often a lot of the price of a particular copy of a baseball book is due not to the book itself but to the signature of the book's subject, usually a major league player. (The autograph market for baseball players is so strong and the mentality of autograph collectors and sellers so fanatical that it is not uncommon for fans to get players to sign baseball books even when the players have only a tangential relationship to the book). Unless the collector collects baseball books signed by players, there is no reason to purchase such a copy and, because of the player's signature, pay a premium price for a common book. The dilemma comes when an uncommon book the collector wants has been signed by the subject, and the collector must decide if it is worth the extra price to acquire the book. On the other hand, when the player is one of the game's immortals, his signature certainly enhances a copy of a book, and even purists who normally attach no extra significance to players' signatures may be tempted to pay extra for such a special copy. In general, when it comes to signing baseball books, authors lag behind subjects (at least when the subjects are major league players) in increasing the prices of the books; despite the fact that many collectors value an author's signature as much as (if not more than) a player's. The main thing to remember is that, while player signatures do inflate prices of baseball books, player-signed copies should not be used to establish prices for unsigned copies of the same books; nor should review copies, associational copies, or any other kind of "special" copy of the book.

Price Guide

While professional bibliographers and book dealers who issue catalogs normally arrange their entries by author's last name, this price guide is arranged by title because the author believes most collectors would prefer such an arrangement and will find it easier to use. This desire to accomodate the typical collector is also responsible for the simplified format of the entries. Consisting of five parts — Title, Author, Publisher, Date of Publication, Price — each entry is meant to provide enough information to accurately identify the book without impeding the user's ability to quickly ascertain each book's price. For more complete bibliographic data and descriptions of content, readers are urged to consult the reference sources mentioned elsewhere in this work, particularly the catalogs of the most prominent used baseball book dealers.

Towards the end of making this price guide as user-friendly as possible, the author has taken a number of liberties, as follows:

- Generally, subtitles are listed only if, and to the extent, they are necessary to identify the subject of the book. In numerous cases, the subtitle of a biography has been included to help distinguish it from other biographies of the same subject.

- When a book has more than two authors (unless one of them is also the subject), the first author on the title page is the one listed in this price guide along with "et al.," to indicate the other authors.

- Many publishers' names have been shortened or simplified in an effort to streamline entries and to maintain consistency, and words such as "Books," "Publishers," and "Press" have been omitted from the names of publishers appearing repeatedly in the guide. For instance, G. P. Putnam's Sons is listed simply as "Putnam," while Greenwood Press and Meckler Books are listed simply as "Greenwood" and "Meckler," respectively.

- The following abbreviations have been used, again, in an effort to streamline entries: Co. (for company), self-pub. (for self-published), Univ. (for University), ed. by (for edited by), Bklt (for Booklet), and PB orig. (for paperback original).

Every price in this guide is for a true first edition copy of the hardback version of a book ... or a paperback original version if a hardback was not issued ... in VG condition with a DJ in the same condition. Prices for copies which exceed this standard or fail to meet it should be adjusted accordingly (see Chapter 5 for particulars).

In some instances, the paperback version of a book published in both a hardback and paperback format is significantly more valuable than is typically the case, and the prices for the paperback version of a number of such books are included in the Guide. In such cases, the paperback price follows the hardback price and is indicated by a lower case abbreviation as in the following example: "85/pb 30."

The price for each book in this guide has been derived from one or more of three sources: catalog asking prices, auction sales, and the estimates of highly qualified colleagues. In the case of differing prices for a title, the author has used his own judgement to arrive at a reconciled price.

In deciding which books to include in the price guide, the author began by incorporating all Casey Award winners and nominees (from 1983 through 2005), as well as the 102 titles which comprise *Diamond Classics*. To this core list he added titles from dealer catalogs, lists of recommended books, and Grobani's *Guide to Baseball Literature*; using his own judgement to determine which books are of the most importance and greatest interest to the average collector. Readers may notice an emphasis on biographies, as they are a staple of baseball literature, including the Young Adult biographies in the highly collectible Putnam, Barnes, and Messner series; a de-emphasis on other genres, such as instructionals, poetry, and adult fiction and on more recent books (i.e., those published after 1990); and an exclusion (or near-exclusion) of juvenile fiction, children's picture books, guides, bargain books, team-issued publications, fantasy and other types of player-ratings books, and a vast assortment of slim publications, chapbooks, and booklets on a wide variety of baseball subjects.

Errors, unintentional omissions, and disagreements are inevitable with a work of this kind and scope, and the author would be pleased to hear from readers about corrections and suggestions for additions and price adjustments to include in future editions of this Price Guide.

A.G. Spalding and the Rise of Baseball, by Peter Levine, Oxford Univ. Press (1985). **15**

Aaron, by Henry Aaron ATT Furman Bisher, Crowell (1974). **15**

Aaron, r.f., by Henry Aaron ATT Furman Bisher, World (1968). **35**

Aaron to Zuverink, by Rich Marazzi w/Len Fiorito, Stein & Day (1982). **20**

Ace: Phil Marchildon, Canada's Pitching Sensation and Wartime Hero, by Brian Kendall, Viking (1993). **15**

Addie Joss: King of Pitchers, by Scott Longert, SABR (1998), PB orig. **10**

Adios to Ghosts, by Christy Walsh, self-pub. (1937). **75**

After the Miracle: The Amazin' Mets Twenty Years Later, by Maury Allen, Watts (1989). **10**

Al Kaline and the Detroit Tigers, by Hal Butler, Regnery (1973). **60**

The Al Kaline Story, by Al Hirshberg, Messner (1964). **125**

All-Star Baseball Since 1933, by Robert Obojski, Stein & Day (1980). **15**

The All-Star Game, by Donald Honig, The Sporting News (1987). **15**

All Time All Stars of Black Baseball, by James A. Riley, TK Publishers (1983). **200/pb 75**

All Time Rosters of Major League Baseball Clubs, by S. C. Thompson, Barnes (1967). **12.50**

Alston and the Dodgers, by Walter Alston & Si Burdick, Doubleday (1966). **20**

Always on the Offense, by Mike Schmidt w/Barbara Walder, Atheneum (1982). **15**

Amazing: The Miracle of the Mets, by Joseph Durso, Houghton Mifflin (1970). **15**

The Amazing Mets, by Jerry Mitchell, Grosset & Dunlap (1964). **20**

America through Baseball, by David Q. Voigt, Nelson-Hall (1976). **15**

American Baseball, Vol. 1, by David Q. Voigt, Univ. of Oklahoma Press (1966). **40**

American Baseball, Vol. 2, by David Q. Voigt, Univ. of Oklahoma Press (1970). **40**

American Baseball, Vol. 3, by David Q. Voigt, Pennsylvania State Univ. Press (1983). **30**

The American Diamond, by Branch Rickey w/Robert Riger, Simon & Schuster (1965). **125**

The American Dream and the National Game, by Leverett T. Smith, Jr., Bowling Green Univ. Popular Press (1975). **35**

The American League: An Illustrated History, by Donald Honig, Crown Publishers (1983). **15**

The American League Story, by Lee Allen, Hill & Wang (1962). **25**

America's Dizzy Dean, by Curt Smith, The Bethany Press (1978). **10**

America's National Game, by Albert G. Spalding, American Sports Publishing Co., (1911). **400**

Andy Pafko: The Solid Man, by John Hoffman, Barnes (1951). **75**

The Angels, by Richard Beverage, Deacon (1981), PB orig. **175**

The Annotated Casey at the Bat, by Martin Gardner, Clarkson N. Potter (1967). **12**

The Answer Is Baseball, by Luke Salisbury, Times Books (1989). **10**

The Armchair Book of Baseball, ed. by John Thorn, Scribners (1985). **20**

The Armchair Book of Baseball, II, ed. by John Thorn, Scribners (1987). **20**

Around the World with the Base Ball Bugs, by Jack Regan and Will Stahl, J. Regan & Co. (1910), PB orig. **125**

Price Guide

The Art of Baseball, by Shelly M. Dinhofer, Harmony (1990). **25**

The Art of Pitching and Fielding, by Henry Chadwick (1887). **300**

The Artful Dodger, by Tommy Lasorda & David Fisher, Arbor House (1985). **7.50**

The Artful Dodgers, by Tom Meany et al., Barnes (1953). **75**

At Fenway: Dispatches from Red Sox Nation, by Dan Shaughnessy, Crown (1996). **12**

At the Crack of the Bat, ed. by Lillian Morrison, Hyperion (1992). **15**

Athletic Sports in America, England and Australia by Harry Clay Palmer et al., W. A. Houghton (1889). **575**

The Babe: A Life in Pictures, by Lawrence Ritter & Mark Rucker, Ticknor & Fields (1989). **35**

Babe: The Legend Comes to Life, by Robert Creamer, Simon & Schuster (1974). **35**

The Babe and I, by Claire Ruth, Prentice Hall (1959). **17.50**

The Babe in Red Stockings, by Kerry Keene et al., Sagamore (1997). **15**

Babe Ruth, by Martin Weldon, Crowell (1948). **125**

Babe Ruth, by Tom Meany, Barnes (1947). **35**

Babe Ruth: Baseball Boy, by Guernsey Van Riper Jr., Bobbs-Merrill (1954). **25**

Babe Ruth: His Life and Legend, by Kal Wagenheim, Praeger (1974). **20**

Babe Ruth: His Story in Baseball, Lee Allen, Putnam (1966). **100**

Babe Ruth: The Idol of the American Boy, by Dan Daniel, Whitman (1930). **75**

Babe Ruth and the American Dream, by Ken Sobol, Random House (1974), PB orig. **30/hb 30**

The Babe Ruth Story, by Babe Ruth ATT Bob Considine, Dutton (1948). **65**

Babe Ruth's America, by Robert Smith, Crowell (1974). **25**

Babe Ruth's Baseball Advice, by Babe Ruth, Rand McNally (1936). **100**

Babe Ruth's Big Book of Baseball, by Babe Ruth, Reilly & Lee (1935), PB orig. **85**

Babe Ruth's Own Book of Baseball, by Babe Ruth, Putnam (1928). **70**

Backstage at the Mets, by Lindsey Nelson w/Al Hirshberg, Viking (1966). **17.50**

The Bad Guys Won, by Jeff Pearlman, Harper Collins (2004). **15**

Bad Henry, by Stan Baldwin & Jerry Jenkins in collaboration w/Hank Aaron, Chilton Book Co. (1974). **15**

Ball, Bat and Bishop, by Robert W. Henderson, Rockport Press (1947). **60**

Ball Four, by Jim Bouton, The World Publishing Co. (1970). **35**

Ballads of Baseball, by W. A. Phelon, Metropolitan Syndicate Press (1906), PB orig. **125**

Balldom: The Britannica of Baseball, by George L. Moreland, Balldom Publishing Co. (1914). $150/reprint, Horton Publishing Co. (1989), **pb 20**

Ballpark: Camden Yards and the Building of an American Dream, by Peter Richmond, Simon & Schuster (1993). **10**

Ballpark Figures: The Blue Jays and the Business of Baseball, by Larry Millson, McClelland & Stewart (1987). **20**

The Ballparks, by Bill Shannon & George Kalinsky, Hawthorn (1975). **75**

Ballparks of North America, by Michael Benson, McFarland (1989). **45**

The Ballplayers, ed. by Mike Shatzkin, Morrow (1990). **22.50**

Ballplayers Are Human Too, by Ralph Houk w/Charles Dexter, Putnam (1962). **25**

A Ballplayer's Career, by Adrian "Cap" Anson, Era (1900). **375**

Balls, by Graig Nettles & Peter Golenbock, Putnam (1984). **7.50**

The Baltimore Orioles, by Fred Lieb, Putnam (1955). **125**

The Baltimore Orioles: 40 Years of Magic from 33rd Street to Camden Yards, by Ted Patterson, Taylor (1994). **17.50**

Ban Johnson, by Eugene Murdock, Greenwood Press (1982). **45**

Banana Bats and Dingdong Balls: A Century of Baseball Inventions, by Dan Gutman, Macmillan (1995), PB orig. **10**

Bang the Drum Slowly, by Mark Harris, Knopf (1956). **125**

Barry Bonds: Baseball's Superman, by Steven Travers, Sports Publishing (2002). **15**

Base Ball: How to Become a Player, by John Montgomery Ward, The Atlantic Publishing Co. (1888). **1,035**

Base Ball A.B.C., McLoughlin Brothers (1885). **1,200**

Base Ball in Cincinnati, by Harry Ellard, Press of Johnson and Hardin (1907). **1,100**/ reprint, Ohio Book Store (1987), **hb 95**

Baseball, by Newton Crane, George Bell & Sons (1891). **900**

Baseball, by Richard G. Knowles and Richard Morton, G. Routledge & Sons (1886), PB orig. **900**

Baseball, by Tom Clark, The Figures (1976), PB orig. **25**

Baseball, by Walter Iooss, Jr. & Roger Angell, Abrams, (1984). **20**

Baseball: America's Diamond Mind 1919–1941, by Richard Crepeau, Univ. of Central Florida (1980). **27.50**

Baseball: A Comprehensive Bibliography, by Myron Smith, McFarland (1986). **55**

Baseball: Diamond in the Rough, by Irving Leitner, Criterion Books (1972). **25**

Baseball: The Fan's Game, by Mickey Cochrane, Funk & Wagnall's (1939). **125**

Baseball: From Backyard to Big League, by George "Specs" Toporcer, Sterling (1954). **15**

Baseball: A Historical Narrative of the Game, by Robert Smith, Simon & Schuster (1947). **20**

Baseball: A History of America's Game, by Benjamin G. Rader, Univ. of Illinois Press (1992). **15**

Baseball: An Illustrated History, by Geoffrey C. Ward & Ken Burns, Knopf (1994). **30**

Baseball: Individual Play and Team Strategy, by John Coombs, Prentice-Hall (1938). **20**

Baseball: An Informal History, by Douglas Wallop, Norton (1969). **15**

Baseball: The Lives Behind the Seams, by Maury Allen, Macmillan (1990). **10**

Baseball: The National Game of the Americans, Harry C. Palmer, A. G. Spalding & Brothers (1888), PB orig. **375**

Baseball: The Perfect Game, photographs by Danielle Weil, Rizzoli (1992). **17.50**

Baseball: The Presidents' Game, by William B. Mead and Paul Dickson, Farragut (1993). **22**

Baseball: A Treasury of Art and Literature, ed. by Michael Ruscoe, Hugh Lauter Levin Associates (1993). **28**

Baseball: Vol. 1, The Early Years, by Harold Seymour, Oxford Univ. Press (1960). **50**

Baseball: Vol. 2, The Golden Age, by Harold Seymour, Oxford Univ. Press (1960). **40**

Baseball: Vol. 3, The People's Game, by Harold Seymour, Oxford Univ. Press (1990). **20**

Baseball: The Writers' Game, by Mike Shannon, Diamond Communications (1992). **20**

A Baseball Album, by Gerald Secor Couzens, Lippincott & Crowell (1980). **20**

Baseball America, by Donald Honig, Macmillan (1985). **17.50**

Baseball and Billions, by Andrew Zimbalist, Basic Books (1992). **10**

Baseball and Mr. Spalding, by Arthur Bartlett, Farrar Straus & Young (1951). **17.50**

Baseball and the American Dream, by Joseph Durso, The Sporting News (1986). **10**

Baseball and the Cold War, by Howard Senzel, Harcourt Brace Jovanovich (1977). **15**

Baseball Anecdotes, by Daniel Okrent & Steve Wulf, Oxford Univ. Press (1989). **12.50**

Baseball as I Have Known It, by Fred Lieb, Coward McCann & Geoghegan (1977). **15**

Baseball as Viewed by a Muffin, S. Van Campen, Taber Brothers (1867), PB orig. **750**

Baseball Ballads, by Grantland Rice, Tennessean Co, (1910). **250**

Baseball Before We Knew It, by David Block, Univ. of Nebraska Press (2005). **20**

Baseball Between the Lines, by Donald Honig, Coward McCann & Geoghegan (1976). **15**

Baseball Between the Wars, by Eugene Murdock, Meckler (1992). **20**

The Baseball Bible, by Angel Torres, self-pub. (1984), PB orig. **15**

The Baseball Business, by James E. Miller, Univ. of North Carolina Press (1990). **15**

Baseball by the Books, by Andy McCue, William C. Brown (1991). **20**

Baseball Cartes: The First Baseball Cards, by Mark Rucker, Haymaker Books (1988), PB orig. **12.50**

Baseball Complete, by Russ Hodges, Rudolph Field (1952). **20**

Baseball Confidential, by Arthur Mann, McKay (1951). **25**

Baseball Cyclopedia, by Ernest J. Lanigan, Baseball Magazine (1922), PB orig. **30/supplements 5–10@**

Baseball (1888) from the Newspaper Accounts, by Preston D. Orem, self-pub. (1967). **200**

Baseball, 1845–1871, by Seymour Church, self-pub. (1902). **1,200/** reprint, The Pyne Press (1974), **pb 35**

Baseball (1845–1881) from the Newspaper Accounts, by Preston D. Orem, self-pub. (1961). **45**

The Baseball Encyclopedia, by Information Concepts, Inc., Macmillan (1969). **20**

Baseball Extra, by Frank Graham, Barnes (1954). **17.50**

Baseball Fanthology, ed. by Edward Branch Lyman, self-pub. (1924). **85**

Baseball for the Love of It, by Anthony J. Connor, Macmillan (1982). **12.50**

Baseball Giant Killers: The Spudders of the '20s, by Al Parker, Nortex (1976). **35**

Baseball Graphics, by John Davenport, First Impressions (1979), PB orig. **20**

Baseball Grins, by J. Honus Wagner, Laurel House (1933), Bklt. **650**

The Baseball Hall of Fame 50th Anniversary Book, ed. by Gerald Astor, Prentice Hall (1988). **25**

Baseball History in Limerick, Verse & Sketch, by D. C. Vogt, Greenfield House, (1981), PB orig. **40**

Baseball I Gave You All the Best Years of My Life, ed. by Kevin Kerrane & Richard Grossinger, North Atlantic Books (1977). **30**

Baseball I Love You, by Charlie Grimm w/Ed Prell, Regnery (1968). **22**

Baseball Immortals, by Ed Burkholder, Christopher Publishing House (1955). **65**

Baseball in America: An Illustrated History of Our National Pastime, by Robert Smith, Holt Rinehart Winston (1961). **17.50**

Baseball in America: From Sandlots to Stadiums, A Portrait of Our National Pastime by 50 of Today's Leading Photographers, ed. by Karen Mullarkey, Collins (1991). **20**

Baseball in '41, by Robert W. Creamer, Viking (1991). **25**

Baseball in Old Chicago, by Federal Writers Project, McClurg (1939), PB orig. **75**

Baseball in the Big Leagues, by John J. Evers & Hugh S. Fullerton, Reilly & Britton (1913). **85**

Baseball in the '30s, by Donald Honig, Crown Publishers (1989). **20**

Baseball in the '50s, by Donald Honig, Crown Publishers (1987). **20**

Baseball in the Movies, by Hal Erickson, McFarland (1992). **30**

Baseball Is a Funny Game, by Joe Garagiola & Martin Quigley, J.B. Lippincott (1960). **12.50**

Baseball Is Their Business, ed. by Harold Rosenthal, Random House (1952). **17.50**

Baseball Jokes, Stories and Poems, by James Sullivan, Arthur Westbrook Co. (1906), PB orig. **45**

Baseball Lingo, Zander Hollander, Norton (1967). **22**

Baseball Lives, by Mike Bryan, Pantheon (1989). **10**

Baseball Memorabilia, by Robert Obojski, Sterling (1991). **12.50**

Baseball on the Border: A Tale of Two Laredos, by Alan Klein, Princeton Univ. Press (1997). **15**

Baseball Palace of the World, Douglas Bukowski, Lyceum (1992). **25**

Baseball Personalities, by Jimmy Powers, Rudolph Field (1949). **17.50**

The Baseball Player: An Economic Study, Paul Gregory, Public Affairs Press (1956). **125**

Baseball Players and Their Times: Oral Histories of the Game, 1920–1940, by Eugene Murdock, Meckler (1991). **22.50**

Baseball Player's Pocket Companion, A. Hudge & Son (1859), Bklt. **10,000**

The Baseball Reader: Favorites from the Fireside Books of Baseball, ed. by Charles Einstein, Lippincott & Crowell (1980). **15**

Baseball Records Registry, by Joseph J. Dittmar, McFarland (1997). **22**

The Baseball Story, Fred Lieb, Putnam (1950). **30**

Baseball the Beautiful: Decoding the Diamond, by Marvin Cohen, Links Books (1974). **20/pb 5**

The Baseball Timeline, by Burt Solomon, Avon (1997), PB orig. **12.50**

The Baseball Trade Register, by Joe Reichler, Macmillan (1984). **10**

Baseball Treasures: Memorabilia from the National Pastime, by Douglas Congdon-Martin & John Kashmanian, Schiffer (1992). **25**

Baseball Uniforms of the 20th Century, by Marc Okkonen, Sterling (1991). **65/pb 40**

Baseball When the Grass Was Real, by Donald Honig, Coward McCann & Geoghegan (1975). **17.50**

A Baseball Winter: The Off-Season Life of the Summer Game, ed. by Terry Pluto & Jeffrey Neuman, Macmillan (1986). **15**

Baseballogy, by Edmund Vance Cooke, Forbes (1912). **250**

Baseball's All-Star Game: A Game-by-Game Guide, by Jeff Lenburg, McFarland (1986). **25**

Baseball's Back in Town, by Louis Cauz, Controlled Media (1977). **17.50**

Baseball's Benchmark Boxscores, by Joseph Ditmar, McFarland (1990). **20**

Baseball's Best Managers, by Harold Rosenthal, Randon House (1952). **30**

Baseball's Best, by Dave Masterson & Timm Boyle, Contemporary Books (1985), PB orig. **15**

Baseball's Best: The Hall of Fame Gallery, by Marty Appel & Burt Goldblatt, McGraw-Hill (1977). **15**

Baseball's Famous First Basemen, by Ira Smith, Barnes (1956). **25**

Baseball's 50 Greatest Games, by Lowell Reidenbaugh, The Sporting News (1986). **12.50**

Baseball's Golden Age: The Photographs of Charles M. Conlon, by Neal & Constance McCabe, Abrams (1993). **25**

Baseball's Great Experiment, by Jules Tygiel, Oxford Univ. Press (1983). **22**

Baseball's Great Tragedy, by Bob McGarigle, Exposition (1972). **150**

Baseball's Greatest Catchers, by Al Hirshberg, Putnam (1966). **75**

Baseball's Greatest Drama, by Joseph Krueger, Classic Publishing Co. (1943). **45**

Baseball's Greatest Hitters, by Tom Meany, Barnes (1950). **40**

Baseball's Greatest Lineup, ed. by Christy Walsh, Barnes (1952). **25**

Baseball's Greatest Managers, by Edwin Pope, Doubleday (1960). **12.50**

Baseball's Greatest Managers, by Harvey Frommer, Watts (1985). **15**

Baseball's Greatest Pitchers, by Milton J. Shapiro, Messner (1969). **40**

Baseball's Greatest Pitchers, by Tom Meany, Barnes (1951). **20**

Baseball's Greatest Rivalry, by Harvey Frommer, Atheneum (1982). **25**

Baseball's Greatest Sluggers, by Bill Libby, Random House (1973). **10**

Baseball's Greatest Teams, by Tom Meany, Barnes (1949). **35**

Baseball's Hall of Fame, by Lowell Reidenbaugh, The Sporting News (1983). **17.50**

Baseball's Most Colorful Managers, by Ray Robinson, Putnam (1969). **40**

Baseball's Most Valuable Players, by George Vecsey, Random House (1966). **7.50**

Baseball's Natural: The Story of Eddie Waitkus, by John Theodore, Southern Illinois Univ. Press (2002). **20**

Baseball's 100: A Personal Ranking, by Maury Allen, A & W Publishers (1981). **15**

Baseball's Pennant Races: A Graphic View, by John Davenport, First Impressions (1981), PB orig. **20**

Baseball's Pivotal Era 1945–1951, by William Marshall, The Univ. of Kentucky Press (1999). **15**

Baseball's Radical for All Seasons; A Biography of John Montgomery Ward, by David Stevens, Scarecrow Press (1998). **20**

Baseball's Ten Greatest Games, by John Thorn, Four Winds Press (1981). **12.50**

Baseball's 10 Greatest Teams, by Donald Honig, Macmillan (1982). **15**

Baseball's 25 Greatest Pennant Races, by Lowell Reidenbaugh, The Sporting News (1987). **12.50**

Baseball's Unforgettable Games, by Joe Reichler & Ben Olan, Ronald Press (1960). **15**

Basepaths: The Best of the Minneapolis Review of Baseball, ed. by Ken LaZebnik & Steve Lehman, Wm. C. Brown (1991). **15**

Basepaths: From the Minor Leagues to the Majors and Beyond, by Marc Gunther, Scribners (1984). **15**

Bat Boy of the Giants, by Garth Garreau, Comet (1949), PB orig. **20**

Batboy of the Braves, by Paul Wick ATT Bob Wolf, Greenberg (1957). **25**

Bats, by Davey Johnson & Peter Golenbock, Putnam (1986). **5**

Batting, by F. C. Lane, Baseball Magazine (1925), PB orig. **30**

The Battle of Baseball, by C. H. Claudy, Century Co. (1911). **120**

Beating the Bushes, by Frank Dolson, Icarus Press (1982). **20**

The Beer and Whiskey League, by David Nemec, Lyons & Burford (1994). **20**

Behind the Mask, by Bill Freehan, World (1970). **24**

Behind the Mask, by Dave Pallone w/Alan Steinberg, Viking (1990). **7**

The Best in Baseball, by Robert H. Shoemaker, Crowell (1949). **17.50**

The Best of Baseball, ed. by Sidney Offit, Putnam (1956). **20**

The Best Seat in Baseball, But You Have to Stand, by Lee Gutkind, The Dial Press (1975). **18**

The Best Team Money Could Buy: The Turmoil and Triumph of the 1977 New York Yankees, by Steve Jacobson, Atheneum (1978). **15**

Between the Lines, by Steve Howe, Masters Press (1989). **7.50**

Beyond the Shadows of the Senators: The Untold Story of the Homestead Grays, by Brad Snyder, McGraw-Hill (2003). **22**

Beyond the Sixth Game, by Peter Gammons, Houghton Mifflin (1985). **12.50**

The Big Baseball Book for Boys, by M.G. Bonner, McLoughlin Brothers (1931). **125**

Big League Batting Secrets, by Harvey Kuenn & Jim Smilgoff, Prentice Hall (1958). **24**

Big Red Dynasty, by Greg Rhodes & John Erardi, Road West Publishing (1997). **22**

The Big Red Machine, by Bob Hertzel, Prentice-Hall (1976). **12**

Big Sticks, by William Curran, Morrow (1990). **10**

Big-Time Baseball, by Harold H. Hart & Ralph Tolleris, Hart Publishing (1950). **10**

The Bill James Baseball Abstract, by Bill James, Ballantine Books (1982–1988), PB orig. **1982 30/1983–88 17.50 @**.

The Bill James Historical Baseball Abstract, by Bill James, Villard (1986). **25**

Bill Stern's Favorite Baseball Stories, by Bill Stern, Doubleday (1949). **20**

Bill Veeck: A Baseball Legend, by Gerald Eskenazi, McGraw Hill (1988). **15**

Billy, by Billy Williams & Irv Haag, Rand McNally (1974). **35**

Billy Martin, by Gene Schoor, Doubleday (1980). **15**

The Billy Martin Story, by Joe Archibald, Messner (1959). **100**

Billy Sunday: The Man and His Message, by William T. Ellis, Winston (1914). **125**

Billyball, by Billy Martin w/Phil Pepe, Doubleday (1987). **10**

The Bingo Long Traveling All-Stars and Motor Kings, by William Brashler, Harper & Row (1973). **55**

The Biographical Encyclopedia of the Negro Baseball Leagues, by James A. Riley, Carroll & Graf (1994). **17**

Birds on the Wing, by Gordon Beard, Doubleday (1967). **25**

Black Baseball's National Showcase: The East-West All-Star Game, 1933–1953, by Larry Lester, Univ. of Nebraska Press (2002), PB orig. **17.50**

Black Diamonds, by John Holway, Meckler Books (1989). **20**

Black Writers/Black Baseball, by Jim Reisler, McFarland (1994). **17.50**

Blackball Stars, by John Holway, Meckler Books (1988). **20**

Bleachers, by Lonnie Wheeler, Contemporary Books, (1988). **15**

Bleep! by Larry Bowa w/Barry Bloom, Bonus Books (1988). **8**

Bless You Boys, by Sparky Anderson w/Dan Ewald, Contemporary Books (1984). **5**

The Blooper Man, by Elston Smith, J. Pohl Associates (1981). **85/pb 25**

Blue Ruin: A Novel of the 1919 World Series, by Brendan Boyd, Norton (1991). **10**

Bo: Pitching and Wooing, by Maury Allen, The Dial Press (1973). **20**

The Bob Allison Story, by Hal Butler, Messner (1967). **100**

Bob Feller: Hall of Fame Strikeout Star, by Gene Schoor, Doubleday (1962). **50**

Bob Gibson: Pitching Ace, by David Lipman & Ed Wilks, Putnam (1975). **225**

Bob Lemon: The Workhorse, by Ed McAuley, Barnes (1951). **50**

Bob Turley: Fastball Pitcher, by Gene Schoor, Putnam (1959). **125**

Bobby Bonds: Rising Superstar, by George Sullivan, Putnam (1976). **200**

The Bobby Richardson Story, by Bobby Richardson, Revell (1965). **20**

Bobby Shantz, by Ed Delaney, Barnes (1953). **65**

The Book of American Pastimes, by Charles A. Peverelly (1866). **1,400**

The Book of Baseball, by William Patten & J. W. McSpadden, P. F. Collier & Son (1911). **325**

The Book of Major League Baseball Clubs (2 vols.) by Ed Fitzgerald, Barnes (1952). **30**

Born to Play Ball, by Willie Mays ATT Charles Einstein, Putnam (1955). **200**

The Boston Braves, by Harold Kaese, Putnam (1948). **45**

The Boston Red Sox, by Fred Lieb, Putnam, (1947). **45**

Boston Red Sox, by Henry Berry, Rutledge (1975). **25**

The Boston Red Sox, by Tom Meany et al., Barnes (1956). **40**

The Boston Red Sox: An Illustrated History, by Donald Honig, Prentice-Hall (1990). **15**

The Boston Red Sox: An Illustrated Tribute, by Donald Honig, St. Martin's (1984). **35**

The Boston Red Sox: Memories and Memorabilia of New England's Team, by Bruce Chadwick, Abbeville Press (1992). **15**

Boston Red Sox: 75th Anniversary History 1901–75, by Ellery H. Clark Jr., Exposition (1975). **20**

The Boston Red Sox of 1955, by E. James Chouinard, Meador Publishing Co. (1956). **55**

The Boys of Spring: Timeless Portraits from the Grapefruit League, by Ozzie Sweet, Sport Classic Books (2005). **25**

The Boys of Summer, by Roger Kahn, Harper & Row (1971). **30**

The Boys Who Would Be Cubs, by Joseph Bosco, Morrow (1990). **12**

Branch Rickey, by Murray Polner, Atheneum (1982). **27.50**

Branch Rickey: American in Action, by Arthur Mann, Houghton Mifflin (1957). **35**

The Braves First Fifteen Years in Atlanta, by J. Hudson Couch, The Other Alligator Creek Co. (1984), PB orig. **12**

The Braves The Pick and the Shovel, by Al Hirshberg, Waverly House (1948). **50**

Breaking the Slump: Baseball in the Depression Era, by Charles Alexander, Columbia Univ. Press (2002). **12**

Breakout: From Prison to the Big Leagues, by Ron LeFlore w/Jim Hawkins, Harper & Row (1978). **10**

Breakthrough to the Big League, by Jackie Robinson & Alfred Duckett, Harper & Row (1965). **37.50**

A Brief History of Baseball, by Francis Richter, Sporting Life Publishing Co. (1909). **1,250**

Brittle Innings, by Michael Bishop, Bantam (1994). **15**

The Broadcasters, by Red Barber, Dial Press (1970). **17.50**

The Bronx Bombers: Memories and Memorabilia of the New York Yankees, by Bruce Chadwick, Abbeville Press (1991). **15**

The Bronx Zoo, by Sparky Lyle & Peter Golenbock, Crown (1979). **10**

The Brooklyn Dodgers, by Frank Graham, Putnam (1945). **40**

The Brooklyn Dodgers: An Illustrated Tribute, by Donald Honig, St. Martin's (1981). **40**

Brooklyn's Babe: The Life and Legend of Babe Herman, by Tot Holmes, Holmes Publishing (1990), PB orig. **10**

The Brooks Robinson Story, by Jack Zanger, Messner (1967). **100**

The Brothers K, by David James Duncan, Doubleday (1992). **35**

Brushing Back Jim Crow, by Bruce Adelson, Univ. of Virginia Press (1999). **15**

Buck Leonard: The Black Lou Gehrig, by Buck Leonard w/James Riley, Carroll & Graf (1995). **10.50**

Bud Harrelson, by Bill Libby, Putnam (1975). **100**

Bullet Bob Comes to Louisville, by John Morris, Diamond Communications (1999). **10**

Bullet Joe and the Monarchs, by John Holway, Capital Press (1984), PB orig. **300**

Bums: An Oral History of the Brooklyn Dodgers, by Peter Golenbock, Putnam (1984). **15**

Bush League: A History of Minor League Baseball, by Robert Obojski, Macmillan (1975). **25**

Bushville: Life and Time in Amateur Baseball, by Jerry Kelly, McFarland (2001), PB orig. **15**

The Business of Major League Baseball, by Gerald W. Scully, The Univ. of Chicago Press (1989). **10**

Busting 'Em, by Ty Cobb, E. J. Clode (1914). **450**

Butchered Baseball, by F. S. Pearson, Barnes (1952). **15**

The California Angels: The Complete History, by Ross Newhan, Simon & Schuster (1982). **15**

Calvin: Baseball's Last Dinosaur, by Jon Kerr, Wm. C. Brown (1990). **10**

Can't Anybody Here Play This Game? by Jimmy Breslin, Viking (1963). **45**

Card Sharks, by Pete Williams, Macmillan (1995). **12.50**

Cardinal Classics, by Robert L. Tiemann, Baseball Histories (1984). **20**

Price Guide

Carew, by Rod Carew w/Ira Berkow, Simon & Schuster (1979). **15**

Casey: The Life and Legend of Charles Dillon Stengel, by Joseph Durso, Prentice Hall (1967). **30**

Casey & Mr. McGraw, by Joseph Durso, The Sporting News (1989). **10**

Casey at the Bat, by Casey Stengel ATT Harry T. Paxton, Random House (1962). **25**

Casey at the Bat, by Ernest Thayer, McClurg & Co. (1912). **2,300**

Casey at the Bat, by Ernest Thayer, New Amsterdam Book Co. (1901), PB orig. **6,250**

Casey at the Bat: A Centennial Edition, by Ernest Lawrence Thayer (illustrations by Barry Moser), David R. Godine (1988). **20**

Casey on the Loose: What Really Might Have Happened, by Frank Deford, Viking (1989). **8**

Casey Stengel, by Frank Graham, John Day (1958). **50**

Casey Stengel, by Norman MacLean, Drake (1976). **20**

Casey Stengel: Baseball's Greatest Manager, by Gene Schoor, Messner (1953). **55**

Casey Stengel's Secret, by Clay Felker, Walker (1961). **28**

Catch: A Major League Life, by Ernie Whitt & Greg Cable, McGraw-Hill (1989). **15**

Catch You Later, by Johnny Bench & William Brashler, Harper & Row (1979). **20**

Catcher in the Rye, by Bob Uecker & Mickey Herskowitz, Putnam (1982). **18**

The Catcher Was a Lady: The Clem Dreisewerd Story, by Edna Dreisewerd, Exposition (1978). **50**

The Catcher Was a Spy, by Nicholas Dawidoff, Pantheon (1994). **15**

Catching, by Elston Howard, Viking (1966). **30**

Catching Dreams, by Frazier "Slow" Robinson w/Paul Bauer, Syracuse Univ. Press (1999). **45**

Catfish, by Jim Hunter w/Armen Keteyian, McGraw Hill (1988). **12**

Catfish: The Three Million Dollar Pitcher, by Bill Libby, Coward McCann & Geoghegan (1976). **20**

Catfish Hunter, by Irwin Stambler, Putnam (1976). **50**

Caught Short, by Donald Davidson w/Jesse Outlar, Atheneum (1972). **20**

The Celebrant, by Eric Rolfe Greenberg, Everest House (1983). **100**

Center Field Grasses: Poems from Baseball, by Gene Fehler, McFarland (1991). **12.50**

Champagne and Baloney, by Tom Clark, Harper & Row (1976). **25**

Champions of the Bat, by Milton Shapiro, Messner (1967). **22**

Charley Hustle, by Pete Rose w/Bob Hertzel, Prentice Hall (1975). **18**

Charlie O: Charles Oscar Finley Vs. the Baseball Establishment, by Herbert Michelson, Bobbs Merrill (1975). **15**

Charlie O. and the Angry A's, by Bill Libby, Doubleday (1975). **15**

Chasing October: The Dodgers-Giants Pennant Race of 1962, by David Plaut, Diamond Communications (1994). **15**

Cheering for the Home Team: The Story of Baseball in Canada, by William Humber, Boston Mills (1983). **35/pb 15**

Chicago Cubs, by Jim Enright, Macmillan (1975). **17**

The Chicago Cubs, by Warren Brown, Putnam (1946). **35**

The Chicago Cubs: An Illustrated History, by Donald Honig, Prentice Hall (1991). **15**

The Chicago Cubs: Memories and Memorabilia of the Wrigley Wonders, by Bruce Chadwick, Abbeville Press (1994). **20**

The Chicago White Sox, by Warren Brown, Putnam (1952). **35**

Chris Von der Ahe and the St. Louis Browns, by J. Thomas Hetrick, Scarecrow (1999). **27**

Christy Mathewson, by Gene Schoor w/Henry Gilfond, Messner (1955). **75**

The Chrysanthemum and the Bat, by Robert Whiting, Dodd Mead (1977). **35/pb (The Permanent Press) 22**

Cincinnati and the Big Red Machine, by Robert Walker, Indiana Univ. Press (1988). **15**

The Cincinnati Game, by Lonnie Wheeler & John Baskin, Orange Frazer Press (1988). **175/pb 60**

The Cincinnati Reds: An Illustrated History, by Donald Honig, Simon & Schuster (1992). **40**

The Cincinnati Reds: An Informal History, by Lee Allen, Putnam (1948). **65**

The Cincinnati Reds: Memories and Memorabilia of the Big Red Machine, by Bruce Chadwick, Abbeville Press (1994). **20**

The Cincinnati Reds: A Pictorial History of Professional Baseball's Oldest Team, by Ritter Collett, Jordan-Powers (1976). **30**

Cincinnati Reds Horoscope, Ira Cook & D. Modin, self-pub. (1971), PB orig. **100**

Cincinnati Reds Scrapbook, by Bob Rathgeber, JCP (1982). **25**

Cincinnati Seasons, by Earl Lawson, Diamond Communications (1987). **15**

The Cinema of Baseball, by Gary E. Dickerson, Meckler (1991). **15**

Circling the Bases, by Bill Werber, self-pub. (1978). **45**

Clemente! by Kal Wagenheim, Praeger Publishing (1973). **22**

Cleon, by Cleon Jones, Coward McCann (1970). **18**

The Cleveland Indian, by Luke Salisbury, The Smith, (1992). **12**

The Cleveland Indians, by Franklin Lewis, Putnam (1949). **85**

The Cleveland Indians Flagpole Sitter, by Charles Lupica, Jr., self-pub. (1997), PB orig. **20**

A Clever Base-Ballist: The Life and Times of John Montgomery Ward, by Bryan Di Salvatore, Pantheon (1999). **17**

Clout! The Top Home Runs in Baseball History, by Dan Valenti, Stephen Greene Press (1989), PB orig. **10**

Clowning through Baseball, by Al Schacht, Barnes (1941). **20**

Cobb, by Al Stump, Algonquin Books, (1994). **10**

Cobb Would Have Caught It, by Richard Bak, Wayne State Univ. Press (1991). **25**

The College World Series: A Baseball History 1947–2003, by W. C. Madden & Patrick J. Stewart, McFarland (2004). **22**

Collision at Home Plate: The Lives of Pete Rose and Bart Giamatti, by James Reston Jr., HarperCollins (1991). **12**

Colorado Rockies: The Inagural Season, by Rich Clarkson, Fulcrum (1993). **10**

Comeback, by Dave Dravecky w/Tim Stafford, Zondervan (1990). **7.50**

The Comeback, by Ryne Duren w/Robert Drury, Lorenz Press (1978). **25**

Coming Apart at the Seams, by Jack Sands & Peter Gammons, Macmillan (1993). **7**

Coming Back with the Spitball, by James Hopper, Harper & Brothers (1914). **60**

Commy, by G. W. Axelson, Reilly & Lee (1919). **300**

Connie Mack, by Fred Lieb, Putnam (1945). **45**

Connie Mack's Baseball Book, by Connie Mack, Knopf (1950). **35**

Cooperstown: Where Legends Live Forever, by Lowell Reidenbaugh, The Sporting News (1983). **15**

Cooperstown Verses: Poems about Each Hall of Famer, by Mark W. Schraf, McFarland (2001), PB orig. **20**

Country Hardball, by Enos Slaughter w/Kevin Reid, Tudor Publishers (1991). **25**

Covering All the Bases, by Lou Boudreau w/Russell Schneider, Sagamore (1993). **12**

Covering the Outfield, by Terry Moore, Ziff Davis (1948). **35**

Crash: The Life and Times of Dick Allen, by Dick Allen & Tim Whitaker, Ticknor & Fields (1989). **18**

The Crooked Pitch: The Curveball in American Baseball History, by Martin Quigley, Algonquin Books (1984). **25**

Crosley Field: An Illustrated History of a Classic Ballpark, by Greg Rhodes & John Erardi, Road West Publishing (1995), PB orig. **15**

The Cubs of '69, by Rick Talley, Contemporary (1989). **15**

Cult Baseball Players, ed. by Danny Peary, Simon & Schuster (1990), PB orig. **12.50**

The Curious Case of Sidd Finch, by George Plimpton, Macmillan (1987). **15**

The Curse of Rocky Colavito, by Terry Pluto, Simon & Schuster (1994). **13**

The Curse of the Bambino, by Dan Shaughnessy, Dutton (1990). **15**

The Cutoff, by Jay Rogoff, The Word Works (1995), Bklt. **12**

Cutting the Corners, by Tex Millard, Barnes (1966). **16**

Cy Young: A Baseball Life, by Reed Browning, Univ. of Massachusetts Press (2000). **18**

Cy Young: Baseball's Legendary Giant, by Ralph Romig, Dorrance (1964). **125/pb 20**

Damn Yankee, by Maury Allen, Times (1980). **10**

Dandy, Day and the Devil, by James A. Riley, TK Publishers (1987), **125/pb 50**

Dave Winfield: The 23 Million Dollar Man, by Gene Schoor, Stein & Day (1982). **15**

Day by Day in Cincinnati Reds History, by Floyd Conner & John Snyder, Leisure Press (1983), PB orig. **35**

Day by Day in Cleveland Indians History, by Morris Eckhouse, Leisure Press (1983), PB orig. **45**

A Day in the Bleachers, by Arnold Hano, Thomas Y. Crowell (1955). **100**

A Day in the Season of the Los Angeles Dodgers, by Tom Zimmerman, Shapolssky (1990). **12**

Day with the Giants, by Laraine Day, Doubleday (1952). **30**

The Days of Mr. McGraw, by Joseph Durso, Prentice Hall (1969). **15**

Dead Pull Hitter, by Alison Gordon, McClelland & Stewart (1988). **20**

The Decline and Fall of the New York Yankees, by Jack Mann, Simon & Schuster (1967). **15**

The Denver Bears, by Mark Foster, Pruett (1983). **60**

Destiny's Darlings, by Martin Ralbovsky, Hawthorne Books (1974). **18**

The Detroit Tigers, by Fred Lieb, Putnam (1946). **45**

Detroit Tigers, by Joe Falls, Macmillan (1975). **17.50**

The Detroit Tigers: An Illustrated History, by Joe Falls, Walker (1989). **18**

The Detroit Tigers: A Pictorial Celebration of the Greatest Players and Moments in Tigers' History, by William M. Anderson, Diamond Communications (1991). **18**

The Devils' Coach, by Jim Brock & Joe Gilmartin, David C. Cook (1977). **18**

The Diamond Appraised, by Craig R. Wright & Tom House, Simon & Schuster (1989). **12**

Diamond Classics: Essays on 100 of the Best Baseball Books Ever Published, by Mike Shannon, McFarland (1989). **40**/reprint, McFarland (2003), **pb 15**

Diamond Greats, by Rich Westcott, Meckler (1988). **12**

Diamonds: The Evolution of the Ballpark, by Michael Gershman, Houghton Mifflin (1993). **25/pb 12.50**

Diamonds Are Forever: Artists and Writers on Baseball, ed. by Peter H. Gordon, Chronicle Books (1987). **35/pb 15**

Diamonds Around the Globe: The Encyclopedia of International Baseball, by Peter C. Bjarkman, Greenwood (2005). **27.50**

Diamonds in the Rough: The Legend and Legacy of Tony Lucadello, One of Baseball's Greatest Scouts, by David V. Hanneman, Diamond Books (1989), PB orig. **12.50**

Diamonds in the Rough: Life in Baseball's Minor Leagues, by Ken Rappoport, Tempo Books (1979), PB orig. **20**

Diamonds in the Rough: The Untold History of Baseball, by Joel Zoss & John Bowman, Macmillan (1989). **20**

Diary of a Yankee Hater, by Bob Marshall, Watts (1981), PB Orig. **7**

The Dickson Baseball Dictionary, by Paul Dickson, Facts on File (1989). **20**

Dictionary of Baseball, by Parke Cummings, Barnes (1950). **25**

DiMaggio: An Illustrated Life, by Dick Johnson & Glenn Stout, Walker (1995). **15**

The DiMaggio Albums, ed. by Richard Whittingham, Putnam (1989). **20**

The Dixon Cornbelt League, by W. P. Kinsella, Harper Collins (1995). **15**

Diz, by Robert Gregory, Viking Penguin (1992). **25**

The Dizziest Season, by G. H. Fleming, Morrow (1984). **27.50**

Dizzy Baseball: A Gay and Amusing Glossary of Baseball Terms Used by Radio Broadcasters, by Jerome H. Dizzy Dean, Greenberg (1952), Bklt. **27.50**

Dizzy Dean: His Story in Baseball, by Lee Allen, Putnam (1967). **85**

The Dizzy Dean Story, by Milton Shapiro, Messner (1963). **125**

Do You Know Your Baseball? by Bill Brandt, Grosby Press (1947). **28**

Do You Know Your Baseball? by Hy Gittlitz, Grosby Press (1955). **25**

Dock Ellis in the Country of Baseball, by Donald Hall w/Dock Ellis, Coward McCann & Geoghegan (1976). **15**

Dodger Classics, by Robert L. Tiemann, Baseball Histories (1983). **20**

Dodger Daze and Knights, by Tommy Holmes, McKay (1953). **70**

Dodger Dogs to Fenway Franks, by Bob Wood, McGraw-Hill (1988). **5**

The Dodgers, by John Durant, Hastings House (1948). **70**

The Dodgers, by Tommy Holmes, Collier (1975). **18**

The Dodgers: Memories and Memorabilia from Brooklyn to L.A., by Bruce Chadwick, Abbeville Press (1993). **20**

The Dodgers and Me, by Leo Durocher, Ziff-Davis (1948). **32**

The Dodgers Move West, by Neil Sullivan, Oxford Univ. Press (1987). **17**

Dog Days: The New York Yankees' Fall from Grace and Return to Glory, 1964–1976, by Philip Bashe, Random House (1994). **12**

Dollar Sign on the Muscle, by Kevin Kerrane, Beaufort Books (1984). **25**

Don Baylor, by Don Baylor w/Claire Smith, St. Martin's (1989). **7.50**

The Don Drysdale Story, by Milton Shapiro, Messner (1964). **85**

Don't Kill the Umpire, by Hy Gittlitz, Grosby Press (1957). **30**

Don't Knock the Rock, by Gordon Cobbledick, World (1966). **175**

Don't Let Baseball Die, by Art Hill, Avery (1978), PB orig. **85**

Double X: Jimmie Foxx: Baseball's Forgotten Slugger, by Bob Gorman, Holy Name Society Diocese of Camden NJ (1990), PB orig. **35**

A Dream Season, by Gary Carter & John Hough, Jr., Harcourt Brace Jovanovich (1987). **10**

The Dreamlife of Johnny Baseball, ed. by Richard Grossinger, North Atlantic Books (1987). **27.50/pb 7.50**

The Duke of Flatbush, by Duke Snider w/Bill Gilbert, Zebra Books (1988). **10**

The Duke of Havana, by Steve Fainaru & Ray Sanchez, Villard (2001). **15**

The Duke Snider Story, by Irwin Winehouse, Messner (1964). **85**

Dynasty: The New York Yankees 1949–1964, by Peter Golenbock, Prentice Hall (1975). **27.50**

The Eastern Shore Baseball League, by William W. Mowbray, Tidewater (1989). **20**

The Eddie Mathews Story, by Al Hirshberg, Messner (1960). **120**

The Education of a Baseball Player, by Mickey Mantle, Simon & Schuster (1967). **30**

Effa Manley and the Newark Eagles, by James Overmyer, Scarecrow (1993). **25**

Eight Men Out, by Eliot Asinof, Holt Reinhart and Winston (1963). **85**

El Beisbol, by John Krich, Atlantic Monthly Press (1989). **12.50**

El Tiante, by Luis Tiant & Joe Fitzgerald, Doubleday (1976). **15**

Encyclopedia of Major League Baseball Team Histories: American League, ed. by Peter C. Bjarkman, Meckler (1991). **30**/Encyclopedia: National League (1991). **30**

The Encyclopedia of Minor League Baseball, by Lloyd Johnson, Baseball America (1993). **17.50**

Endless Summers: The Fall and Rise of the Cleveland Indians, by Jack Torry, Diamond Communications (1995). **12**

The Era 1947–1957, by Roger Kahn, Ticknor & Fields (1993). **10**

Even the Browns, by William Mead, Contemporary (1978). **15**

Every Diamond Doesn't Sparkle, by Fresco Thompson w/Cy Rice, McKay (1964). **20**

Everything Baseball, by James Mote, Prentice Hall (1989), PB orig. **15**

Ewell Blackwell, by Lou Smith, Barnes (1951). **55**

Explosion: Mickey Mantle's Legendary Home Runs, by Mark Gallagher, Arbor House (1987). **65**

The Expos Inside Out, by Dan Turner, McClelland & Steward (1983). **22**

Extra Innings, by Frank Robinson & Berry Stainback, McGraw Hill (1988). **10**

Extra Innings, by Minnie Minoso w/Fernando Fernandez, Regnery (1983). **45**

Extra Innings: A Season in the Senior League, by David Whitford, Harper Collins (1991). **10**

The Face of Baseball, photography by John Weiss, Thomasson-Grant (1990). **18**

The Fairport Nine, by Noah Brooks, Scribner's (1880). **600**

The Fall of the Roman Umpire, by Ron Luciano & David Fisher, Bantam Books (1986). **10**

A False Spring, by Pat Jordan, Dodd Mead (1975). **20**

Famous Baseball Stars, by Dan Gutman, Dodd Mead (1973). **12.50**

Fan Poems, by Tom Clark, North Atlantic Books (1976), Bklt. **15**

Fathers Playing Catch with Sons, by Donald Hall, North Point Press (1985), PB orig. **13**

Fear Strikes Out, by Jim Piersall & Al Hirshberg, Atlantic-Little Brown (1955). **35**

Fenway, by Peter Golenbock, Putnam (1992). **12**

Fenway: A Biography in Words and Pictures, by Dan Shaughnessy, Houghton Mifflin (1999). **15**

Fenway Park: A Stadium Pop-Up Book, by John Boswell & David Fisher, Little Brown (1992). **17.50**

Fenway Voices, by Jack Lautier, Yankee Books (1990), PB orig. **10**

Ferguson Jenkins: The Quiet Winner, by Stanley Pashko, Putnam (1975). **65**

Fielder's Choice, ed. by Jerome Holtzman, Harcourt Brace Jovanovich (1979). **15**

The Final Season: Fathers, Sons, and One Last Season in a Classic American Ballpark, by Tom Stanton, Thomas Dunne Books (2001). **12**

Fireballers: Baseball's Fastest Pitchers, by Jack Newcombe, Putnam (1964). **75**

The Fireside Book of Baseball, ed. by Charles Einstein, Simon & Schuster, (1956). **45**

The Fireside Book of Baseball, 4th Edition (actually Vol. 4) ed. by Charles Einstein, Simon & Schuster (1987), PB orig. **14**

The First One Hundred Years of Baseball, by George Moreland (1929), PB orig. **225**

Fisk of Fenway Park, by Robert B. Jackson, Henry Z. Walck (1976). **65**

Five O'Clock Comes Early, by Bob Welch & George Vecsey, Morrow (1982). **15**

Five O'Clock Lightning, by Tommy Henrich, Birch Lane (1992). **10**

Five Seasons, by Roger Angell, Simon & Schuster (1977). **10**

Five Straight Errors on Ladies' Day, by Walter Nagle ATT Bryson Reinhardt, Caxton (1965). **55**

A Flag for San Francisco, by Charles Einstein, Simon & Schuster (1962). **40**

Fleet Walker's Divided Heart, by David Zang, Univ. of Nebraska Press (1995). **25**

The Forever Boys, by Peter Golenbock, Carol Publishing Group (1991). **10**

The Forgotten Championships: Postseason Baseball, 1882–1981, by Jerry Lansche, McFarland (1989). **20**

Forgotten Fields, by Paul Green, Parker Publications (1984), PB orig. **10**

Forty Years a Fan, by Ed Doyle, Dorrance (1972). **30**

Foul Ball! Five Years in the American League, by Alison Gordon, Dodd Mead (1984). **15**

Foul Ball: My Life and Hard Times Trying to Save an Old Ballpark, by Jim Bouton, Bulldog Publishing (2003). **15**

Frank: The First Year, by Frank Robinson, Holt, Reinhart, Winston (1976). **15**

Frank Frisch: The Fordham Flash, by Frank Frisch ATT J. Roy Stockton, Doubleday (1962). **40**

Frank Robinson: The Making of a Manager, by Russell J. Schneider, Coward McCann & Geoghegan (1976). **20**

Fred Lynn: Young Star, by Bill Libby, Putnam (1977). **10**

Fridays with Red, by Bob Edwards, Simon & Schuster (1993). **7**

From Behind the Plate, by Johnny Bench, Prentice Hall (1972). **17.50**

From Cobb to Catfish, ed. by John Kuenster, Rand McNally (1975). **12.50**

From Ghetto to Glory, by Bob Gibson w/Phil Pepe, Prentice Hall (1968). **25**

From Sandlot to Big League, by Connie Mack, Knopf (1960). **30**

From Scratch, by the KGB Chicken, Joyce Press (1978). **20**

Full Count: Inside Cuban Baseball, by Milton H. Jamail, Southern Illinois Univ. Press (2000). **12.50**

Fun and Frolic with an Indian Ball Team, by Guy Green, self-pub. (1900). **175**/reprint, Amereon (1992), **hb 30**

The Further Adventures of Slugger McBatt, by W. P. Kinsella, Houghton Mifflin (1988). **20**

G. I. Had Fun, by Al Schacht & Murray Goodman, Putnam (1945). **35**

The Gabby Hartnett Story, by James M. Murphy, Exposition Press (1983). **75**

The Game and the Glory, ed. by Joseph Reichler, Prentice-Hall (1976). **15**

The Game for All America, by John Thorn, The Sporting News (1988). **17.50**

The Game Is Never Over: An Appreciative History of the Chicago Cubs, by Jim Langford, Icarus Press (1980). **15**

The Game of Baseball, by Gil Hodges & Frank Slocum, Crown (1969). **22.50**

The Game of Baseball, by Henry Chadwick, George Munro & Co. (1868). **7,000**/reprint, Camden House (1983), **hb 125**

The Game That Was: The George Brace Baseball Photo Collection, by Richard Cahan & Mark Jacob, Contemporary (1996). **22.50**

The Gamer, by Gary Carter, Word (1993). **12**

Games, Asterisks, and People, by Ford C. Frick, Crown (1973). **10**

The Garry: A Book of Humorous Cartoons: Pickings from the Diamond, J. F. Collins (1904). **2,200**

Garvey, by Steve Garvey w/Skip Rozin, Times (1986). **5**

The Gashouse Gang, by J. Roy Stockton, Barnes (1945). **35**

The Gashouse Gang, by Robert E. Hood, Morrow (1976). **25**

Gateway to the Majors: Williamsport and Minor League Baseball, by James P. Quigel Jr. & Louis E. Hunsinger Jr., Pennsylvania State Univ. Press (2001). **17.50**

General Baseball Doubleday, by Robert S. Holzman, Longmans (1955). **18**

George Brett: From Here to Cooperstown, by George Brett w/Steve Cameron, Addax Publishing Group (1999). **15**

George Brett: Last of a Breed, by Steve Cameron, Taylor (1993). **15**

The George Brett Story, by John Garrity, Coward McCann & Geoghegan (1981). **20**

The George Foster Story, by George Foster & Malka Drucker, Holiday House (1979). **20**

George Wright's Record Book of the Boston Club, by George Wright (1875), Bklt. **1,500**

The Georgia-Florida League 1935–1958, by Bobby Dews, self-pub. (1985), PB orig. **25**

Get That Nigger Off the Field, by Art Rust Jr., Delacorte Press (1976). **50**

The Giants: Memories and Memorabilia from a Century of Baseball, by Bruce Chadwick, Abbeville Press (1993). **20**

The Giants and the Dodgers, by Lee Allen, Putnam (1964). **75**

The Giants of San Francisco, by Art Rosenbaum & Bob Stevens, Coward-McCann (1963). **25**

The Giants of the Polo Grounds, by Noel Hynd, Doubleday (1988). **18**

"The Giants Win the Pennant! The Giants Win the Pennant!" by Bobby Thomson w/Lee Heiman & Bill Gutman, Zebra (1991). **15**

The Gil Hodges Story, by Milton Shapiro, Messner (1960). **75**

The Ginger Kid: The Buck Weaver Story, by Irving M. Stein, Elysian Fields Press (1992). **20**

The Girls of Summer, by Lois Browne, Harper Collins (1992). **12.50**

Glory Days with the Dodgers, by John Roseboro w/Bill Libby, Atheneum (1978). **25**

Glory Fades Away: The Nineteenth Century World Series Rediscovered, by Jerry Lansche, Taylor (1991). **15**

The Glory of Their Times, by Lawrence Ritter, Macmillan (1966). **65**

Glove Affairs, by Noah Liberman, Triumph Books (2003). **15**

The Go-Go Chicago White Sox, by Dave Condon, Coward McCann (1960). **60**

The Golden Era Cubs 1876–1940, by Eddie Gold & Art Ahrens, Bonus Books (1985). **12.50**

Good Enough to Dream, by Roger Kahn, Doubleday (1985). **12**

Goodbye Old Friend: A Pictorial Essay on the Final Season at Old Comiskey Park, by Frank Budreck, Aland Corporation (1991). **15**

The Great American Baseball Card Flipping Trading and Bubble Gum Book, by Brendan C. Boyd & Fred C. Harris, Little Brown (1973). **25**

The Great American Baseball Scrapbook, by A. D. Suehsdorf, Random House (1978). **17.50**

The Great American Novel, by Philip Roth, Holt, Rinehart and Winston (1973). **55**

Great Baseball Managers, by Charles Cleveland, Crowell (1950). **20**

The Great Baseball Mystery: The 1919 World Series, by Victor Luhrs, Barnes (1966). **45**

Great Baseball Pitchers, by Jim Brosnan, Random House (1965). **10**

The Great Encyclopedia of 19th Century Major League Baseball, by David Nemec, Donald I. Fine (1997). **20**

Great Infielders of the Major Leagues, by Dave Klein, Random House (1972). **7.50**

Great Negro Baseball Stars, by A. S. "Doc" Young, Barnes (1953). **85/pb 40**

Great Rookies of the Major Leagues, by Jim Brosnan, Random House (1966). **10**

Great Time Coming, by David Falkner, Simon & Schuster (1995). **12.50**

The Greatest American Leaguers, by Al Hirshberg, Putnam (1970). **55**

The Greatest Cardinals of Them All, John Devaney, Putnam (1968). **125**

The Greatest Dodgers of Them All, by Steve Gelman, Putnam (1968). **125**

The Greatest Game Ever Played, by Jerry Izenberg, Henry Holt (1987). **25**

The Greatest Giants of Them All, by Arnold Hano, Putnam (1967). **125**

The Greatest of All: The 1927 NY Yankees, by John Mosedale, Dial (1974). **20**

The Greatest Summer: The Remarkable Story of Jim Bouton's Comeback to Major League Baseball, by Terry Pluto, Prentice Hall (1979). **10**

Greatest World Series Thrillers, by Ray Robinson, Random House (1965). **7.50**

The Greatest Yankees of Them All, by Ray Robinson, Putnam (1969). **125**

Green Cathedrals, by Philip J. Lowry, SABR (1986), PB orig. **30**

Green Cathedrals: The Ultimate Celebration of All 271 Major League and Negro League Ballparks Past and Present, by Philip J. Lowry, Addison-Wesley (1992) **17.50**

Green Fields and White Lines: Baseball Poems, by Robert L. Harrison, McFarland (1995). **12.50**

Guide to Baseball Literature, by Anton Grobani, Gale Research (1975). **175**

Guidry, by Ron Guidry & Peter Golenbock, Crown (1980). **12.50**

Hack, by Robert Boone & Gerald Grunska, Highland (1978). **35**

Hal Chase: The Defiant Life and Turbulent Times of Baseball's Biggest Crook, by Martin Donell Kohout, McFarland (2001), PB orig. **17.50**

Hall of Fame Cartoons of Major League Ball Parks, by Gene Mack, Boston Globe Newspaper Co. (1947), PB orig. **60**

The Hank Aaron Story, by Milton Shapiro, Messner (1961). **150**

Hank Greenberg: The Story of My Life, by Hank Greenberg, Times Books (1989). **20**

Hank Sauer, by John C. Hoffman, Barnes (1953). **35**

Hardball, by George Bell & Bob Elliott, Key Porter (1990). **22**

Hardball: The Education of a Baseball Commissioner, by Bowie Kuhn, Times Books (1987). **7.50**

Hardball: A Season in the Projects, by Daniel Coyle, Putnam (1994). **12.50**

Harmon Killebrew: Baseball's Superstar, by Wayne J. Anderson, Deseret Book Company (1971). **65**

The Harmon Killebrew Story, by Hal Butler, Messner (1966). **100**

Harry Hooper, by Paul J. Zingg, Univ. of Illinois Press (1993). **12**

Havana Heat, by Darryl Brock, Total Sports Publishing (2000). **12**

Hawk, by Andre Dawson w/Tom Bird, Zondervan (1994). **10**

Hawk, by Ken Harrelson w/Al Hirshberg, Viking (1969). **20**

The Head Game, by Roger Kahn, Harcourt (2000). **10**

The Heart of the Game, by Paul Hemphill, Simon & Schuster (1996). **10**

Heart of the Order, by Tony Ardizonne, Holt (1986). **12.50**

The Heart of the Order, Tom Boswell, Doubleday (1989). **10**

Henry Aaron: A Quiet Superstar, by Al Hirshberg, Putnam (1969). **85**

Heroes Behind the Mask, by Milton Shapiro, Messner (1969). **65**

Heroes of Baseball, by Robert Smith, World (1952). **25**

Heroes of the Bullpen, by Milton Shapiro, Messner (1967). **65**

Heroes of the Major Leagues, by Alexander Peters, Randon House (1967). **7.50**

Heroes, Plain Folks, and Skunks, by Happy Chandler w/Vance Trimble, Bonus Books (1989). **10**

The Hidden Game of Baseball, by John Thorn & Pete Palmer w/David Reuther, Doubleday (1984). **85/pb 35**

High and Inside: A Chronicle of 1987's Daze of Autumn from the Metrodome to Kent Hrbek's Duck Blind, by Jim Klobuchar, Voyageur Press (1987). **27.50**

High & Inside: Orlando Cepeda's Story, by Orlando Cepeda w/Bob Markus, Icarus Press (1983). **50**

The High Hard One, by Kirby Higbe w/Martin Gardner, Viking (1967). **30**

High Inside: Memoirs of a Baseball Wife, by Danielle Gagnon Torrez & Ken Lizotte, Putnam (1983). **7.50**

The History of American League Baseball Since 1901, by Glenn Dickey, Stein & Day (1980). **15**

History of Baseball in California and the Pacific Coast Leagues 1847–1938, by Fred W. Lange, self-pub. (1938), PB orig. **85**

The History of National League Baseball Since 1876, by Glenn Dickey, Stein & Day (1979). **20**

A History of the Boston Baseball Club, by George V. Tuohey, M. F. Quinn (1897). **1,400**

The History of the International League 1919–1960 Part 1, by David F. Chrisman, self-pub. (1981), PB orig. **35**/Part 2 (1982), PB orig. **35;** Part 3 (1983), PB orig. **35**

History of the Junior World Series, by Bob Bailey, Scarecrow Press (2004). **15**

The History of the Piedmont League (1920–1955), by David F. Chrisman, self-pub. (1986), PB orig. **35**

History of the Virginia League, by David Chrisman, self-pub. (1988). **35**

The History of the World Series Since 1903, by Glenn Dickey, Stein and Day (1984). **15**

History of the World's Tour, by Ted Sullivan, M. A. Donohue & Co. (1914). **275**

Hitter: The Life and Turmoils of Ted Williams, by Ed Linn, Harcourt Brace (1993). **12**

The Hollywood Stars, by Richard E. Beverage, The Deacon Press (1984), PB orig. **125**

Holy Cow! by Harry Caray w/Bob Verdi, Villard (1989). **12.50**

Home Games, by Bobbie Bouton & Nancy Marshall, St. Martin's/Marek (1983). **7.50**

The Home Run Heard 'Round the World, by Ray Robinson, Harper Collins (1991). **10**

The Home Run Story, by Zander Hollander, Norton (1966). **15**

The Home Team: 100 Years of Baseball in Baltimore, by James Bready, self-pub. (1958). **75/pb 20**

Honus: The Life and Times of a Baseball Hero, by William Hageman, Sagamore (1996). **10**

Honus Wagner: A Biography, by Dennis & Jeanne DeValeria, Henry Holt (1996). **12.50**

Honus Wagner: The Life of Baseball's "Flying Dutchman," by Arthur D. Hittner, McFarland (1996). **40**

Hoopla, by Harry Stein, Knopf (1983). **26**

The Horse that Played Center Field, by Hal Higdon, Holt Rinehart & Winston (1969). **7.50**

The Hot Stove League, by Lee Allen, Barnes (1955). **65**

How Life Imitates the World Series, by Thomas Boswell, Doubleday (1982). **22.50**

How to Get to First Base, by Marc Simont & Red Smith, Schuman (1952), PB orig. **17.50**

How to Hit, by Johnny Mize ATT Murray Kaufman, Holt (1953). **30**

How to Pitch Real Curves, by Henry Buser, B & N Publishing (1924), PB orig. **65**

How to Play Baseball, by Babe Ruth, Cosmopolitan (1931). **550**

How to Play Baseball, by Connie Mack, Drexel Biddle (1903), PB orig. **55**

How to Steal a Pennant, by Maury Wills & Don Freeman, Putnam (1976). **15**

How to Talk Baseball, by Mike Whitford, Dembner Books (1983), PB. orig. **10**

How to Umpire, by William G. (Billy) Evans, (1917). **35**

The Humming Bird, by Owen Johnson, Baker & Taylor (1910). **85**

Hustle: The Myth, Life, and Lies of Pete Rose, by Michael Sokolove, Simon & Schuster (1990). **10**

The Hustler's Handbook, by Bill Veeck w/Ed Linn, Putnam (1965). **40**

Hygiene for Baseball Players, by A. H. P. Leuf, A. J. Reach & Co. (1888), PB orig. **900**

I Ain't an Athlete, Lady, by John Kruk w/Paul Hagen, Simon & Schuster (1994). **7.50**

I Don't Care If I Never Come Back, by Art Hill, Simon & Schuster (1980). **12**

I Had a Hammer, by Hank Aaron w/Lonnie Wheeler, Harper Collins (1991). **12**

I Hit and Ran, by Dick Groat & Frank Dascenzo, Moore Publishing Co. (1978). **75**

I Love This Game! by Kirby Puckett w/Mike Bryan, HarperCollins (1993). **10**

I Managed Good, But Boy Did They Play Bad, by Jim Bouton, Playboy Press (1973). **7.50**

I Never Had It Made, by Jackie Robinson ATT Alfred Duckett, Putnam (1972). **10**

I Was Right on Time, by Buck O'Neal, Simon & Schuster (1996). **10**

I'd Rather Be a Yankee, by John Tullius, Macmillan (1986). **7.50**

If at First, by Keith Hernandez & Mike Bryan, McGraw-Hill (1986). **7.50**

If I Never Get Back, by Darryl Brock, Crown (1990). **18**

If They Don't Win It's a Shame, by Dave Rosenbaum, McGregor (1998). **12.50**

The Illustrated Book of Baseball Folklore, by Tristram Potter Coffin, The Seabury Press (1975). **20**

I'm Glad You Didn't Take It Personally, by Jim Bouton, Morrow (1971). **7.50**

The Image of Their Greatness, by Lawrence Ritter & Donald Honig, Crown (1979). **20**

Imagining Baseball: America's Pastime and Popular Culture, by David McGimpsey, Indiana Univ. Press (2000). **12**

The Imperfect Diamond, by Lee Lowenfish & Tony Lupien, Stein & Day (1980). **17.50**

The Impossible Dream, by Bill McSweeny, Coward McCann (1968). **25**

The Impossible Dream Remembered: The 1967 Red Sox, by Ken Coleman & Dan Valenti, Stephen Greene (1987). **15**

The Impossible Takes a Little Longer: The Texas Rangers from Pretenders to Contenders, Phil Rogers, Taylor (1990). **10**

The Incredible Giants, by Tom Meany, Barnes (1955). **40**

The Indianapolis ABCs, by Paul Debono, McFarland (1997). **35**

Innings Ago: Recollections by Kansas City Ballplayers of Their Days in the Game, by Jack Etkin, Normandy Square Publications (1987), PB orig. **15**

Inside Big League Baseball, by Roger Kahn, Macmillan (1962). **15**

Inside Corner: Talks with Tom Seaver, ed. by Joel H. Cohen, Atheneum (1974). **15**

Inside Pitch, by Roger Craig w/Vern Plagenhoef, Eerdmans (1984). **7.50**

Inside Pitching, by Ferguson Jenkins, Regnery (1972). **22.50**

Inside the Strike Zone, by Randall A. Hendricks, Eakin Press (1994). **17.50**

Inside the Yankees, by Ed Linn, Ballantine (1978). **15**

Insider's Baseball, ed. by L. Robert Davids, Scribners (1983). **30**

Into the Temple of Baseball, ed. by Richard Grossinger & Kevin Kerrane, Celestial Arts (1990), PB orig. **12.50**

Invisible Men, by Donn Rogosin, Atheneum (1983). **35**

The Iowa Baseball Confederacy, by W. P. Kinsella, Houghton Mifflin (1986). **10**

Iron Horse, by Ray Robinson, Norton (1990). **12**

Iron Man: The Cal Ripken Story, by Harvey Rosenfeld, St. Martin's (1995). **10**

It Pays to Steal, by Maury Wills & Steve Gardner, Prentice Hall (1963). **17.50**

It Takes Heart, by Mel Allen, Harper (1959). **25**

It's Anybody's Ball Game, by Joe Garagiola, Contemporary (1988). **6**

It's Gone ... No, Wait a Minute, by Ken Levine, Villard Books (1993). **7.50**

It's Good to Be Alive, by Roy Campanella, Little Brown (1959). **27.50**

It's What You Learn After You Know It All That Counts, by Earl Weaver w/Berry Stainback, Doubleday (1982). **15**

The Jackie Jensen Story, by Al Hirshberg, Messner (1961). **75**

Jackie Robinson, by Bill Roeder, Barnes (1950). **65**

Jackie Robinson: A Biography, by Arnold Rampersad, Knopf (1997). **15**

Jackie Robinson: An Intimate Portrait, by Rachel Robinson w/Lee Daniels, Abrams (1996). **17.50**

Jackie Robinson: A Life Remembered, by Maury Allen, Watts (1987). **20**

Jackie Robinson: My Own Story, by Jackie Robinson ATT Wendell Smith, Greenberg (1948). **175/pb 25; Avon pb (1949) 25**

Jackie Robinson of the Brooklyn Dodgers, by Milton Shapiro, Messner (1957). **85**

The Jackie Robinson Story, by Arthur Mann, F. J. Low (1950), PB orig. **75**

Japan Is Big League in Thrills, by John Holway, Tokyo News Service (1955), PB orig. **375**

Japanese Baseball: A Fan's Guide, by Brian Maitland, Charles E. Tuttle (1991), PB orig. **20**

The Jersey Game, by James DiClerico & Barry Pavelec, Rutgers Univ. Press (1991). **8**

Jewish Baseball Stars, by Harold U. Ribalow & Meir Z. Ribalow, Hippocrene Books (1984). **10**

Jim Bunning: Baseball and Beyond, by Frank Dolson, Temple Univ. Press (1998). **12.50**

Jim Konstanty, by Frank Yeutter, Barnes (1951). **45**

Jim Palmer: Great Comeback Competitor, by Joel Cohen, Putnam (1978). **25**

Jocko, by Jocko Conlan w/Robert Creamer, J. B. Lippincott (1967). **25**

The Jock's Itch, by Tom House, Contemporary (1989). **12.50**

Joe: Rounding Third and Heading for Home, by Greg Hoard, Orange Frazer Press (2004). **15**

Joe & Marilyn: A Memory of Love, by Roger Kahn, Morrow (1986). **7.50**

Joe DiMaggio, by Gene Schoor, Doubleday (1980). **20**

Joe DiMaggio, by George DeGregorio, Scarborough (1983). **15**

Joe DiMaggio: Baseball's Yankee Clipper, by Jack B. Moore, Praeger (1987). **20**

Joe DiMaggio: A Bio-Bibliography, by Jack B. Moore, Greenwood (1986). **30**

Joe DiMaggio: The Golden Year 1941, by Al Silverman, Prentice Hall (1969). **70**

Joe DiMaggio: The Hero's Life, by Richard Ben Cramer, Simon & Schuster (2000). **15**

Joe DiMaggio: Yankee Clipper, by Tom Meany, Barnes (1951). **40**

Joe Morgan: A Baseball Life, by Joe Morgan & David Falkner, Morrow (1993). **7.50**

The Joe Williams Baseball Reader, ed. by Peter Williams, Algonquin Books (1989). **10**

Joe, You Coulda Made Us Proud, by Joe Pepitone w/Berry Stainback, Playboy Press (1975). **10**

John McGraw, by Charles Alexander, Viking (1988). **12**

Johnny Bench: Catching and Power Hitting, ed. by John Sammis, Viking (1975). **17.50**

Johnny Bench: King of the Catchers, by Lou Sabin, Putnam (1977). **17.50**

Josh and Satch, by John Holway, Meckler (1991). **12.50**

Josh Gibson, by William Brashler, Harper & Row (1978). **30**

Joy in Mudville, by George Vecsey, McCall (1970). **10**

The Joy of Keeping Score, by Paul Dickson, Walker (1996). **10**

Judge and Jury, by David Pietrusza, Diamond Communications (1998). **15**

Judge Landis and 25 Years of Baseball, by J. G. Taylor Spink, Thomas Y. Crowell (1947). **17.50**

Juicing the Game, by Howard Bryant, Viking Penguin (2005). **14**

July 2, 1903: The Mysterious Death of Hall-of-Famer Big Ed Delahanty, by Mike Sowell, Macmillan (1992). **10**

Junior: Griffey on Griffey, by Ken Griffey Jr., Harper Collins (1997). **15**

The Kansas City Athletics, by Ernest Mehl, Holt (1956). **17.50**

The Kansas City Monarchs, by Janet Bruce, Univ. Press of Kansas (1985). **100**

Ken Boyer, by David Lipman, Putnam (1967). **125**

Ken Boyer: Guardian of the Hot Corner, by Jack Zanger, Rutledge (1965). **65**

The Kid from Cuba: Zolio Versalles, by James Terzian, Doubleday (1967). **25**

Kill the Ump, by Dusty Boggess ATT Ernie Helm, Lone Star (1966), PB orig. **15**

Kiner's Korner, by Ralph Kiner w/Joe Gergen, Arbor House (1987). **10**

King of Swat, ed. by Father Ted, Society of St. Paul (1951), PB orig. **35**

Kings of the Diamond, by Lee Allen & Tom Meany, Putnam (1965). **15**

Kings of the Home Run by Arthur Daley, Putnam (1962). **15**

Kiss It Goodbye, by Shelby Whitfield, Abelard Schuman (1973). **15**

Know Your Vols, by John Sabbatini, self-pub. (1950), Bklt. **40**

Knuckle Balls, by Phil Niekro & Tom Bird, Freundlich Books (1986). **10**

Knuckler: The Phil Niekro Story, by Wilfred Binette, Hallux Brothers (1970). **15**

Koufax, by Edward Gruver, Taylor (2000). **12**

Koufax, by Sandy Koufax w/Ed Linn, Viking (1966). **25**

The Krank: His Language and What It Means, by Thomas W. Lawson, Rand Avery Co. (1888), PB orig. **1,500**

Lady in the Locker Room, by Susan Fornoff, Sagamore Publishing (1993). **12**

The Last Best League, by Jim Collins, Da Capo Press (2004). **17**

The Last .400 Hitter, by John Holway, Wm. C. Brown (1991). **10**

The Last Hero: The Life of Mickey Mantle, by David Falkner, Simon & Schuster (1995). **15**

The Last Night of the Yankee Dynasty, by Buster Olney, Ecco (2004). **12**

The Last Rebel Yell, by Ken Brooks, Seneca Park (1986), PB orig. **25**

Last to First: The Story of the Mets, by Larry Fox, Harper (1970). **25**

The Last Yankee, by David Falkner, Simon & Schuster (1992). **15**

Late Innings, by Roger Angell, Simon & Schuster (1982). **12.50**

Laughs from the Dugout, by Milton J. Shapiro, Messner (1966). **20**

Leagues Apart: The Men and Times of the Negro Baseball Leagues, by Lawrence Ritter, Morrow Junior Books (1995). **15**

Lefty Grove: American Original, by Jim Kaplan, SABR (2000), PB orig. **10**

A Legend for the Legendary, by James Vlasich, Bowling Green State Univ. Press (1990). **10**

A Legend in the Making: The New York Yankees in 1939, by Richard J. Tofel, Ivan R. Dee (2002). **12**

Legends at the Stick, by Tom Rodrigues, Rodrigues Studio (1993), PB orig. **15**

Leonardo Knows Baseball, by Charles Hobson, Chronicle Books (1991), PB orig. **10**

Let's Play Ball!: Inside the Perfect Game, by William Humber, Lester & Orpen Dennys (1989), PB orig. **7.50**

Letters from a Baseball Fan to His Son, by S. DeWitt Clough, Backbone Publishing Co. (1910), PB orig. **225**

Lew Burdette of the Braves, by Gene Schoor, Putnam (1960). **100**

The Life That Ruth Built, by Marshall Smelser, Quadrangle/The New York Times Book Co. (1975). **25**

Like Nobody Else, by Ferguson Jenkins ATT George Vass, Regnery (1973). **40**

The Lip: A Biography of Leo Durocher, by Gerald Eskenazi, Morrow (1993). **10**

Little League to Big League, by Jim Brosnan, Random House (1968). **10**

The Long Season, by Jim Brosnan, Harper & Brothers (1960). **30**

The Lords of Baseball, by Harold Parrott, Praeger (1976). **25**

Lords of the Realm, by John Helyar, Villard (1994). **22**

Lore and Legends of Baseball, by Mac Davis, Lantern Press (1953). **18**

The Los Angeles Dodgers, by Paul Zimmerman, Coward McCann (1960). **65**

The Los Angeles Dodgers: The First Quarter Century, by Donald Honig, St. Martin's (1983). **12.50**

The Los Angeles Dodgers: The First Twenty Years, by Frank Finch, Jordan and Co. (1977). **25**

The Los Angeles Dodgers: An Illustrated History, by Richard Whittingham, Harper (1982). **12.50**

Lights On! The Wild Century-Long Saga of Night Baseball, by David Pietrusza, Scarecrow (1997). **12.50**

Lost Ballparks, by Lawrence Ritter, Viking Penguin (1992). **25**

Lou Gehrig: An American Classic, by Richard Bak, Taylor (1995). **12.50**

Lou Gehrig: Courageous Star, by Robert Rubin, Putnam (1979). **30**

Lou Gehrig: The Iron Horse of Baseball, by Richard Hubler, Houghton Mifflin (1941). **35**

Lou Gehrig: Pride of the Yankees, by Paul Gallico, Grosset & Dunlap (1942). **35**

Lou Gehrig: A Quiet Hero, by Frank Graham, Putnam (1942). **35**

Louis Sockalexis: The First Cleveland Indian, by David L. Fleitz, McFarland (2002), PB orig. **15**

Louisville Slugger: The Making of a Baseball Bat, by Jan Arnow, Pantheon Books (1984). **15**

Love Letters to the Mets, by Bill Adler & George Price, Simon & Schuster (1965). **15**

Low & Inside, by Ira Smith & H. Allen Smith, Doubleday (1949). **17.50**

Low & Outside, by Jerry Kettle & Ed Addeo, Coward McCann (1965). **20**

Luckiest Man: The Life and Death of Lou Gehrig, by Jonathan Eig, Simon & Schuster (2005). **18**

Lucky to Be a Yankee, by Joe DiMaggio, Field (1946). **25**

The Mackmen, by Rev. Jerome C. Romanowski, self-pub. (1979). **20**

The Magic of Indians' Baseball, by David Reddick & Kim Rogers, Indianapolis Indians (1988), PB orig. **20**

A Magic Summer: The '69 Mets, by Stanley Cohen, Harcourt Brace Jovanovich (1988). **7.50**

The Magnificent Yankees, by Tom Meany, Barnes (1952). **35**

The Main Spark, by Sparky Anderson, Doubleday (1978). **15**

Major League Baseball, by Ethan Allen, Macmillan (1938). **50**

Major Leagues, by David Pietrusza, McFarland (1991). **25**

A Man and His Diamonds: A Story of Andrew "Rube" Foster..., by Charles E. Whitehead, Vantage Press (1980). **220**

The Man in the Dugout, by Donald Honig, Follett (1977). **12.50**

The Man in the Dugout, by Leonard Koppett, Crown (1993). **10**

Man on Spikes, by Eliot Asinof, McGraw-Hill (1955). **75**

The Man Who Invented Baseball, by Harold Peterson, Scribner's (1973). **15**

Manny Sanguillen: Jolly Pirate, by Joel H. Cohen, Putnam (1975). **60**

Manual of Cricket and Base Ball, Mayhew & Baker (1858). **1,900**

Marketing Your Dreams: Business and Life Lessons from Bill Veeck, by Pat Williams, Sports Publishing (2001). **10**

Marquard and Seeley, by Noel Hynd, Parnassus (1996). **12**

Matty: An American Hero, by Ray Robinson, Oxford Univ. Press (1993). **12.50**

Maybe I'll Pitch Forever, by Leroy (Satchel) Paige w/David Lipman, Doubleday (1962). **35**

Mays, Mantle, Snider, by Donald Honig, Macmillan (1987). **30**

McGraw of the Giants, by Frank Graham, Putnam (1944). **45**

Me and DiMaggio, C. Lehmann-Haupt, Simon & Schuster (1986). **7.50**

Me and My Dad, by Paul O'Neill w/Burton Rocks, Morrow (2003). **10**

Me and the Spitter, by Gaylord Perry w/Bob Sudyk, Saturday Review Press/Dutton (1974). **17.50**

The Meaning of Nolan Ryan, by Nick Trujilo, Texas A & M Univ. Press (1994). **24**

The Mel Ott Story, Milton Shapiro, Messner (1959). **125**

Memories of Summer, Roger Kahn, Hyperion (1997). **10**

Men at Work, by George Will, Macmillan (1990). **5**

The Men in Blue, by Larry Gerlach, Viking (1980). **20**

The Men of Autumn: An Oral History of the 1949–53 World Champion New York Yankees, by Dom Forker, Taylor (1989). **10**

Men of the Machine, by Ritter Collett, Landfill Press (1977). **25**

The Mets from Mobile: Cleon Jones and Tommie Agee, by A. S. "Doc" Young, Harcourt (1970). **20**

The Mets Will Win the Pennant, by William Cox, Putnam (1964). **35**

The Mick, by Mickey Mantle w/Herb Gluck, Doubleday (1985). **10**

Mickey Mantle: America's Prodigal Son, by Tony Castro, Brassey's (2002). **17**

Mickey Mantle: Mr. Yankee, by Al Silverman, Putnam (1963). **65**

Mickey Mantle: Yankee Slugger, by Milton Shapiro, Messner (1962). **85**

Mickey Mantle: The Yankee Years: The Classic Photography of Ozzie Sweet, by Larry Canale, Tuff Stuff Books (1998). **20**

The Mickey Mantle Album, by Howard Liss, Hawthorn (1966). **45**

Mickey Mantle of the Yankees, by Gene Schoor, Putnam, (1958). **75**

The Mickey Mantle Story, by Mickey Mantle ATT Ben Epstein, Holt (1953). **75**

Mighty Casey: All American, by Eugene Murdock, Greenwood (1984). **25**

Mike Schmidt: Baseball's Young Lion, by Jim Wright, Putnam (1979). **37.50**

Mile High Madness: A Year with the Colorado Rockies, by Bob Kravitz, Times Books (1994). **7.50**

The Milwaukee Braves, by Bob Buege, Douglas American Sports Publications (1988). **17.50**

The Milwaukee Braves, by Harold Kaese and R. G. Lynch, Putnam (1954). **75**

Milwaukee's Miracle Braves, by Tom Meany et al., Barnes (1954). **25**

Minor Miracles: The Legend & Lure of Minor League Baseball, by David Pietrusza, Diamond Communications (1995). **15**

The Minors, by Neil J. Sullivan, St. Martin's (1990). **10**

The Miracle at Coogan's Bluff, Thomas Kiernan, Thomas Y. Crowell (1975). **25**

Miracle in Atlanta, by Furman Bisher, World (1966). **12.50**

Miracle in Buffalo, by Anthony Violanti, St. Martin's (1991). **10**

Miracle Man, by Nolan Ryan, Word (1992). **7.50**

The Miracle New York Yankees, by Phil Rizzuto & Al Silverman, Coward McCann (1962). **70**

Miracle on 35th Street, by Bob Logan, Icarus (1983), PB orig. **5**

Misfits! The Cleveland Spiders in 1899, by J. Thomas Hetrick, McFarland (1991). **15**

Mr. Baseball: The Story of Branch Rickey, by David Lipman, Putnam (1966). **125**

Mr. Cub, by Ernie Banks & Jim Enright, Follett Publishing Co. (1971). **30**

Mr. October, by Maury Allen, Times (1981). **10**

Mr. Ump, by Babe Pinelli, Westminster (1953). **30**

Mitts: A Celebration of the Art of Fielding, by William Curran, Morrow (1985). **15**

Modern Baseball Science, by E. B. Rankin, National Baseball Registration Bureau (1915), PB orig. **220**

Moe Berg: Athlete, Scholar, Spy, by Louis Kaufman et al., Little Brown (1974). **17.50**

Moneyball: The Art of Winning an Unfair Game, by Michael Lewis, Norton (2003). **12**

More Strange but True Baseball Stories, by Howard Liss, Random House (1972). **7.50**

Mostly Baseball, by Tom Meany et al. Barnes (1958). **15**

Murder at Fenway Park, by Troy Soos, Kensington Books (1994). **60**

Murderers' Row: The 1927 New York Yankees, by G. H. Fleming, Morrow (1985). **65**

Murph, by Dale Murphy w/Brad Rock, Bookcraft (1986). **18**

The Museum of Clear Ideas, by Donald Hall, Ticknor & Fields (1993). **12**

Musial: From Stash to Stan the Man, by James N. Giglio, Univ. of Missouri Press (2001). **15**

My Baseball Diary, by James T. Farrell, Barnes (1957). **25**

My Brother Morris Berg: The Real Moe, by Ethel Berg, self-pub. (1976), PB orig. **60**

My Dad, the Babe, by Dorothy Ruth Pirone w/Chris Martens, Quinlan Press (1988). **12.50**

My Favorite Summer, by Mickey Mantle, Doubleday (1991). **10**

My 50 Years in Baseball, by Edward Grant Barrow w/James M. Kahn, Coward McCann (1951). **60**

My Giants, by Russ Hodges, Doubleday (1963). **17.50**

My Greatest Baseball Game, ed. by Don Schiffer, Barnes (1950). **25**

My Greatest Day in Baseball, ed. by John. P. Carmichael, Grosset & Dunlap (1945). **20**

My Kind of Baseball, by Rogers Hornsby, David McKay (1953). **30**

My Life and Baseball, by Felipe Alou, Word (1967). **20**

My Life as a Fan, by Wilfred Sheed, Simon & Schuster (1993). **10**

My Life In and Out of Baseball, by Willie Mays ATT Charles Einstein, Dutton (1966). **20**

My Life in Baseball: The True Record, by Ty Cobb w/Al Stump, Doubleday (1961). **35**

My Life in the Negro Leagues, by Wilmer Fields, Meckler (1992). **17.50**

My Life Is Baseball, by Frank Robinson w/Al Silverman, Doubleday (1968). **15**

My Luke and I, by Eleanor Gehrig & Joe Durso, Crowell (1976). **15**

My 9 Innings, by Lee MacPhail, Meckler (1989). **10**

My Own Particular Screwball, by Al Schacht, Doubleday (1955). **17.50**

My 66 Years in the Big Leagues, by Connie Mack, The John C. Winston Co. (1950). **50**

My Thirty Years in Baseball, by John McGraw, Boni & Livelight (1923). **200**

My Turn at Bat, by Ted Williams w/John Underwood, Simon & Schuster (1969). **30**

My Ups and Downs in Baseball, by Orlando Cepeda w/Charles Einstein, Putnam (1968). **100**

My War with Baseball, by Rogers Hornsby & Bill Surface, Coward McCann (1962). **50**

Nails, by Lenny Dykstra w/Marty Noble, Doubleday (1987). **25**

Napoleon Lajoie: Modern Baseball's First Superstar, by J. M. Murphy, SABR (1988), PB orig. **45**

National Association of Professional Baseball Leagues Silver Jubilee 1902–1926, ed. by John Foster, Nat. Assoc. of Prof. Bb. Lgs. (1926). **75**

The National Game, by Alfred Spink, National Game Publishing Co. (1910). **600**

The National League: An Illustrated History, by Donald Honig, Crown (1983). **15**

The National League Story, by Lee Allen, Hill & Wang (1961). **25**

The Natural, by Bernard Malamud, Harcourt, Brace (1952). **1,250**

Negro Baseball before Integration, by Effa Manley & Leon Hardwick, Adams (1976), PB orig. **175**

The Negro Baseball Leagues: A Photographic History, by Phil Dixon, Amereon (1992). **75**

Negro League Baseball: The Rise and Ruin of a Black Institution, by Neil Lanctot, Univ. of Pennsylvania Press (2004). **17**

The Neighborhood of Baseball, by Barry Gifford, Dutton (1981). **15**

The New Chicago White Sox, by Arch Ward, Regnery (1951), PB orig. **40**

The New Era Cubs 1941–1985, by Eddie Gold & Art Ahrens, Bonus Books (1985). **15**

New York City Baseball: The Last Golden Era 1947–1957, by Harvey Frommer, Macmillan (1980). **15**

The New York Giants, by Frank Graham, Putnam (1952). **45**

The New York Mets: The First Quarter Century, by Donald Honig, Crown (1986). **15**

The New York Mets: Twenty-Five Years of Baseball Magic, by Jack Lang & Peter Simon, Henry Holt (1986). **15**

The New York Mets: The Whole Story, by Leonard Koppett, Macmillan (1970). **45**

The New York Yankees, by Donald Honig, Crown (1987). **15**

The New York Yankees, by Frank Graham, Putnam (1943). **45**

Newark Bears, by Randolph Linthurst, self-pub. (1978), PB orig. **25**

Newark Bears: The Final Years, by Randolph Linthurst, self-pub. (1981), PB orig. **25**

Newark Bears: The Middle Years, by Randolph Linthurst, self-pub. (1979), PB orig. **25**

Nice Guys Finish First, by Monte Irvin w/James Riley, Carroll & Graf (1996). **7.50**

Nice Guys Finish Last, by Leo Durocher w/Ed Linn, Simon & Schuster, (1975). **20**

A Nice Tuesday, by Pat Jordan, Golden Books (1999). **10**

The Niekro Files, by Phil & Joe Niekro w/Ken Picking, Contemporary (1988). **10**

Nine Innings, by Daniel Okrent, Ticknor & Fields (1985). **7.50**

Nine Sides of the Diamond, by David Falkner, Times Books (1990). **12**

The 1937 Newark Bears, by Ronald Mayer, Wise (1980). **35**

The 1947 Trenton Giants, by Randolph Linthurst, self-pub. (1982), PB orig. **40**

1947: When All Hell Broke Loose, by Red Barber, Doubleday (1982). **25**

No Big Deal, by Mark Fidrych & Tom Clark, Lippincott (1977). **10**

No Cheering in the Press Box, by Jerome Holtzman, Holt Rinehart Winston (1973). **15**

No Joy in Mudville, by Ralph Andreano, Schenkman Publishing (1965). **7.50**

Nobody's Perfect, by Denny McLain w/Dave Diles, Dial Press (1975). **10**

The No-Hit Hall of Fame, by Rich Coberly, Triple Play Publications (1985), PB orig. **17.50**

Nolan Ryan: The Authorized Pictorial History, The Summit Group (1991). **25**

Nolan Ryan: The Road to Cooperstown, by Nolan Ryan w/T. R. Sullivan & Mickey Herskowitz, Addax (1999). **10**

Nolan Ryan Fireballer, by Bill Libby, Putnam (1975). **50**

Nothing to Prove: The Jim Abbott Story, by Bob Bernotas, Kodansha (1995). **8**

Now I Can Die in Peace: How ESPN's Sports Guy Found Salvation..., by Bill Simmons, ESPN Books (2005). **10**

Now Pitching Bob Feller, by Bob Feller w/Bill Gilbert, Birch Lane (1990). **7.50**

Now Pitching for the Yankees, by Marty Appel, Total Sports Publishing (2001). **12.50**

Now Wait a Minute Casey, by Maury Allen, Doubleday (1965). **10**

Number 1, by Billy Martin & Peter Golenbock, Delacorte Press (1980). **5**

The Numbers Game: Baseball's Lifelong Fascination with Statistics, by Alan Schwarz, Thomas Dunne (2004). **15**

The October Heroes, by Donald Honig, Simon & Schuster (1979). **15**

October 1964, by David Halberstam, Villard (1994). **7.50**

Off Base: Confessions of a Thief, by Rickey Henderson w/John Shea, Harper (1992). **7.50**

Off the Record, by Buzzie Bavasi w/John Strege, Contemporary (1987). **7.50**

The Official Encyclopedia of Baseball, Hy Turkin and S. C. Thompson, Barnes (1951). **15**

The Official History of the National League (75th Anniversary), ed. by Charles Segar, Jay Publishing (1951). **40**

The Old Ball Game: Baseball in Folklore and Fiction, by Tristram Potter Coffin, Herder and Herder (1971). **12**

Old Baseball Scout and His Players, Joe E. Palmer, Remlap (1987), PB orig. **15**

The Oldest Rookie, by Jim Morris & Joel Engel, Little Brown and Co. (2001). **13**

On Days Like This: Poems, by Dan Quisenberry, Helicon Nine Editions (1998), PB orig. **15**

On the Run, by Maury Wills & Mike Celizic, Carroll & Graf (1991). **7.50**

On to Nicollet: The Glory and Fame of the Minneapolis Millers, by Stew Thornley, Nodin Press (1988). **20**

Once a Bum Always a Dodger, by Don Drysdale w/Bob Verdi, St. Martin's (1990). **10**

Once Upon the Polo Grounds: The Mets That Were, by Leonard Shecter, The Dial Press (1970). **20**

One for the Record, by George Plimpton, Harper & Row (1974). **20**

The 100 Greatest Baseball Players of All Time, by Lawrence Ritter & Donald Honig, Crown (1981). **10**

The 100 Seasons of Buffalo Baseball, by Joseph M. Overfield, Partners' Press (1985), PB orig. **100**

100 Years of Baseball, by Lee Allen, Bartholomew House (1950). **25**

100 Years of National League Baseball, by Lowell Reidenbaugh, The Sporting News (1976), PB orig. **15**

One Last Round for the Shuffler, by Tom Clark, Truck Books (1979). **35/pb 35**

One Pitch Away, by Mike Sowell, Macmillan (1995). **8**

One Strike Away: The Story of the 1986 Red Sox, by Dan Shaughnessy, Beaufort Books (1987). **12**

The Only Game in Town, by Charles Einstein, Dell Publishing (1954), PB orig. **20**

The Only One: The Babe, by Ed "Dutch" Doyle, Adams Press (1974), PB orig. **40.**

Only the Ball Was White, by Robert Peterson, Prentice Hall (1970). **50**

The Other Game, by Nolan Ryan w/Bill Libby, Word (1977). **35**

Our Baseball Club, by Noah Brooks, Dutton (1884). **550**

Our Game: An American Baseball History, by Charles C. Alexander, Henry Holt (1991). **10**

Our Lugnuts, Year One! by Bob Roth, self-pub. (1996), PB orig. **15**

Our Tribe, by Terry Pluto, Simon & Schuster (1999). **7.50**

Out of Left Field: Willie Stargell and the Pittsburgh Pirates, by Bob Adelman & Susan Hall, Two Continents (1976). **30**

Out of My League, by George Plimpton, Harper & Row (1961). **22.50**

Out of the Blue, by Orel Hershiser & Jerry Jenkins, Wolgemuth & Hyatt (1989). **7.50**

Over the Edge, by Jay Johnstone & Rick Talley, Contemporary (1987). **5**

The Pacific Coast League: One Man's Memories 1938–1957, by Ken Stadler, Marbek Publications (1984), PB orig. **60**

Paul Molitor: Good Timing, by Stuart Broomer, ECW (1994), PB orig. **25**

Peanuts and Crackerjack, by David Cataneo, Rutledge Hill Press (1991). **10**

The Pee Wee Reese Story, by Gene Schoor, Messner (1956). **85**

Pen Men, by Bob Cairns, St. Martin's (1992). **10**

A Pennant for the Kremlin, by Paul Molloy, Doubleday (1964). **10**

Pennant Race, by Jim Brosnan, Harper & Brothers (1962). **35**

Percentage Baseball and the Computer, by Earnshaw Cook, Waverly Press (1971). **75**

Percentage Baseball, by Earnshaw Cook and Wendell R. Garner, Williams and Wilkins (1964). **75**/reprint, MIT Press (1966), **pb 45**

The Perfect Game: America Looks at Baseball, by Elizabeth V. Warren, Abrams (2003). **17.50**

The Perfect Game: Tom Seaver and the Mets, by Tom Seaver w/Dick Schaap, Dutton (1970). **23**

Pete Rose: 4,192, by John G. Erardi, The Cincinnati Enquirer (1985), PB orig. **7.50**

Pete Rose: Mr. .300, by Keith Brandt, Putnam (1977). **200**

Pete Rose: My Life in Baseball, by Pete Rose, Doubleday (1979). **12.50**

Pete Rose: My Story, by Roger Kahn, Macmillan (1989). **7.50**

Pete Rose: They Call Him Charlie Hustle, by Bill Libby, Putnam (1972). **85**

The Pete Rose Story, by Pete Rose, World (1970). **15**

Phil Regan, by Phil Regan & James Hefley, Zondervan (1968). **25**

Phil Rizzuto, by Joe Trimble, Barnes (1951). **40**

Phil Rizzuto: A Yankee Tradition, by Dan Hirshberg, Sagamore (1993). **12.50**

The Phil Rizzuto Story, by Milton Shapiro, Messner (1959). **70**

The Philadelphia Phillies, by Fred Lieb & Stan Baumgartner, Putnam (1953). **150**

The Philadelphia Phillies: A Pictorial History, by Allen Lewis, JCP (1981). **25**

The Philadelphia Phillies: An Illustrated History, by Donald Honig, Simon & Schuster (1992). **40**

Philip K. Wrigley, by Paul Angle, Rand McNally (1975). **25**

The Physics of Baseball, by Robert Kemp Adair, Harper & Row (1990), PB orig. **15**

Pictorial History of the Dodgers, by Gene Schoor, Leisure (1984). **15**

Pictorial Negro League Legends Album, by Robert D. Retort, self-pub. (1992), PB orig. **35**

Picture History of the Boston Red Sox, George Sullivan, Bobbs-Merrill (1979). **30**

The Pilot Light and the Gas House Gang, by Bob Broeg, The Bethany Press (1980). **20**

Pine-Tarred and Feathered: A Year on the Baseball Beat, by Jim Kaplan, Algonquin Books (1985). **7.50**

Pinstriped Pandemonium: A Season with the Yankees, by Geoffrey Stokes, Harper & Row (1984). **10**

Pinstriped Summers, by Dick Lally, Arbor House (1985). **10**

Pioneers of Baseball, by Robert Smith, Little Brown (1978). **22.50**

The Pirates, by Lou Sahadi, Times (1980). **17.50**

The Pitch That Killed, by Mike Sowell, Macmillan (1989). **45**

The Pitcher, by John Thorn & John Holway, Prentice Hall (1987). **20**

A Pitcher's Story, by Juan Marichal & Charles Einstein, Doubleday, (1967). **75**

Pitchin' Man, by Leroy Satchel Paige ATT Hal Lebovitz, Cleveland News (1948), Bklt. **45**

Pitching in a Pinch, by Christy Mathewson, Putnam (1912). **275**

The Pitching Staff, by Steve Jacobson, Crowell (1975). **10**

Pittsburgh Baseball through the Years, by A. K. Roswell, Fort Pitt Brewing Co. (1952), Bklt. **30**

The Pittsburgh Crawfords, by James Bankes, Wm. C. Brown (1991), PB orig. **12**

The Pittsburgh Pirates, by Fred Lieb, Putnam (1948). **65**

The Pittsburgh Pirates: A Pictorial History, by Richard L. Burtt, Jordan and Co. (1977). **25**

The Pittsburgh Pirates: An Illustrated History, by Bob Smizik, Walker (1990). **15**

A Place for Summer: A Narrative History of Tiger Stadium, by Richard Bak, Wayne State Univ. Press (1998). **15**

Play Ball: Stories of the Ball Field, by Mike Kelly, Press of Emery and Hughes (1888). **700**

Play for a Kingdom, by Thomas Dyja, Harcourt Brace (1997). **16**

Player for a Moment: Notes from Fenway, by John Hough Jr., Harcourt Brace Jovanovich (1988). **10**

Player-Manager, by Lou Boudreau w/Ed Fitzgerald, Little Brown (1949). **50**

Players' Choice: Major League Baseball Players Vote on the All-Time Greats, by Eugene V. McCaffrey & Roger A. McCaffrey, Facts on File (1987). **10**

Playing Around: The Million Dollar Infield Goes to Florida, by Donald Hall et al., Little Brown (1974). **17**

Playing for Keeps: A History of Early Baseball, by Warren Goldstein, Cornell Univ. Press (1989). **12.50**

Playing the Field: Why Defense Is the Most Fascinating Art in Major League Baseball, by Jim Kaplan, Algonquin Books (1987), PB orig. **10**

Playing the Game: From Mine Boy to Manager, by Stanley "Bucky" Harris, Frederick A. Stokes (1925). **300**

The Politics of Glory, by Bill James, Macmillan (1994). **12.50**

The Power Hitters, by Donald Honig, The Sporting News (1989). **10**

Pride Against Prejudice: The Biography of Larry Doby, by Joseph Thomas Moore, Praeger (1988), PB orig. **40**

The Pride of Havana: A History of Cuban Baseball, by Roberto Gonzalez Echevarria, Oxford Univ. Press (1999). **12.50**

Primitive Baseball: The First Quarter Century, by Harvey Frommer, Atheneum (1988). **15**

Professional Baseball Franchises, by Peter Filichia, Facts on File (1993). **30**

The Progress of the Seasons: Forty Years of Baseball in Our Town, by George V. Higgins, Henry Holt (1989). **7.50**

Prophet of the Sandlots, by Mark Winegardner, Atlantic Monthly Press (1990). **15**

The Psychologist at Bat, by David Tracy, Sterling (1951). **35**

Puck! Kirby Puckett: Baseball's Last Warrior, by Chuck Carlson, Addax (1997). **20**

Putting It All Together, by Brooks Robinson w/Fred Bauer, Hawthorn (1971). **25**

The Quality of Courage, by Mickey Mantle ATT Robert Creamer, Doubleday (1964). **25**

Queen of Diamonds: The Tiger Stadium Story, by Mike Betzold & Ethan Casey, A & M Publishing (1992), PB orig. **17.50**

Rain Delays: An Anecdotal History of Baseball ..., by Burt Randolph Sugar, St. Martin's (1990). **10**

Ralph Kiner: The Heir Apparent, by Tom Meany, Barnes (1951). **60**

The Real Babe Ruth, by Dan Daniel, C. C. Spink (1948). **125/pb (1963) 25**

The Real Baseball Story, by Howard Palmer, Pageant Press (1953). **65**

The Real Billy Sunday, by Elijah P. Brown, Fleming H. Revell Co. (1914). **55**

Real Grass/Real Heroes, by Dom DiMaggio & Bill Gilbert, Zebra (1990). **10**

The Real McGraw, by Mrs. John McGraw & Arthur Mann, McKay (1953). **30**

Rebel Baseball, by Steve Perlstein, Onion Press (1994), PB orig. **15**

Record of the Boston Baseball Club, 1871–74, by George Wright, Rockwell and Churchill (1974). **1,500**

Red: A Biography of Red Smith, by Ira Berkow, Times Books (1986). **7.50**

Red Schoendienst: The Man Who Fought Back, by Al Hirshberg, Messner (1961). **180**

Red Sox Century, by Glenn Stout & Richard A. Johnson, Houghton Mifflin (2000). **22**

Red Sox Drawing Board: 25 Years of Cartoons, by Eddie Germano, Stephen Greene Press (1989), PB orig. **10**

Red Sox Fever! Ellery H. Clark Jr., Exposition Press (1979). **26**

Red Sox Forever, by Ellery H. Clark Jr., Exposition Press (1977). **26**

The Red Sox the Bean and the Cod, by Al Hirshberg, Waverly (1947). **60**

Redbirds: A Century of Cardinals' Baseball, by Bob Broeg, River City (1981). **25**

Redbirds Revisited, by David Craft & Tom Owens, Bonus Books (1990). **10**

Redleg Journal: Year by Year and Day by Day with the Cincinnati Reds Since 1866, by Greg Rhodes & John Snyder, Road West (2001). **17**

Reggie, by Reggie Jackson w/Mike Lupica, Villard (1984). **15**

Reggie: A Season with a Superstar, by Reggie Jackson w/Bill Libby, Playboy Press (1975). **10**

Reggie Jackson: The $3 Million Man, by Maury Allen, Harvey (1978). **10**

Reggie Jackson: The True Life Story of Baseball's Greatest Clutch Hitter, by Eddie Stone, Holloway (1980), PB orig. **20**

The Reggie Jackson Story, by Bill Libby, Lothrop (1979). **10**

Reggie Jackson's Scrapbook, ed. by Robert Kraus, Dutton (1978). **15**

The Relentless Reds, by Hal McCoy, Press Co (1976), PB orig. **35**

The Relief Pitcher, by John Thorn, Dutton (1979). **15**

Remembering the Soos, by David Evans, Plains Press (1986), PB orig. **20**

Remembering the Vees, by Elliott Irving, Cumberland (1979), PB orig. **65**

Remembrance of Swings Past, by Ron Luciano & David Fisher, Bantam Books (1988). **10**

The Return of Billy the Kid, by Norman Lewis Smith, Coward McCann & Geoghegan (1977). **12.50**

Rex Barney's Thank Youuuu, by Rex Barney w/Norman Macht, Tidewater Publishers (1993). **10**

Rhubarb, by H. Allen Smith, Doubleday (1946). **15**

Rhubarb in the Catbird Seat, by Red Barber w/Robert Creamer, Doubleday (1968). **27.50**

The Rhubarb Patch, by Red Barber & Barney Stein, Simon & Schuster (1954). **85**

The Richie Ashburn Story, by Joe Archibald, Messner (1962). **135**

Richter's History and Records of Baseball, by Francis Richter, Dando (1914). **1,255**

Rickey and Robinson, by Harvey Frommer, Macmillan (1982). **20**

Right Off the Bat, by William F. Kirk, G. W. Dillingham (1911). **150**

The Ripening of Pinstripes, by Rodney Torreson, Story Line Press (1998), Bklt. **12**

The Rise of Japanese Baseball Power, by Robert Obojski, Chilton (1975). **65**

The Road to Cooperstown, by Tom Stanton, St. Martin's (2003). **12**

The Roar of the Crowd, by William R. Burnett, Clarkson N. Potter (1964). **10**

The Roaring Redhead: Larry MacPhail, by Don Warfield, Diamond Communications (1987). **17.50**

Roberto Clemente: Batting King, by Arnold Hano, Putnam (1968). **75**

The Rock Springs Chronicles, by William J. McGill, Fithian Press (1999), PB orig. **10**

Rocket Man, by Roger Clemens w/Peter Gammons, The Stephen Greene Press (1987). **20**

Roger Maris: A Man for All Seasons, by Maury Allen, Donald I. Fine (1986). **22.50**

Roger Maris: A Title to Fame, by Harvey Rosenfeld, Prairie House (1991). **17.50**

Roger Maris: Home Run Hero, by Leonard Shecter, Bartholomew (1961), PB orig. **20**

Roger Maris at Bat, by Roger Maris & Jim Ogle, Duell, Sloan & Pearce (1962). **150/pb 30**

Rogers Hornsby, by Charles Alexander, Henry Holt (1995). **10**

Romancing the Horsehide: Baseball Poems on Players and the Game, by Gene Carney, McFarland (1993). **15**

Ron Santo: For Love of Ivy, by Ron Santo & Randy Minkoff, Bonus (1993). **12.50**

Ron Santo, 3rd Baseman, by Jim Brosnan, Putnam (1974). **100**

Rookie, by Dwight Gooden w/Richard Woodley, Doubleday (1985). **10**

Rookie Season: A Year with the West Michigan Whitecaps, by Branson Wright, Eerdmans (1995), PB orig. **12.50**

The Rookies, by Ed Walton, Stein & Day (1982). **10**

Rowdy Richard, by Dick Bartell w/Norman L. Macht, North Atlantic Press (1987). **17.50**

Roy Campanella, by Dick Young, Barnes (1952). **85**

Roy Campanella: Man of Courage, by Gene Schoor, Putnam (1959). **140**

The Roy Campanella Story, by Milton Shapiro, Messner (1958). **80**

The Royal Reds, by Hal McCoy et al., Pressco (1977), PB orig. **35**

Run, Rabbit, Run, by Rabbit Maranville, SABR (1991), PB orig. **10**

Runner Mack, by Barry Beckham, Morrow (1972). **65**

Rusty Staub of the Expos, by John Robertson, Prentice Hall (1971). **30**

S.F. Giants: An Oral History, by Mike Mandel, self-pub. (1979), PB orig. **50**

Sadaharu Oh, by Sadaharu Oh & David Falkner, Times Books (1984). **27.50**

Safe at Home, by Sharon Hargrove & Richard Hauer Costa, Texas A & M Univ. Press (1989). **9**

The St. Louis Cardinals, by Fred Lieb, Putnam (1944). **55**

The St. Louis Cardinals: An Illustrated History, by Donald Honig, Prentice Hall (1991). **15**

The Sal Maglie Story, by Milton Shapiro, Messner (1957). **125**

The San Francisco Giants, by Joe King, Prentice Hall (1958). **32.50**

Sandlot Peanuts, by Charles M. Schulz, Holt Rinehart and Winston (1977). **30**

Sandlot Seasons, by Rob Ruck, Univ. of Illinois Press (1987). **25**

Sandy Koufax, by Jerry Mitchell, Grosett & Dunlap (1966). **17.50**

Sandy Koufax: A Lefty's Legacy, by Jane Leavy, HarperCollins (2002). **12**

Sandy Koufax: Strikeout King, by Arnold Hano, Putnam (1964). **70**

The Sandy Koufax Album, by Howard Liss, Hawthorn (1966). **30**

Satchel Paige's America, by William Price Fox, Univ. of Alabama Press (2005), PB orig. **10**

Say Hey, by Willie Mays w/Lou Sahadi, Simon & Schuster (1988). **10**

Say It Ain't So, Joe! by Donald Gropman, Little Brown (1979). **25**

The Science of Baseball, by Byrd Douglas, Thomas E. Wilson (1922). **30**

The Science of Hitting, by Ted Williams w/John Underwood, Simon & Schuster (1968). **50**

The Scooter, by Gene Schoor, Scribner's (1982). **30**

Score by Innings, by Charles Van Loan, George H. Doran (1919). **55**

The Scrapbook History of Baseball, by Jordan A. Deutsch et al., Bobbs-Merrill (1975). **15**

Screwball, by Tug McGraw & Joseph Durso, Houghton Mifflin (1974). **15**

A Season in the Sun, by Roger Kahn, Harper & Row (1977). **10**

Season of Dreams: The Minnesota Twins' Drive to the 1991 World Championship, by Tom Kelly & Ted Robinson, Voyageur Press (1992). **22.50**

Season of Glory, by Ralph Houk w/Robert Creamer, Putnam (1988). **17.50**

Season Ticket, by Roger Angell, Houghton Mifflin (1988). **12.50**

Seasons in Hell, by Mike Shropshire, Donald I. Fine (1996). **15**

The Seattle Pilots Story, by Carson Van Lindt, Marabou Publishing (1993), PB orig. **20**

Seaver, by Gene Schoor, Contemporary (1986). **10**

The Second Fireside Book of Baseball, ed. by Charles Einstein, Simon & Schuster (1958). **60**

Second to Home, by Ryne Sandberg w/Barry Rozner, Bonus Books (1995). **15**

Second to None, by Roberto Alomar w/Stephen Brunt, Viking (1993). **12**

Seeing It Through: The Story of a Comeback, by Tony Conigliaro w/Jack Zanger, Macmillan (1970). **22.50**

Seeking the Perfect Game: Baseball in American Literature, by Cordelia Candelaria, Greenwood Press, (1989). **17.50**

The Series: An Illustrated History of Baseball's Postseason Showcase 1903–1989, by Joe Hoppel, The Sporting News (1989), PB orig. **12.50**

The Shadows of Summer: Classic Baseball Photographs 1869–1947, by Donald Honig, Viking Studio Books (1994). **15**

Shoeless Joe, by W. P. Kinsella, Houghton-Mifflin (1982). **125**

Shoeless Joe and Ragtime Baseball, by Harvey Frommer, Taylor (1992). **20**

Shoeless Summer, by John Bell, Vabella Publishing (2001), PB orig. **10**

The Short Season, by David Falkner, Times Books (1986). **17.50**

Shut Out: A Story of Race and Baseball in Boston, by Howard Bryant, Routledge (2002). **15**

Sights around the World with the Baseball Boys, by Harry C. Palmer, Edgewood Publishing Co. (1892). **280**

The Sinister First Baseman & Other Observations, by Eric Walker, Celestial Arts (1982), PB orig. **17.50**

A Six-Gun Salute: An Illustrated History of the Houston Colt .45s, by Robert Reed, Lone Star Books (1999). **15**

The Six Perfect Games of Baseball History and Almost the Seventh, by Bill Shelton, self-pub. (1955), PB orig. **35**

Sixty-One: The Team, The Record, The Men, by Tony Kubek, Macmillan (1987). **22.50**

Sketchbook of the Cleveland Indians, by W. R. Blackwood, Davis & Cannon Printers (1918), Bklt. **1,000**

Slick, by Whitey Ford & Phil Pepe, Morrow (1987). **12.50**

Slide, Kelly Slide, by Marty Appel, Scarecrow (1996). **20**

Slouching Toward Fargo, by Neal Karlen, Spike (1999). **15**

Slugging It Out in Japan, by Warren Cromartie w/Robert Whiting, Kodansha (1991). **12**

Smithsonian Baseball: Inside the World's Finest Private Collections, by Stephen Wong, HarperCollins (2005). **22**

Smoke: The Romance and Lore of Cuban Baseball, by Mark Rucker & Peter Bjarkman, Total/Sports Illustrated (1999). **12.50**

Snap Me Perfect, by Darrell Porter & Williams Deerfield, Nelson (1984). **10**

Sol White's Baseball Guide, by Sol White, H. Walter Schlicter (1907), PB orig. **8,000**/reprint, Camden House (1984), **hb 125**

Some Are Called Clowns, by Bill Heward w/Dimitri V. Gat, Thomas Y. Crowell (1974). **50**

Some of My Best Friends Are Crazy, by Jay Johnstone w/Rick Talley, Macmillan (1990). **5**

The Southern League, by Bill O' Neal, Eakin Press (1994). **25**

The Southpaw, by Mark Harris, Bobbs Merrill (1953). **125**

Sparky! by Sparky Anderson & Dan Ewald, Prentice Hall (1990). **5**

Spartan Seasons, by Richard Goldstein, Macmillan (1980). **12.50**

Speed Kings of the Base Paths, by Ray Robinson, Putnam (1964). **50**

Sphere and Ash, by Jacob Morse, J. F. Spofford & Co. (1888), PB orig. **1,240**/reprint, Camden House (1984), **hb 85**

The Spirit of St. Louis: A History of the St. Louis Cardinals and Browns, by Peter Golenbock, Spike (2000). **12.50**

Sports Hero: Fred Lynn, by Marshall Burchard, Putnam (1976). **10**

Sports Hero: Joe Morgan, by Marshall Burchard, Putnam (1978). **15**

Sports Hero: Johnny Bench, by Marshall Burchard, Putnam (1973). **15**

Spring Training, by William Zinsser, Harper & Row (1989). **8**

Stan Musial: Baseball's Durable Man, by Ray Robinson, Putnam (1963). **100**

Stan Musial: The Man, by Irv Goodman, Nelson (1961). **95**

Stan Musial: The Man, by Tom Meany, Putnam (1951). **25**

Stan Musial: The Man's Own Story, by Stan Musial & Bob Broeg, Doubleday (1964). **35**

The Stan Musial Story, by Gene Schoor w/Henry Gilfond, Messner (1955). **125**

Stan the Man Musial: Born to Be a Ballplayer, by Jerry Lansche, Taylor (1994). **12.50**

Stan the Man Musial: Then ... and Now, by Stan Musial w/Bob Broeg, Bethany Press (1977), PB orig. **30**

Standing the Gaff, by Harry "Steamboat" Johnson, Parthenon Press (1935). **75**

Star Pitchers of the Major Leagues, by Bill Libby, Random House (1977). **7.50**

Stars of the Series, by Joseph Gies & Robert Shoemaker, Crowell (1964). **15**

Stealing Is My Game, by Lou Brock & Franz Schulze, Prentice-Hall (1976). **75**

Steinbrenner! by Dick Schaap, Putnam (1982). **7.50**

Steinbrenner's Yankees, by Ed Linn, Holt Rinehart Winston (1982). **12.50**

Stengel: His Life and Times, by Robert Creamer, Simon & Schuster (1984). **15**

Steve Garvey: Storybook Star, by Joel H. Cohen, Putnam (1977). **20**

Stolen Season, by David Lamb, Random House (1991). **10**

Stories of the Baseball Field, by Harry C. Palmer, Rand McNally (1890), PB orig. **400**

Stormin' Norm Cash, by Hal Butler, Messner (1968). **200**

The Story of Baseball, by John Rosenberg, Random House (1962). **7.50**

The Story of Baseball, by Lawrence Ritter, Morrow (1983). **15**

The Story of Baseball in Words and Pictures, by John Durant, Hastings House (1947). **40**

The Story of Bobby Shantz, by Bobby Shantz w/Ralph Bernstein, Lippincott (1953). **50**

The Story of Jim Bunning, by Jim Bunning w/Ralph Bernstein, Lippincott (1965). **75**

The Story of Minor League Baseball, by Robert L. Finch et al. The National Association of Professional Baseball Leagues (1953). **50**

The Story of the World Series, by Fred Lieb, Putnam (1949). **35**

The Story of Ty Cobb, by Gene Schoor, Messner (1952). **65**

The Story of Yogi Berra, by Gene Schoor, Doubleday (1976). **25**

Strange but True Baseball Stories, by Furman Bisher, Random House (1966). **7.50**

Stranger to the Game, by Bob Gibson & Lonnie Wheeler, Viking Penguin (1994). **12**

Price Guide

Streak: Joe DiMaggio and the Summer of '41, by Michael Seidel, McGraw-Hill (1988). **12**

Strike Three, You're Dead, by R. D. Rosen, Walker (1984). **125**

Strike Two, by Ron Luciano & David Fisher, Bantam (1984). **10**

Strikeout, by Denny McLain w/Mike Nahrstedt, The Sporting News (1988). **7.50**

Strikeout: A Celebration of the Art of Pitching, by William Curran, Crown (1995). **15**

Strikeout Story, by Bob Feller, Barnes (1947). **27.50**

The Suitors of Spring, by Pat Jordan, Dodd Mead (1973). **15**

The Summer Game, by Roger Angell, Viking (1972). **25**

The Summer of '49, by David Halberstam, Morrow (1989). **10**

The Sun Field, by Heywood Broun, Putnam (1923). **300**

Super Joe: The Life and Legend of Joe Charboneau, by Joe Charboneau, Burt Graeff, & Terry Pluto, Stein & Day (1981). **35**

Superstars of Baseball, by Bob Broeg, The Sporting News (1971). **15**

Superstars, Stars, and Just Plain Heroes, by Nathan Salant, Stein & Day (1982). **10**

Sweet Lou, by Lou Piniella & Maury Allen, Putnam (1986). **10**

Sweet Seasons: Recollections of the 1955–64 New York Yankees, by Dom Forker, Taylor (1990). **10**

T. J.: My 26 Years in Baseball, by Tommy John w/Dan Valenti, Bantam (1991). **7.50**

Take Me Out to the Ballpark, by Lowell Reidenbaugh, The Sporting News (1983). **25**

Take Time for Paradise, by A. Bartlett Giamatti, Summit (1989). **10**

Take Two and Hit to Right, by Hobe Hays, Univ. of Nebraska Press (1999), PB orig. **8**

Taking on the Yankees: Winning and Losing in the Business of Baseball, by Henry D. Fetter, Norton (2003). **12**

A Tale of Two Cities: The 2004 Yankees-Red Sox Rivalry..., by Tony Massarotti & John Harper, The Lyons Press (2005). **10**

Tales of the Diamonds: Gems of Baseball Fiction, Woodford Press (1991). **12.50**

The Tall Mexican: The Life of Hank Aguirre, by Robert Copley, Pinata (1998). **20**

Taylor Spink: The Legend and the Man, ed. by C. C. Johnson Spink, The Sporting News (1973). **25**

The Team that Wouldn't Die, by Hal Bodley, Serendipity (1981). **25**

The Teammates, by David Halberstam, Hyperion (2003). **10**

Ted "Double Duty" Radcliffe, by Kyle P. McNary, self-pub. (1994), PB orig. **10**

The Ted Simmons Story, by Jim Brosnan, Putnam (1977). **25**

The Ted Williams Story, by Gene Schoor, Messner (1954). **85**

Ted Williams, by Arthur Sampson, Barnes (1950). **45**

Ted Williams: A Baseball Life, by Michael Seidel, Contemporary (1991). **17.50**

Ted Williams: A Portrait in Words and Pictures, by Dick Johnson & Glenn Stout, Walker (1991). **20**

Ted Williams: A Tribute, by Jim Prime & Bill Nowlin, Masters Press (1997). **20**

Ted Williams: Hitting Unlimited, by Tom Meany, Barnes (1951). **55**

Ted Williams: The Biography of an American Hero, by Leigh Montville, Doubleday (2004). **17**

Ted Williams: The Eternal Kid, by Ed Linn, Thomas Nelson & Sons (1961). **180**

Ted Williams: The Golden Year: 1957, by Edwin Pope, Prentice Hall (1957). **50**

Ted Williams: The Seasons of the Kid, by Richard Ben Creamer, Prentice Hall (1991). **25**

Teenagers, Graybeards and 4-Fs, by Harrington Crissey, self-pub. (Part 1 1991; Part 2 1992), PB orig. **20** @

The Temple of Baseball, ed. by Richard Grossinger, North Atlantic Books (1985). **17.50**

Temporary Insanity, by Jay Johnstone, Contemporary (1985). **5**

The Ten Best Years of Baseball, by Harold Rosenthal, Contemporary (1979). **15**

The Texas League, by Bill O'Neal, Eakin Press (1987). **50**

Thanks for Listening, by Jack Brickhouse, Diamond Communications (1986). **20**

That Old Ball Game: Rare Photographs from Baseball's Glorious Past, ed. by David R. Phillips, Regnery (1975). **20**

They Also Served: Baseball and the Home Front 1941–1945, by Bill Gilbert, Crown (1992). **10**

They Call Me Sarge, by Fred Mitchell w/Gary Matthews, Bonus Books (1985), PB orig. **7**

They Played the Game, by Harry Grayson, Barnes (1944). **12.50**

The Thinking Man's Guide to Baseball, by Leonard Koppett, Dutton (1967). **17.50**

Third Base Is My Home, by Brooks Robinson, Word (1974). **20**

The Third Fireside Book of Baseball, by Charles Einstein, Simon & Schuster (1968). **75**

Thirty-One and Six, by Robert Jackson, Henry Z. Walck (1969) **30**

This Great Game, ed. by Doris Townsend, Prentice Hall (1971). **20**

This One and That One: The True Life Story of BoBo "No-hit" Holloman, by Nan Holloman, self-pub. (1975), Bklt. **150**

This Time Let's Not Eat the Bones, by Bill James, Villard (1989). **25**

Those Damn Yankees, by Dean Chadwin, Verso (1999). **18**

Three and Two! by Tom Gorman ATT Jerome Holtzman, Scribner's (1979). **15**

Three Men on Third, by Ira Smith & H. Allen Smith, Doubleday (1951). **15**

3 Nights in August, by Buzz Bissinger, Houghton Mifflin (2005). **12**

The Thrill of the Grass, by W. P. Kinsella, Penguin (1985), PB orig. **20**

The Thrilling Story of Joe DiMaggio, by Gene Schoor, Fell (1951). **25**

Throwing Heat, by Nolan Ryan & Harvey Frommer, Doubelday (1988). **8**

Thurman Munson, by Thurman Munson w/Marty Appel, Coward McCann (1978). **10**

Thurman Munson: Pressure Player, by Bill Libby, Putnam (1978). **30**

The Ticket Out: Darryl Strawberry and the Boys of Crenshaw, by Michael Sokolove, Simon & Schuster (2004). **15**

A Tiger in His Time: Hal Newhouser and the Burden of Wartime Ball, by David M. Jordan, Diamond Communications (1990). **17.50**

Tiger Tales and Trivia, by Fred Smith, self-pub. (1988), PB orig. **7.50**

The Tiger Wore Spikes: An Informal Biography of Ty Cobb, by John McCallum, Barnes (1956). **27.50**

Times at Bat, by Arthur Daley, Random House (1950). **25**

To Everything a Season: Shibe Park and Urban Philadelphia, 1909–1976, by Bruce Kuklick, Princeton Univ. Press (1991). **18**

Today's Game, by Martin Quigley, Viking (1965). **12.50**

Tom Seaver: Portrait of a Pitcher, by Malka Drucker w/Tom Seaver, Holiday House (1978). **25**

Tom Seaver of the Mets, by George Sullivan, Putnam (1971). **50**

The Tommy Davis Story, by Patrick Russell, Doubleday (1969). **200**

The Tommy John Story, by Tommy & Sally John w/Joe Musser, Revell (1978). **5**

Tomorrow I'll Be Perfect, by Dave Stieb w/Kevin Boland, Doubleday (1986). **10**

Tony C: The Triumph and Tragedy of Tony Conigliaro, by David Cataneo, Rutledge Hill Press (1997). **15**

Tony Conigliaro, by Robert Rubin, Putnam (1971). **30**

Tony O! by Tony Oliva & Bob Fowler, Hawthorn (1973). **50**

Topps Baseball Cards, Warner (1985). **85**

Total Baseball, ed. by John Thorn & Pete Palmer, Warner (1989). **20**

Touching Base: Professional Baseball and American Culture in the Progressive Era, by Stephen Riess, Greenwood (1980). **17.50**

Touching Second, by John J. Evers & Hugh S. Fullerton, Reilly & Britten (1910). **85**

The Tour to End All Tours, by James E. Elfers, Univ. of Nebraska Press (2003), PB orig. **10**

Trade Him, ed. by Jim Enright, Follet (1976). **10**

Treasures of the Baseball Hall of Fame, by John Thorn, Villard (1998). **15**

Triumph Born of Tragedy, by Andre Thornton, Harvest House (1983). **10**

The Tropic of Baseball: Baseball in the Dominican Republic, by Rob Ruck, Meckler (1991). **10**

The Truth Hurts, by Jimmy Piersall w/Richard Whittingham, Contemporary (1984). **7.50**

Tuned to Baseball, by Ernie Harwell, Diamond Communications (1985). **7.50**

Turkey Stearnes and the Detroit Stars, by Richard Bak, Wayne State Univ. Press (1994). **20**

Twelve Perfect Innings, Weldon Myers, Commercial Press (1961), Bklt. **85**

20 Years Too Soon, by Quincy Trouppe, S & S Enterprises (1977). 275/reprint. Missouri Historical Society Press (1995), **pb 25**

Twin Killing: The Bill Mazeroski Story, by John Bird, Esmerelda (1995). **25**

Two Spectacular Seasons, by William B. Mead, Macmillan (1990). **7.50**

Ty Cobb, by Charles Alexander, Oxford Univ. Press, (1984). **25**

Ty Cobb, by James McCallum, Praeger (1975). **20**

Ty Cobb: The Greatest, by Robert Rubin, Putnam (1978). **50**

Ty Cobb: The Idol of Baseball Fandom, by Sverre Braathen, Avondale (1928). **400**

The Ultimate Baseball Book, ed. by Daniel Okrent & Harris Lewine, Houghton-Mifflin (1979). **30**

The Umpire Story, by James M. Kahn, Putnam (1953). **45**

The Umpire Strikes Back, by Ron Luciano & David Fisher, Bantam (1982). **10**

Umpiring from the Inside, by Billy Evans, self-pub. (1947). **75**

Under Coogan's Bluff, Fred Stein, Chapter & Cask (1981), PB orig. **15**

The Unforgettable Season, by G. H. Fleming, Holt Rinehart Winston (1981). **17.50**

The Universal Baseball Association, by Robert Coover, Random House (1968). **125**

Up from the Minor Leagues, by Donald Honig, Cowles (1970). **45**

Veeck, as in Wreck, by Bill Veeck w/Ed Linn, Putnam (1962). **35**

The Veracruz Blues, by Mark Winegardner, Viking (1996). **12**

Vida: His Own Story, by Bill Libby & Vida Blue, Prentice Hall (1972). **5**

Vida Blue: Coming Up Again, by Don Kowet, Putnam (1974). **100**

View from the Dugout, by Ed Richter, Chilton (1964). **40**

Viva Baseball: Latin Major Leaguers and Their Special Hunger, by Samuel O. Regalado, Univ. of Illinois Press (1998). **10**

Voices from the Great Black Baseball Leagues, by John Holway, Dodd Mead (1975). **25**

Voices from the Negro Leagues, by Brent Kelley, McFarland (1998). **15**

Voices of the Game, by Curt Smith, Diamond Communications (1987). **12.50**

Vols Feats 1901–1950, by Fred Russell & George Leonard, Nashville Banner (1950), Bklt. **50**

Wait 'Til Next Year: The Yankees, Dodgers, and Giants, 1947–1957, by Christopher Jennison, Norton (1974). **25**

Wait Till I Make the Show, by Bob Ryan, Little Brown (1974). **15**

Waiting Game: Photographs of the Oakland A's, by Debra Heimerdinger (text by John Krich), North Atlantic Books (1982). **15**

Price Guide

Walter Johnson: Baseball's Big Train, by Henry W. Thomas, Phenon Press (1995). **30**

Walter Johnson: King of the Pitchers, by Roger Treat, Messner (1948). **85**

The Warren Spahn Story, by Milton Shapiro, Messner (1958). **100**

The Warsaw Sparks, by Gary Gildner, Univ. of Iowa Press (1990). **65/pb 22.50**

Warsaw to Wrigley, by Joseph A. Reaves, Diamond Communications (1997). **15**

Washington Senators, by Morris Bealle, Columbia Publishing (1947). **85**

The Washington Senators, by Shirley Povich, Putnam (1954). **225**

The Washington Senators 1901–1971, by Tom Deveaux, McFarland (2001). **22**

Waterloo Diamonds, by Richard Panek, St. Martin's (1995). **10**

The Way It Is, by Curt Flood w/Richard Carter, Trident Press (1970). **45**

We Could Have Finished Last without You, by Bob Hope, Longstreet Press (1991). **7.50**

We Played the Game, ed. by Danny Peary, Hyperion (1994). **12.50**

We Saw Stars, by Stan Musial, Jack Buck, & Bob Broeg, Bethany Press (1976). **15**

We Won Today: My Season with the Mets, by Kathryn Parker, Doubleday (1977). **15**

What a Baseball Manager Does, by Roy & Spencer Hoopes, John Day (1970). **125**

What's a Nice Harvard Boy Like You Doing in the Bushes? by Rick Wolff w/Phil Pepe, Prentice-Hall (1975). **20**

What's the Matter with the Red Sox?, by Al Hirshberg, Dodd Mead (1973). **45**

When in Doubt, Fire the Manager, by Alvin Dark & John Underwood, Dutton (1980). **20**

When Johnny Came Sliding Home: The Post-Civil War Baseball Boom, by William J. Ryczek, McFarland (1998). **40**

When the Game Was Black and White: The Illustrated History of Baseball's Negro Leagues, by Bruce Chadwick, Abbeville Press (1992). **12.50**

Where Have You Gone Joe DiMaggio?, by Maury Allen, Dutton (1975). **12.50**

Where They Ain't, by Burt Solomon, The Free Press (1999). **10**

White Rat, by Whitey Herzog & Kevin Horrigan, Harper & Row (1987). **7.50**

The White Sox: A Pictorial History, by Richard Whittingham, Contemporary (1989). **17.50**

Whitey and Mickey, by Whitey Ford, Mickey Mantle & Joseph Durso, Viking (1977). **15**

The Whitey Ford Story, by Milton Shapiro, Messner (1962). **85**

The Whiz Kids, by Harry Paxton, McKay (1950). **200**

The Whiz Kids and the 1950 Pennant, by Robin Roberts & C. Paul Rogers III, Temple Univ. Press (1996). **12.50**

Who Was Roberto? A Biography of Roberto Clemente, by Phil Musick, Doubleday (1974). **25**

The Whole Baseball Catalog, by John Thorn & Bob Carroll, Simon & Schuster (1990), PB orig. **10**

A Whole Different Ballgame, by Marvin Miller, Birch Lane Press (1991). **10**

Who's on Third: The Chicago White Sox Story, by Richard Lindberg, Icarus Press (1983). **17.50**

Who's Who in Major League Baseball, by Harold "Speed" Johnson, Buxton (1933). **400/supplements 25–40@**

Who's Who in Professional Baseball, by Gene Karst & Martin J. Jones, Jr., Arlington House (1973). **12.50**

Why Time Begins on Opening Day, by Thomas Boswell, Doubleday (1984). **15**

A Wife's Guide to Baseball, by Charline Gibson & Michael Rich, Viking (1970). **10**

Wild and Outside, by Stefan Fatsis, Walker (1995). **10**

Wild, High and Tight: The Life and Death of Billy Martin, by Peter Golenbock, St. Martin's (1994). **10**

The Willie Horton Story, by Hal Butler, Messner (1970). **125**

Willie Mays, by Arnold Hano, Grosset & Dunlap (1970). **10**

Willie Mays: Coast-to-Coast Giant, by Charles Einstein, Putnam (1963). **150**

Willie Mays: Modest Champion, by Gene Schoor, Putnam (1960). **100**

Willie Mays: My Life In and Out of Baseball, by Willie Mays & Charles Einstein, Dutton, (1966). **20**

The Willie Mays Album, by Howard Liss, Hawthorn (1966). **75**

The Willie Mays Story, by Ken Smith, Greenberg (1954). **275/pb 65**

The Willie Mays Story, by Milton Shapiro, Messner (1960). **100**

Willie Stargell, by Bill Libby, Putnam (1973). **85**

Willie Stargell, by Willie Stargell & Tom Bird, Harper & Row (1984). **15**

Willie's Throw, by Paul Metcalf, Five Trees Press (1979), Bklt. **65**; Pequod Press (1981), Bklt. **45**; Mad River Press (1989), Bklt. **30**

Willie's Time, by Charles Einstein, J. B. Lippincott (1979). **20**

Winfield, by Dave Winfield w/Tom Parker, Norton (1988). **7.50**

Winning! by Earl Weaver, Morrow (1972). **10**

The Wit and Wisdom of Yogi Berra, by Phil Pepe, Hawthorn (1974). **7.50**

Wizard, by Ozzie Smith w/Rob Rains, Contemporary (1988). **17.50**

Women at Play: The Story of Women in Baseball, by Barbara Gregorich, Harcourt Brace (1993), PB. orig. **12.50**

Won in the Ninth, by Christy Mathewson, R. J. Bodner Co. (1910). **250**

The Wonder Team: The True Story of the Incomparable 1927 New York Yankees, by Leo Trachtenberg, Bowling Green State Univ. Popular Press (1995). **15**

Working at the Stadium, by Tom Zimmerman, Pacific Tides Press (1989), PB orig. **10**

Working the Plate, by Eric Gregg & Marty Appel, William Morrow (1990). **5**

The World Champion Pittsburgh Pirates, by Dick Groat & Bill Surface, Coward McCann (1961). **50**

The World Series, by John Devaney & Burt Goldblatt, Rand McNally (1972). **45**

The World Series: A History of Baseball's Fall Classic, by Ron Fimrite, Oxmoor House (1993). **12.50**

The World Series: An Illustrated History, by Donald Honig, Crown Publishers (1986). **12.50**

The World Series: Complete Play-by-Play of Every Game, 1903–1975..., by Richard M. Cohen et al. The Dial Press (1976). **30/pb 15**

The World Series: The Story of Baseball's Annual Championship, by Lee Allen, Putnam (1969). **20**

The World Series and Highlights of Baseball, by Lamont Buchanan, Dutton (1951). **20**

World Series Classics, by Bill Gutman, Random House (1973). **7.50**

The World Series, 75th Anniversary Edition, ed. by Joseph L. Reichler, Simon & Schuster (1979). **10**

World Series Thrills, by Joseph Bell, Messner (1962). **75**

The Worst Team Money Could Buy: The Collapse of the New York Mets, by Bob Klapisch & John Harper, Random House (1993). **10**

Wrigleyville, by Peter Golenbock, St. Martin's (1996). **10**

The Wrong Season, by Joel Oppenheimer, Bobbs-Merrill (1973). **15**

The Wrong Stuff, by Bill Lee w/Dick Lally, Viking (1984). **7.50**

Yankee Batboy, by Joe Carrieri & Zander Hollander, Prentice Hall (1955). **15**

Yankee Doodles, by Milton Gross, House of Kent (1948). **35**

Yankee Stadium, by Ray Robinson & Christopher Jennison, Penguin/Studio (1998). **15**

Yankee Stadium: Fifty Years of Drama, by Joseph Durso, Houghton Mifflin (1972). **22.50**

The Yankee Story, by Tom Meany, Dutton (1960). **35**

Yankee Stranger, by Ed Figueroa & Dorothy Harshman, Exposition Press (1982). **35**

The Yankees, by John Durant, Hastings House (1949). **75**

Yankees: An Illustrated History, by George Sullivan & John Powers, Prentice Hall (1982). **25**

The Yankees: The Four Fabulous Eras of Baseball's Most Famous Team, by Dave Anderson et al., Random House, (1979). **12**

Yankees Century: 100 Years of New York Yankees Baseball, by Glenn Stout & Richard A. Johnson, Houghton Mifflin (2002). **15**

Yaz, by Carl Yastrzemski & Al Hirshberg, Viking (1968). **25**

Yaz: Baseball, the Wall and Me, by Carl Yastrzemski & Gerald Eskenazi, Doubleday (1990). **15**

Yaz 2: The Ultimate Collector of Carl Yastrzemski Memorabilia, by Richard Henry Grabowski, self-pub., (1995), PB orig. **7.50**

A Year at a Time, by Walter Alston w/Jack Tobin, Word (1976). **25**

A Year in the Minors, by Richard A. Lyttle, Doubleday (1975). **17.50**

Year of the Tiger, by Jerry Green, Coward McCann & Geoghegan (1969). **45**

The Year the Mets Lost Last Place, by Paul Zimmerman & Dick Schaap, World (1969). **10**

The Year the Yankees Lost the Pennant, Douglas Wallop, Norton (1954). **100**

The Year They Called Off the World Series, by Benton Stark, Avery (1991). **15**

Yesterday's Heroes, by Marty Appel, Morrow (1988). **7.50**

Yogi, by Yogi Berra & Ed Fitzgerald, Doubleday (1961). **35**

Yogi: It Ain't Over, by Yogi Berra & Tom Horton, McGraw-Hill (1989). **10**

Yogi Berra, by Joe Trimble, Barnes (1952). **50**

Yogi Berra: The Muscle Man, by Ben Epstein, Barnes (1951). **75**

The Yogi Berra Story, by Gene Roswell, Messner (1958). **55**

You Can't Beat the Hours, by Mel Allen & Ed Fitzgerald, Harper & Row (1964). **25**

You Can't Hit the Ball with the Bat on Your Shoulder, by Bobby Bragan ATT Jeff Guinn, Summit (1992). **15**

You Can't Steal First Base, by Jimmie Dykes & Charles O. Dexter, Lippincott (1967). **25**

You Could Look It Up: The Life of Casey Stengel, by Maury Allen, Times Books (1979). **10**

You Gotta Have Heart: Dallas Green's Rebuilding of the Cubs, by Ned Colletti, Diamond Communications (1985). **10**

You Gotta Have Wa, by Robert Whiting, Macmillan (1989). **15**

You Know Me Al, Ring Lardner, Scribner's (1916). **800**

Your Lookouts Since 1885, by Wirt Gammon, Chattanooga Publishing Co. (1955), Bklt. **65**

You're Missing a Great Game, by Whitey Herzog & Jonathan Pitts, Simon & Schuster (1992). **7.50**

You've Got to Have Balls to Make It in This League, by Pam Postema & Gene Wojciechowski, Simon & Schuster (1992). **10**

The Zen of Base and Ball, by Tom Zeigler & Hal Barnell, Simon & Schuster (1964). **17.50**

GLOSSARY

acid free paper—as the name indicates, paper free (for the most part) of the acids that cause the paper in books to disintegrate. With the world's great libraries full of books that are literally turning to dust because of the acidic paper in such books, this problem has received a lot of attention recently. To ameliorate the problem for future generations, some publishers, particularly ones which publish scholarly books, have begun using acid free paper. The symbol used to designate acid free paper is the sign for infinity inside a circle, and it is usually found on the verso of the title page. McFarland & Company, Inc., Publishers and the University of Nebraska Press are examples of publishers of baseball books who use acid free paper.

Abstract—the abbreviated form of the name Bill James gave to his annual books (e.g., *The Bill James Baseball Abstract*, Ballantine Books, 1982), which were technical analyses of records and statistics in an attempt to arrive at provable baseball knowledge.

addendum—something that is added, after the fact, to a book. An addendum could be something forgotten, a correction, or new material that the author wanted to add after the book was finished. The publisher of *Collision at Home Plate: The Lives of Pete Rose and Bart Giamatti* (1991), Harper Collins, issued an addendum to that book correcting four statements about the activities of John Dowd, the man who served as Special Counsel to the Commissioner of Baseball in the investigation of Pete Rose.

advance reading copy—a bound paperback copy of a book produced in the second stage of printing, following the sequence: galleys or proofs, advance reading copy, finished book. Often but not always appearing with a plain cover, advance reading copies are sent to reviewers and booksellers and sometimes to the author himself (for final corrections) prior to the release of the finished book. Advance reading copies are prized by some collectors, as they are a pre-first edition copy of a book and thus more difficult to obtain than the book itself. Since corrections and changes are still possible at this stage, reviewers are sometimes cautioned not to quote from advance copies. Although advance reading copies should be distinguished from proofs or galleys, the term is widely used interchangeably (even by publishers) with one of the several synonyms for proofs; especially "uncorrected proof."

almanac— in baseball literature, a reference book full of information, such as records, statistics, rosters, rules, historical accounts, and previews of an upcoming season, usually intended to be an annual publication. Prior to his fame as the author of the *Boys of Summer* (Harper & Row, 1971), Roger Kahn co-authored the *Mutual Baseball Almanac* (Doubleday & Co.) in 1954 and 1955. Although Anton Grobani (*Guide to Baseball Literature*, Gale Research Co., 1975) lists almanacs under "Record Books," there is often not a very clear line to be drawn between almanacs and guides, annuals, and some books which have the word "Yearbook" in the title. *USA Today's Sports Weekly* (formerly *Baseball Weekly*) and *Baseball America* both began publishing fine almanacs in the early 1990s.

annotation— an explanatory or evaluative comment added to something else, such as to the books in a bibliography. In *The Annotated Casey at the Bat* (Clarkson N. Potter, Inc., 1967) Martin Gardner provides extensive annotations for the 28 "Casey" poems (most of them parodies, of course) included in the book.

annual— any baseball book which appears on a yearly basis. The invention of Rotisserie League Baseball (and related variants falling under the heading of "Fantasy Baseball") gave rise to a number of different player analysis annuals, which were notorious for lasting five years or less. The entries which Grobani listed under "Annuals" are almost exclusively magazines, not books, and several magazine annuals are still going strong today: e.g., *Street & Smith Baseball*, *Athlon Sports Baseball*, and *Lindy's Baseball Scouting Report*.

anthology— a collection of written pieces, usually literary in nature, by various authors. Technically, an anthology is a collection of previously-published pieces, but the term is often applied to compilations which are properly called "collections." The classic anthology of baseball literature is *The Fireside Book of Baseball* (Simon & Schuster), edited by Charles Einstein and published in four volumes in 1956, 1958, 1968, and 1987. *Baseball, I Gave You All the Best Years of My Life* (North Atlantic Books, 1980; edited by Kevin Kerrane and Richard Grossinger) is also outstanding, as it contains the most diverse types of baseball writing to be found in any baseball anthology.

appendix— supplementary material placed at the end of a book. The first edition of *The Baseball Encyclopedia* (Macmillan, 1969) contains four appendices: Appendix A: Sources; Appendix B: Decisions of the Special Baseball Records Committee; Appendix C: Major Changes in Playing Rules and Scoring Rules; and Appendix D: 1969 Summary.

association copy— a copy of a book that can be connected to (or "associated with") a famous person or a person of note (at least in his own field) through an inscription or some indication of ownership. Such copies presumably have added value, although it is difficult to determine how much that extra value should be (cf. presentation copy). An example from the catalog of R. Plapinger describing a copy of *Baseball Giant Killers* by Al Parker (Nortex, 1976): "ASSOCIATION COPY, SIGNED by Robert Obojski (who literally "wrote the book" on minor league baseball)."

ATT— short for "as told to"; a phrase used to acknowledge the role of the author of an "autobiography" while allowing the publisher to emphasize the name of the subject; as in *The Babe Ruth Story* (E.P. Dutton, 1948) by Babe Ruth as told to Bob Considine and *Maybe I'll Pitch Forever* (Doubleday & Co., 1962) by LeRoy (Satchel) Paige as told to David Lipman. In such collaborative autobiographies "with" or "and" has in most cases come to replace ATT; as in *Garvey* (Times Books, 1986) by Steve Garvey with Skip Rozin and *Crash: The Life* *and Times of Dick Allen* (Ticknor & Fields, 1989) by Dick Allen and Tim Whitaker.

bibliography— meaning "the study of books" in its narrowest sense, bibliography is commonly understood to mean a list of books on a particular subject. Most baseball books of a scholarly or academic nature include bibliographies; in which cases, the bibliography is books (and usually articles as well) that were consulted by the author as he researched and wrote his own book. Such bibliographies are useful for readers who wish to follow in an author's footsteps or learn more about the subject covered in the author's book. The three great bibliographies of baseball literature which are themselves book-length works are those produced by Anton Grobani (*Guide to Baseball Literature*), Myron J. Smith, Jr. (*Baseball: A Comprehensive Bibliography*), and Andy McCue (*Baseball by the Books*). Shorter, more narrowly-focused baseball bibliographies have also been published, such as *The Dodgers Bibliography: From Brooklyn to Los Angeles* (Meckler, 1988) by Myron J. Smith, Jr. and Kevin Grace's *A Checklist of Books on Cincinnati Baseball* (Archives & Rare Books Department University of Cincinnati, 1988). There is a clear need for additional bibliographies on specific baseball topics, as well as bibliographies devoted to individual baseball authors.

blurb— a description and summary of a book produced by the publisher and printed on the inside flaps of the book's dust jacket. There is an art to writing a good blurb: the trick being to explain, in a very few words, why the book should be bought and read, without resorting to outlandish claims which only tend to irritate sophisticated readers and book buyers. The first paragraph of the blurb for *Bo: Pitching and Wooing* reads: "The sexiest sports book ever—makes others look like kid stuff—this is the inside, unvarnished story of Bo 'No-Hitter' Belinsky, the lefthander who got more press than any other player of his time, who laughed his way through his baseball years, enjoying the nights as much as the days in one of the last bastions of male chauvinism."

boards— in reference to modern hardback books, the stiff part of the front and back covers.

Glossary

book club edition—a book offered at a substantial savings to members of a book club. Book club editions are anathema to collectors because of the cheap paper and binding used to produce the books. Normally, book club editions are easily identified by a designation to that effect on the dust jacket, but used baseball book dealer R. Plapinger warns that many a collector owns a copy of *The Boys of Summer* which states that the copy is a First Edition when, in fact, it is a book club edition copy.

bookplate—a decorated label with a person's name either printed or written on it and affixed (normally) to one of the front end papers of a book as a means of indicating ownership. In 2003 Barnes & Noble published *The Art of the Bookplate* by James P. Keenan, which reproduces and comments on a number of beautifully-done bookplates, many commissioned by famous persons. Interestingly, the Foreword of the book was written by George Plimpton, author of three outstanding baseball books.

book rate—an outdated term, synonymous with "media mail."

Brodart—a clear plastic book jacket cover manufactured by the Brodart Company of Williamsport, Pennsylvania. Although Brodart produces a varied line of products for the library industry, it is best known among the public and book collectors for its book jacket covers, which come in a variety of sizes and two qualities: standard or archival. The founder of the company, Arthur Brody, invented the plastic dust jacket cover in 1939 while he was a student at Columbia University studying architectural photography.

Casey Award—the oldest of the three major annual awards given specifically to baseball books. Inaugurated in 1983 and sponsored by *Spitball: The Literary Baseball Magazine*, the Casey Award competition is open to baseball books of all types and is not limited to certain kinds of baseball books. For more information on the Casey, as well as the Seymour Medal and the Dave Moore Award, see Chapter 2, as well as Appendix A.

catalog—an extensive, often annotated list of books for sale, offered by a serious, if not always full-time, used book dealer. A catalog should provide detailed bibliographic and condition information about each book it includes, and collectors should pay close attention to this information, as well as to explanations about condition terminology, shipping charges, return and exchange policies, and other technical and practical matters which may be discussed by the dealer in the front of the catalog. Many catalogs are issued irregularly, but a very few used baseball book dealers, such as R. Plapinger and Wayne Green, have been issuing catalogs on a regular basis — usually twice a year — for several years. One should expect to pay a few dollars for the biggest catalogs as they are not produced without real expense to the dealers. The price of the catalog is usually applied to one's first purchase anyway. The biggest and best catalogs (Plapinger, Green, Mike's Baseball Books) are extremely useful bibliographically, and Plapinger's catalogs have long been recognized as the most consulted reference for determining values.

chapbook— a thin cheaply-produced book, bound (almost always) with one to three staples. While chapbooks can be prose or poetry, the term chapbook in regard to baseball literature refers usually to brief volumes of poetry, usually 20 pages or fewer in length. Since baseball poetry chapbooks do not receive wide distribution, they can be a challenge to collect. Moreover, they are appealing to collectors because they often represent the first publication of writers who later become important figures in the field of baseball poetry. Two baseball poetry chapbooks by poets of note are: *The Long Ball* by Jim Daniels (Pig in a Poke Press, 1988), 24 pages; and *What Do You Have to Lose?* by William Heyen (William B. Ewert, Publisher, 1987), 13 pages.

cloth— publishers' term for hardcover; synonymous with hardback and hardbound.

condition— the physical state of a book and all its parts. condition is the most important factor in determining the value of a book other than the demand for the book. See Chapter 5 for a full discussion of condition, including a list of common defects and their definitions.

copyright page— the recto of the title page where important information about a book is to be found, including Library of Congress Cataloging-in-Publication Data, the copyright date, and indications of edition. Publishers sometimes state on this page that the copy of the book is a First Edition, but not always. In lieu of that clear statement, publishers usually use a numbering system, such as 1 to 10 or 1 to 20; with the edition indicated by the lowest number remaining. For example, if the 1 and 2 are missing, then the copy in hand is from the third edition (more properly speaking, from the third printing of the first edition).

dust jacket— the removable, paper cover of a book. While the ostensible purpose of a dust jacket (DJ) is to protect the book, its actual purpose is to help sell the book; and an attractive DJ is one of the most effective tools at the disposal of a publisher's marketing department. A wonderful dust jacket (employing great design, typography, photography, and/or artwork) cannot redeem a bad book, but such a jacket combined with a good book will certainly enhance the pleasure of most readers and collectors. DJs are extremely important from a collecting perspective, and as a general rule the absence of one lowers a book's value by one half. Imperfections to a DJ also affect value, to a lesser degree, and should always be noted by a seller. It may seem a bit ironic, but dust jackets meant to protect books themselves require protection. The most effective method of protecting DJs is to cover them in the clear plastic material produced for that purpose by the Gaylord Brothers Company of Rochester, New York, and Los Angeles and the Brodart Company of Williamsport, Pennsylvania. Occasionally, soft cover books also have removable dust jackets. Examples are the Japanese version of *The Chrysanthemum and the Bat* (The Permanent Press, 1971) and *Fathers Playing Catch with Sons* (North Point Press, 1985) by Donald Hall.

edition— all copies of a book produced from the same printing plates. Unless something about the book changes, future printings are still technically from the same first edition. When changes are made (and it is not simply a case of more copies being printed), then subsequent editions are created, and it is proper to use terms such as "second edition" and "revised edition" (cf. printing). Nevertheless, for collecting purposes, the all-important term "first edition" refers to the first printing of the first edition.

ex library— a pejorative term used to refer to a book which has been discarded or otherwise officially removed from an institutional, usually public or school, library. Such books, properly called "library discards," are anathema to collectors because of the tell-tale marks of ownership that libraries permanently affix to them and because of the excessive wear the books endure in service to a large population of readers, many of whom have little regard for the aesthetics of a book. An ex library book (i.e., a library discard) can serve until a replacement in collectible condition can be found and thereafter as a reading copy. Books in the Putnam, Messner, and Barnes Young Adult biography series of the 1950s, for example, are difficult to find in non-ex library condition. Note: it is possible that the overall condition of an ex library book could be superior to that of a reading copy; however, even an ex library book in otherwise Fine condition, except for ownership marks, is not a collectible book. Synonymous with Ex Lib and X Lib.

ex libris— meaning "from the library of," the term is often confused with "ex library" but properly refers to books which belong to or have been removed from a private collection. The term is non-pejorative and is usually printed on bookplates. When a baseball book has a bookplate that confirms it is an ex libris copy from the library of a notable or important person, the distinction should increase, not decrease, the book's value.

fly leaf—" fly leaves" are blank pages at the beginning and end of a book. It is common for an author to sign on the front fly leaf of his book.

fore-edge— the side of a book opposite the spine. As a decorative novelty, fore-edge paintings were done to books as early as the sixteenth century. In this method some scene or picture is painted onto the edges of a book's leaves as the leaves are fanned out and held in place by a special press. The picture is visible only when the book is open. Since fore-edge painting reached its zenith of popularity in Britain in the eighteenth century, it would seem to have little relevance to the subject of his book, yet at least one example of a baseball fore-edge painting is known to exist. A fore-edge-painted copy of the *Works of John Greenleaf Whittier* from the 1890's was offered in a 2002

MastroNet, Inc. auction; and this book featured, not one, but two nineteenth century baseball scenes on its fore-edges. A scene of a runner sliding into home appears when the pages of the book are fanned in one direction; a panoramic view of a game in progress appears when the pages are fanned in the other direction. The book carried a minimum bid of $500, and should any other fore-edge paintings of a baseball nature be discovered they would certainly command similar interest among collectors.

foreword—an introduction to a book by someone other than the author himself, the main purpose of which is to recommend the book to the public. It is common for baseball books to have forewords by major league players, but such forewords are often ghost-written. More trustworthy (not to mention usually more worth reading) are forewords by other, distinguished writers. In the foreword to Henry W. Thomas' great biography of Walter Johnson (Phenom Press, 1995), for instance, Shirley Povich writes: "For years Walter Johnson was identified by baseball writers, in the slang of the time, as 'The Big Swede.' Despite no Swedes in his ancestry, Johnson accepted the appellation without protest. 'I didn't want to offend anybody,' Johnson once told me. 'There are a lot of Swedes I know who are nice people.' This book is about that kind of man."

galleys—the first state of a book, sometimes printed in long continuous sheets of paper that are used by the printer and proofreaders to make corrections. Galley pages, usually unbound, are usually also sent to authors for their corrections. Synonymous with proofs, galley proofs, uncorrected proofs, and page proofs.

ghost—a professional writer who writes for and under the name of another real person, usually a celebrity. Ghost-writing or ghosting—not to be confused with using a nom de plume—is rarely done today, but it was fairly common in the first half of the twentieth century. Major league stars, such as Babe Ruth, Christy Mathewson, John McGraw, and Dizzy Dean, put their names to countless newspaper articles and even autobiographies under ghost-writing arrangements. The most famous and most successful baseball ghost writer was Christy Walsh, one of five writers to ghost for Babe Ruth. Walsh tells his story and that of the ghosting profession he helped develop into an industry in a thin 1937 biography called *Adios to Ghosts*. On the last page of the book Walsh adds the following P.S.: "The author guarantees that this book (unfortunately) was not ghost-written."

guide—a pre-season reference publication intended to be published on an annual basis that is full of information regarding game scores, averages, rules and regulations, past season's results, rosters, statistics and records, and previews of a coming season. Guides (almost always issued in softcover) were among the first baseball books ever published; famous (and valuable) examples are *Beadle's Dime Baseball Player, Dewitt's Baseball Guide, Spalding's Official Baseball Guide*, and *Reach Baseball Guide*. The longest-running guide is *The Sporting News Baseball Guide* which began in 1942.

half title page—a page set before the title page, with only the book's title printed on it. The additional room on the half title page makes it a handy place for authors' or subjects' signatures.

illustrations—although typically meaning photos in reference to baseball books, illustrations refer to any pictures, artwork, diagrams, and non-text items used to clarify the text or for decoration. "Illustrated" means that a book has such items. Illustrated baseball books often have the word in their titles but not always. In the latter cases, catalog issuers are careful to identify their illustrated books as such. *This Great Game* edited by Doris Townsend (Rutledge Books, 1971) is an example of a wonderful baseball book which does not, by its title, indicate that it is a heavily-illustrated book.

index—an alphabetical listing of topics (with corresponding page numbers) at the end of a book. Once hit-or-miss propositions, indexes for baseball books are becoming more common than they once were; probably due to the influence of academic presses in baseball book publishing. The presence of an index probably does not add much to a book's monetary value, but baseball researchers and writers value indexes highly. The increasing prevalence of indexes may be illustrated by the three Honus Wagner biographies which were all published in 1996: *Honus Wagner: A Biography* by Dennis & Jeanne Burke DeValeria, *Honus Wagner: The Life of Baseball's "Flying Dutchman"* by Arthur D. Hittner, and

Honus: The Life and Times of a Baseball Hero by William Hageman. Only the latter volume appeared without an index.

inscription—a message or greeting written by the author or subject of a book in addition to a mere signature. Inscribed copies presumably have more value than merely signed copies, but the extra value depends on the length and nature of the inscription. In the sports collecting world inscriptions are often referred to as "personalizations," and so a baseball card dealer might offer for sale baseball books which he describes as being "personalized" rather than inscribed.

inspirational—a baseball book, usually an autobiography, with a religious, usually Christian, outlook and message. The first of several Sunday biographies, Theodore T. Frankenburg's *Spectacular Career of Rev. Billy Sunday, Famous Baseball Evangelist* (McClelland & Co., 1913) might be considered the first such book. Although inspirational baseball books are seldom cited in lists of best baseball books, they sometimes sell very well: e.g., *Comeback* (Zondervan Publishing House/Harper & Row, 1990) by Dave Dravecky with Tim Stafford.

instructional—a how-to-play baseball book. As a rule, instructionals inspire little excitement among collectors; however, as with juveniles, collectors may be interested in instructionals done by their favorite players, especially when few if any biographies of the players exist. For example, Johnny Mize has not been the subject of a biography, but he did "author" with help from Murray Kaufman (in an ATT format) an instructional: *How to Hit* (Holt, Rinehart & Winston, 1953). The book illustrates why instructionals can be of interest, apart from the playing advice proffered. *How to Hit* includes a fair amount of biographical material and many photos of the subject and other players, such as Mickey Mantle and Phil Rizzuto; not to mention Mize's inadequately explained or proven claim that he was cousin to both Ty Cobb and Babe Ruth! The most famous instructional is Ted Williams' *The Science of Hitting* (Simon & Schuster, 1971). The book is also the most sought-after instructional, by book collectors and major league players who live by its prescriptions.

introduction—usually, although not always, a prefatory piece written by the author himself. If written by a celebrity, an introduction is not much different than a foreword, the main purpose of which is to recommend the book. If the introduction is written by the author himself, the piece may have some or all of the following purposes: to acknowledge assistance rendered, to set the scene of the book, to explain how or why the book came to be written, and to outline methods, sources, or parameters that were used in the writing of the book. In other words, introductions often contain information that is useful to a proper understanding of the work. It is probably impossible to appreciate *No Big Deal* by Mark Fidrych and Tom Clark without first reading the book's Introduction wherein Clark explains how he mined the material for the book (mostly during intensive interviews with Fidrych over a four-day period) and went to great pains to preserve the subject's language and natural speech patterns.

juvenile—a descriptive, non-pejorative term, which indicates that a baseball book was written for a younger, "juvenile" audience. It is an especially helpful indicator for collectors in reference to fiction and biographies. Some juvenile novels, particularly older ones, appeal to collectors not normally interested in juvenile baseball literature or fiction simply for their attractive picture covers. Some juvenile biographies are of interest because they are the only biographies published of the subjects: for example, the juvenile biographies of Jim Konstanty (published as part of the Barnes' All-Star series), Jackie Jensen (as part of the Messner series), and Bobby Bonds (as part of Putnams' Sports Shelf series).

laid in—referring to anything such as photos, maps, or newspaper clippings which are placed inside a book, not glued or sewn in. Publicity releases are a common "laid in" item. An example from the catalog of Wayne Greene in connection with *All My Octobers* by Mickey Mantle with Mickey Herskowitz (Harper, 1994): "Review copy with 5"×7" promotional photo of Mantle and a 4 page press release laid in."

library binding—a superior, reinforced type of stitched binding meant to make the binding last longer than normal. Presumably, a selling point for libraries whose books are subject to excessive use.

limited edition—a book of which only a certain number of copies are printed. In order to have a true limited edition, the number of copies printed must be indicated in each copy of the book, which is itself identified as to its place in the sequence of printing (or numbering), as in #12 of 100 (or 12/100). Limited edition books usually are also signed, by the author, an illustrator, a subject, or some combination of the principals involved. Many baseball poetry chapbooks are printed in limited editions, but major commercial houses also occasionally do limited, signed & numbered editions (usually with special covers) prior to the regular book's release. "Casey And the Bat," an anonymous erotic parody of Ernest Thayer's famous poem, in which the word "Bat" is a euphemism for prostitute, was printed by Polo Grounds Press (1988) in a limited edition of 100 copies, signed and numbered by illustrator Blair Gibeau.

list—a compilation of books for sale, too short to be a catalog. Lists are normally offered by other collectors, not full-time used book dealers.

mass market paperback—(see pocket books). The smaller and cheaper of the two standard-sized paperbacks commonly issued by American publishers, mass market paperbacks are usually released after a hardback version of the same book has had its chance to sell. *Where Have You Gone, Vince DiMaggio?* (Bantam Books, 1983) by Edward Kiersh is an example of a worthwhile baseball book that was issued as an original mass market paperback.

media guide—team produced booklets issued annually, usually in digest form or brochure shape, that contain all manner of information about the team, its personnel, and history. Originally intended exclusively for and still given free of charge to accredited members of the newspaper, radio, and television media, the guides are now routinely sold to the public by the issuing teams. Media guides are popular with team collectors, many of whom are not baseball book collectors per se. For decades media guides were rather slim publications, but in recent years they have ballooned to full-length book proportions. For example, the San Francisco Giants media guide for 1978 came out with 84 pages; by 2004 the page count for the Giants media guide had risen to 408.

media mail—the reduction in price by which books may be sent through the United States Postal System. The reduced price also means slower delivery. Used baseball books dealers often automatically send out orders by media mail but are willing to use faster service when the customer is willing to pay extra for it.

octavo— the name for the most common size of hardback books, roughly 6×9 inches. Such a book is made by folding a book sheet into eight leaves or sixteen pages. Other common book sizes: duodecimo (5×7), quarto (9×12), and folio (17×22).

o.p.— short for Out of Print, the eventual fate of all but the most tenacious of books. Baseball books from academic and scholarly publishers often remain in print longer than their counterparts from commercial houses. Only a handful of baseball books issued by commercial publishers stay in print for more than a single year.

oral history— the remembrances of a person whose life story and times are supposed to be of historical significance, tape recorded and transcribed in the first person. Lawrence Ritter was the first person to apply the oral history technique to baseball subjects; and his seminal volume in the field (*The Glory of Their Times,* Macmillan, 1966), which has been widely imitated, remains unsurpassed. While oral history has made significant contributions to baseball history and literature — the literature of the Negro Leagues is highly dependent on oral history — professional historians, who know that nothing is more fallible than human memory, have cautioned against its misuse. Charles Alexander, for one, feels that too often baseball oral historians accept any and all claims of their subjects and rush them into print without checking their accuracy. Sometimes, too, amateur oral historians forget about the art necessary to transform unrehearsed recorded speech into literate narrative, and more than a few dreadful baseball oral histories have been published.

oversized— a catch-all term for books larger than the typical octavo size. Books with lots of photos are often published in this format.

paperback— a book with a paper or cardboard cover. Synonymous with softcover.

paperback original— a book which is published "originally" as a paperback, not a hardback. On occasion, a paperback original is followed by a hardback version of the same book, but usually the paperback original is the only version of the book to ever be published. *Diamonds in the Rough: Life in Baseball's Minor Leagues* by Ken Rappoport (Tempo Books, 1979) is an example of an interesting paperback original.

perfect binding— basically, binding a book by gluing the pages together at the spine; the normal method of binding for paperback books.

personalization— a signature that is addressed or personalized to a specific person, presumably the book's owner. An example from the catalog of R. Plapinger describing a copy of *The Comeback* by Ryne Duren with Robert Drury (Lorenz Press, 1978): "SIGNED by Duren (pers. to "Mrs. Siegle ...")."

picture book— an oversized illustrated children's book for which the appeal of the artwork is crucial. In other words, while the text of such a book should tell the story effectively, if the artwork is not exceptional there is no point in publishing (or collecting) the book. Two examples of picture books with art work so outstanding as to captivate any adult baseball fan are: *My Dad's Baseball* (written and illustrated by Ron Cohen) and *Leagues Apart: The Men and Times of the Negro Baseball Leagues* (written by Lawrence S. Ritter and illustrated by Richard Merkin).

picture cover— a hardback book with either engraved art or a photo reproduced on its board cover. Sometimes a book with a picture cover also comes with a dust jacket that has an identical picture on it —*Baseballogy* by Edmund Vance Cooke (Forbes & Co., 1912) is a good example — but more often the picture cover is meant to take the place of a dust jacket. Most baseball books with picture covers have been juveniles. Examples of baseball books with picture covers: the baseball books in Clair Bee's Chip Hilton series of sports novels; Random House's Major League Library series (e.g., *Great Rookies of the Major Leagues* by Jim Brosnan, 1966); and *Baseball's Strangest Moments* (Sterling Publishing, 1988) by Robert Obojski. Particularly attractive picture covers were done for Chelsea House's series of juvenile biographies, "Baseball Legends," which were done in the style of baseball cards.

plates—a term used to describe illustrations printed separately from the text. Many early baseball books, such as Alfred Spinks' *The National Game* (National Game Publishing Company, 1911), were published with plates; and it is a challenge to find copies of such books with all plates intact, as readers often could not resist the temptation to cut the plates out of the books. Not to be confused with a "bookplate."

pocket book—the smallest, standard size of paperback book, more commonly known today as a "mass market" paperback, that derives its name from the fact that such a book fits into the back pocket of a pair of pants. Technically, mass market paperbacks are slightly larger than true pocket books. While some collectors eschew pocket books or mass market paperbacks, some baseball books have been published only in that form, as paperback originals. Examples of true pocket books are *Bill Stern's Favorite Baseball Stories*, published in 1949 by Pocket Books, Inc.; and *The Only Game in Town: An Original Novel* by Charles Einstein, published in 1955 by Dell Publishing Company, Inc.

pop-up book—a book containing cardboard figures or constructions which, when opened, stand or "pop up." While pop-up books are nominally made for children, adults, who appreciate the genius of the design of such books, sometimes collect them. At least one baseball pop-up book has been published: *Fenway Park: Legendary Home of the Boston Red Sox* (Little, brown, 1992). According to the publisher the scale model of Fenway (made of 50 separate pieces) which pops up "is the most complex pop-up ever created."

preface—the introductory remarks of an author. Most readers skip the preface and go right to the first page of the book proper, and many of them never go back to read the preface later. This can be a mistake, as authors sometimes convey important information and memorable sentiments in their prefaces. Who, for instance, would not want to read the preface to *Baseball: The People's Game* (Oxford University Press, 1990) in which Harold Seymour writes: "A book of this length and range of topics is bound to invite some honest criticism, which is to be expected but I scorn the nit-pickers and scrap nibblers, not to mention a few plagiarizers, who, without citing me as their source, like yipping jackals snatch chunks from the disdainful tiger's kill. One even had the gall to complain of the taste of a chunk he gulped from one of my books."

presentation copy—supposedly, a copy of a book given as a present from the author's own stock; inscribed, of course. The only way to tell a presentation copy is by the wording of the inscription, and this method is not always foolproof. Few, if any, collectors of baseball books put a premium on such copies (cf. association copy).

printing—all the copies of a book produced during one run through the presses. The concept is important in regard to First Editions, in that what is really meant by the term is the first *printing* of the first edition. A copy of a book that comes from the second printing of a first edition is not a First Edition.

proofs—correctly another term for "galleys" which are typically unbound, "proofs" are commonly used synonymously with "advance reading copies." Most baseball book collectors do not seem to attach any special significance to these so-called "proofs" or advance reading copies. In the general book collecting world proofs and advance reading copies are sometimes highly prized, especially when they are for books by highly collected authors of fiction. The existence or the possibility of the existence of text in proofs or advance reading copies that is not in the finished book is what creates the collectibility of those proofs or advance reading copies; as collectors loyal to their author want all states of the books published by the author. Although R. Plapinger has not had much success selling proofs or advance reading copies to his customers, he reports that he did sell an advance reading copy of Robert Creamer's *Babe* for more than $100 ... probably due to the existence in the advance reading copy of unflattering comments about Claire Ruth that did not appear in the first edition.

publicity release—a document of one to several pages written by a book's publicity department that accompanies review copies of the book. Besides praising the book, publicity releases also often summarize the book, highlight quotations from it, and provide biographical information about the author, as well as pertinent facts relating to the publication of the book (such as cost, format, publication date, marketing strategy, and size of the initial print run). The presence of this release adds some value to a copy of the book. As sometimes happens, a publicist at Crown Publishers got a little carried away while writing the publicity release for a 1993 book. "Kevin Baker's first novel, *Sometimes You See It Coming*, is one of the finest baseball book I have ever read," she gushed. "Reminiscent of *The Natural* and *Shoeless Joe*, it stretches its focus well beyond the sport and captures the magic of a game that perennially reminds us of our youth."

publicity slip—a small piece of paper inserted into the front of a review copy of a book by the publisher's publicity department. It is sometimes accompanied by a press release. A slip, which usually states the book's publication date and asks that the reviewer send one or two copies of any published review to the publisher, is of interest to collectors because it identifies the book as a review copy.

Putnam—a volume from the series of team histories published in the late 1940s and early 1950s by G. P. Putnam's Sons. The books were authored by some of the leading sportswriters of the day (such as Lee Allen, Warren Brown, Frank Graham, Frederick Lieb, and Shirley Povich) and are highly prized by most baseball book collectors. The volumes on the Philadelphia Phillies and Washington Senators are the scarcest and most expensive, but even the more common volumes can rarely be found today for sale for less than $50. Southern Illinois University Press has embarked upon a program to reprint these volumes as part of their "Writing Baseball" series.

reading copy—a used book dealer's term meant to indicate that a book so described is fit for reading but not collecting. In other words, the condition of such a book is not good. Reading copies of expensive books can serve a purpose, even after they have been replaced by collectible copies, in that they allow the latter to remain on the shelf undisturbed, its satisfactory condition undiminished by the rigors of reading.

remainder—when publishers decide to take a book out of print, they often sell their remaining stock of such a book to used book wholesalers or large bookstore chains at a very large discount, sometimes

Glossary

pennies on the dollar. The wholesaler or bookstore chain then offers the title as a bargain book; often putting a "remainder mark," such as a red dot or black slash, on the bottom pages to indicate its status. Remainders are obviously welcome to bargain hunters, but they can be irritating when collectors have previously paid full price for the same book.

reprint—a book that is re-published after it has been out of print. For a discussion of reprinting as an indication of quality, see Chapter 2.

review copy—a copy of a book sent compliments of the publisher to a reviewer, a publisher, or a bookseller in the hope that a review of the book will be done or assigned by the recipient or ordered by a book seller. While review copies in the past could often be identified as such by a printed designation on the cover, today there is normally no way to tell if a book is a review copy other than the publicity release or slip that may still accompany and be laid in the book.

roundup review—a review of three or more baseball books in the same article by the same writer. Such reviews often appear in the spring, in the pages of daily newspapers; in journals devoted to the book trade, such as *Publishers' Weekly*; and in baseball publications, such as *Baseball America* and *USA Today's Sports Weekly*. Rather than in-depth analysis of any particular book, roundup reviews usually strive to bring some attention to as many books as possible. Also known as "omnibus" reviews.

SABR—an organization of 6,000+ members dedicated to the study of baseball history and statistical analysis. Founded in Cooperstown, New York, on August 10, 1971, the Society for American Baseball Research states that its constitutional objectives are "to foster the study of baseball, stimulate interest in baseball, establish an accurate historical account of baseball, and disseminate baseball information." Responsible for many additions and corrections to the historical baseball record, SABR is respected and recognized by Major League Baseball. SABR members are avid baseball book buyers and collectors; many SABR members are authors of baseball books; and SABR itself does a great deal of baseball publishing, in the form of newsletters, journals (such as, *Baseball Research Journal* and *The National Pas-*

time), and books, such as *Nineteenth Century Stars* (Robert Tiemann and Mark Rucker, 1989) and *Addie Joss: King of Pitchers* (Scott Longert, 1998).

sabermetrics—"Sabermetrics is a coined word, the first part honoring SABR (Society for American Baseball Research), the second part indicating measurement. Sabermetrics is the mathematical and statistical analysis of baseball records."—*The Bill James Baseball Abstract.* Although Bill James is the author most readily identified as a sabermetrician, many other authors have written sabermetrical type books; some of them, such as Earnshaw Cook (*Percentage Baseball*, Waverley Press, 1964), before the term sabermetrics was invented. *The Hidden Game of Baseball* (Doubleday, 1984) by John Thorn and Pete Palmer is an important history of sabermetrical endeavor.

SASE—self-addressed, stamped envelope. Often required with orders to used baseball books dealers for the return of refunds and with queries to ensure a reply.

saddle stitching—binding by staples through the spine. Obviously, the number of pages that can be bound by saddle stitching is limited, and some collectors may classify saddle-stitched publications as "booklets" rather than books. Baseball poetry chapbooks are almost always saddle stitched.

series—a group of books connected to each other by subject matter and format (and possibly author, as well) and issued over time by the same publisher. Two outstanding recent series of baseball books: Bruce Chadwick and David M. Spindel's "Memories and Memorabilia" series of team histories (published by Abbeville Press) and "The World of Baseball" series published by Redefinition, Inc. The latter series was sold by subscription and ran to ten unnumbered volumes, including *The Old Ball Game: Baseball's Beginnings*; *The Lively Ball: Baseball in the Roaring Twenties*; *Low and Outside: Baseball in the Depression, 1930–1939*; *The Sluggers: Those Fabulous Long Ball Hitters*; *The Explosive Sixties: Baseball's Decade of Expansion*; *The Hurlers: Pitching Power and Precision*; *October's Game: The World Series*; *The New Professionals: Baseball in the 1970s*; *The Fielders: The Game's Greatest Gloves*; and *Speed: Baseball in High Gear.*

Glossary

signed copy— a copy of a book containing the signature of the author or subject or both. The more famous and collectible the author, the more value the signature adds to the book.

slip case— a papered cardboard box with one end open that houses and protects a book or books. It is always highly desirable to retain and preserve in top condition a book's slip case, just as it is desirable to do the same with dust jackets. Examples of baseball books that were published with slip cases: *The Baseball Encyclopedia* (1st ed.); the first two volumes of Harold Seymour's history, *Baseball*; and *The DiMaggio Albums* (Putnam, 1989, compiled and edited by Richard Whittingham).

title page— the recto side of the copyright page and following the half-title page, the title page states, in addition to the name of the book, the author and the publisher. It is common for the title page to include also the place of publication and the publisher's logo. Authors and subjects sometimes choose to sign on this page.

trade paperback— paperback books which are larger and more expensive than their mass market counterparts. It is not uncommon for trade paperbacks to be as tall as hardback books. Today most baseball books issued as paperback originals are manufactured as trade paperbacks.

uncorrected proof— the first, trial printing of a book, almost always unbound, which is used by the publisher and proofreader to make corrections. Synonymous with advance proof, page proof, proofs, galleys, and galley proofs. Although technically incorrect to do so, uncorrected proof is often used to refer to what is produced in the second stage of printing, an advance reading copy.

volume— used informally to mean "book," as in a "volume of poetry," the word technically refers to each one of several books in a set or series. It is sometimes confused with "edition," even by publishers. For instance, in 1987 Simon & Schuster proclaimed the fourth volume of the *Fireside Book of Baseball* to be the fourth edition, much to the disgust of editor Charles Einstein.

want list— serious collectors often compile a list of baseball books they most want to add to their collection; hence, the term "want list." The value of a want list is two-fold. When given to a dealer, it allows the dealer to give the collector first crack at a book, before the dealer puts it in his catalog. A want list, particularly in an abbreviated "cheat sheet" form of authors' last names, can also be useful when the collector is searching book store shelves himself; not so much perhaps when the non-fiction baseball book section is being searched, but exceedingly so when a large general fiction section is being searched for unsegregated (and often unrecognized as such by the shop owner) baseball fiction.

weeding— permanently removing books from a collection. While sometimes difficult to do from an emotional point of view, weeding is often necessary and should result in a stronger collection.

wraps— the cover of a paperback book, and a term used mostly by those inhabiting the antiquarian book world. The term is NOT synonymous with "dust wrapper," which is sometimes used (carelessly) as a synonym for dust jacket.

yearbook— more magazines than books, these over-sized, paperback, team-issued annual publications are sold as souvenirs and are heavy on photos of the team's players. As with media guides, yearbooks are extremely popular with many team collectors who are not otherwise much interested in baseball book collecting.

APPENDIX A: BASEBALL BOOK AWARDS

Casey Award Winners

1983 — *The Celebrant* by Eric Rolfe Greenberg (Everest House)

1984 — *Bums: An Oral History of the Brooklyn Dodgers* by Peter Golenbock (Putnam)

1985 — *Good Enough to Dream* by Roger Kahn (Doubleday)

1986 — *The Bill James Historical Baseball Abstract* by Bill James (Villard)

1987 — *Diamonds Are Forever: Artists and Writers on Baseball* by Peter H. Gordon, ed. (Chronicle Books)

1988 — *Blackball Stars* by John Holway (Meckler)

1989 — *The Pitch that Killed* by Mike Sowell (Macmillan)

1990 — *Baseball: The People's Game* by Harold Seymour (Oxford University Press)

1991 — *To Everything a Season: Shibe Park and Urban Philadelphia, 1909–1976* by Bruce Kuklick (Princeton University Press)

1992 — *The Negro Baseball Leagues: A Photographic History* by Phil Dixon (Amereon)

1993 — *Diamonds: The Evolution of the Ballpark* by Michael Gershman (Houghton Mifflin)

1994 — *Lords of the Realm* by John Helyar (Villard)

Appendix A

1995 — *Walter Johnson: Baseball's Big Train* by Henry W. Thomas (Phenom Press)

1996 — *Slide, Kelly, Slide* by Marty Appel (Scarecrow Press)

1997 — *Play for a Kingdom* by Thomas Dyja (Harcourt Brace)

1998 — *Judge and Jury* by David Pietrusza (Diamond Communications)

1999 — *Slouching Toward Fargo* by Neal Karlen (Spike)

2000 — *Cy Young: A Baseball Life* by Reed Browning (University of Massachusetts Press)

2001 — *The Final Season: Fathers, Sons, and One Last Season in a Classic American Ballpark* by Tom Stanton (Thomas Dunne Books)

2002 — *Shut Out: A Story of Race and Baseball in Boston* by Howard Bryant (Routledge)

2003 — *Moneyball: The Art of Winning an Unfair Game* by Michael Lewis (Norton)

2004 — *Ted Williams: The Biography of an American Hero* by Leigh Montville (Doubleday)

2005 — *Luckiest Man: The Life and Death of Lou Gehrig* by Jonathan Eig (Simon & Schuster)

2006 — *A Game of Inches: The Stories Behind the Innovations That Shaped Baseball* by Peter Morris (Ivan R. Dee)

Seymour Medal Winners

1996 — *Fleet Walker's Divided Heart* by David Zang (University of Nebraska Press)

1997 — *Honus Wagner: The Life of Baseball's "Flying Dutchman"* by Arthur D. Hittner (McFarland)

1998 — *The Detroit Tigers: Club and Community, 1945–95* by Patrick Harrigan (University of Toronto Press)

1999 — *Baseball's Last Dynasty: Charlie Finley's Oakland A's* by Bruce Markusen (Masters Press)

2000 — *Baseball's Pivotal Era: 1945–51* by William Marshall (University Press of Kentucky)

2001 — *Past Time: Baseball as History* by Jules Tygiel (Oxford University Press)

2002 — *Early Baseball and the Rise of the National League* by Tom Melville (McFarland)

2003 — *Breaking the Slump: Baseball in the Depression Era* by Charles C. Alexander (Columbia University Press)

2004 — *Baseball Fever: Early Baseball in Michigan* by Peter Morris (University of Michigan Press)

2005 — *Negro League Baseball: The Rise and Ruin of a Black Institution* by Neil Lanctot (Uiversity of Pennsylvania Press)

2006 — *Baseball Before We Knew It: A Search for the Roots of the Game* by David Block (University of Nebraska Press)

Dave Moore Award Winners

1999 — *The Pride of Havana: A History of Cuban Baseball* by Roberto Gonzalez Echevarria (Oxford University Press)

2000 — *Havana Heat* by Darryl Brock (Total Sports Publishing)

2001 — *The Final Season* by Tom Stanton (Thomas Dunne Books)

2002 — *The End of Baseball as We Knew It: The Players Union, 1960–81* by Charles Korr (University of Illinois Press)

2003 — *Foul Ball: My Life and Hard Times Trying to Save an Old Ballpark* by Jim Bouton (Bulldog Press)

2004 — *September Swoon: Richie Allen, the '64 Phillies, and Racial Integration* by William C. Kashatus (Pennsylvania State University Press)

Appendix A

2005 — *The Greatest Ballpark Ever: Ebbets Field and the Story of the Brooklyn Dodgers* by Bob McGee (Rutgers University Press)

2006 — *A Well-Paid Slave: Curt Flood's Fight for Free Agency in Professional Sports* by Brad Snyder (Viking Penguin)

APPENDIX B:
INTERVIEW WITH WILLIS MONIE

The owner and proprietor of Willis Monie Books in Cooperstown, New York, Willis Monie was born in New York City and was raised in Westchester County. After graduating from Hartwick College (BA 1967), he earned a Master's Degree (1970) and a Ph.D (1973) in literature from the University of New Hampshire. He taught for three years in the West Virginia state University system and moved to Cooperstown in 1975. After working for antiquarian book dealer Roger Butterfield for four years, he started his own business in 1979. A member of the Antiquarian Booksellers Association of America and the American Antiquarian Society, Monie is a life-long fan of the Philadelphia-Kansas City-Oakland A's. He served as a Judge for the 2004 Casey Award competition and has been doing business at the same location (139 Main Street, one block from the Baseball Hall of Fame) since 1989.

While Willis Monie Books is a general store that stocks old and rare books, manuscripts, and ephemera on (potentially) all subjects, it specializes in baseball. The baseball books there can be found immediately to the right of the front door, completely filling (and spilling out of) four long floor-to-ceiling sections with nine shelves per section. Nearby, a filing cabinet and a dozen or so bins resting on the floor bulge with baseball magazines, yearbooks, programs, and ephemera of all kinds. Upstairs, a large stock room (off limits to unescorted customers) houses an even larger cache of baseball books and publications for which there is not room in the store proper. No visit by a baseball book lover to Cooperstown is complete without a lengthy stop at "Monie's." The following brief interview with Willie Monie was conducted by Mike Shannon at his store on Saturday, July 30, 2005, during the annual Hall of Fame Induction Weekend.

What percentage of your business results from the sale of baseball books?

Percentage-wise baseball books are no more than ten percent of the business of the store. We do a large amount of business on-line but don't normally sell any baseball books on-line, although we are beginning to list some of our scarcer baseball items on-line. We also don't take baseball books to book shows. More to the point, it's only as much as ten percent because some of the baseball books we sell are rare books. When you're selling $5 and $10 books, which is what most of our baseball books are priced at, it doesn't add up to a large amount.

What percentage of that ten percent happens on Induction Weekend every year?

The baseball book business is steady all summer, so maybe ten percent of our baseball book sales happen this weekend. We obviously benefit from our proximity to the Hall of Fame, and business at the Hall of Fame is pretty steady all summer, from the time school gets out through Labor Day. And then the weekends are pretty good even through the end of October. The Hall of Fame gets something like 500,000 visitors for the summer, and not all of them are here this weekend, you know, so the percentage of our baseball book sales for this weekend is not as high as you might have expected.

What is your acquisition strategy for baseball books?

Well, you might think I'm being facetious, but I'm not when I say that for the most part the baseball books come to me. Because I'm here in Cooperstown other book sellers, who are interested in baseball, will call me. They will either buy a collection of baseball books and then wholesale the books to me, or they will call me first and let me buy the books directly. For instance, I recently got a call from a book dealer who specializes in fishing. He was looking at a collection in the Long Island home of a well known New York sportswriter, and when he saw the baseball material he thought of me. He said, "There's a lot of baseball media guides and books here ... do you want 'em?" A lot of it is word of mouth from dealer to dealer. The dealer I just spoke of told another dealer about me, so when the second one was helping the widow of a second New York sportswriter liquidate her deceased husband's collection so she could move to a condo in Florida, they called me about the baseball books in the collection.

It also helps that I'm basically the only one here. There are fewer general stores around than there used to be so in that respect I have less and less competition ... at least when it comes to buying books from people who still like to visit used book shops in person. A lot of stuff comes from other areas of the country too. This is a sparsely populated area — the population of the village is only 2,200 — but when people who know I'm here come to town, they often bring me a box of baseball books or several boxes of books that they want to sell me.

How do you price your baseball books?

I try to sell my baseball books ... the common ones, that is, ... for what I consider to be a "low end" retail price: say, $5 to $8 each. The guys who make catalogs would consider my prices low end "wholesale," but I use that low retail price because common baseball books are hard to sell. Take *Men at Work*, for example. It's a good book, but almost all of my customers who want that book already have a copy of it. We have a hundred copies of it in storage, so to have any chance of selling them we need to keep them priced at a fairly low end retail level.

It gets trickier with books that aren't so common. We do as much research on prices as we can, but often there is not that much to go on. We hold onto auction catalogs and get "prices realized" reports from auctions, but auction prices might be retail or they might be wholesale. A single auction price tells you very little, so you really need multiple prices before they become meaningful. In general, what it comes down to is trying to determine fair market value, which is the rule of thumb used by the IRS. And that price is "what a willing buyer and a willing seller can agree on."

Our recent purchase of George Wright's book illustrates the difficulty of pricing rare books. A book scout called about the book, which is actually more of a pamphlet than a book, and she said, "I don't know much about it ... it has no wrappers ... but this is what I want for it." Normally, in a case like that we have to find out what we can sell the book for before we can make an offer for it, but this time that was pretty difficult to do. We could find only two recorded sales of the 1875 version of the book (*George Wright's Book for 1875*), which is the more common version, and only one for the 1874 version (*Record of the Boston Baseball Club, 1871–74*), which is the version she had. The one sale of the 1874 book we could document came in the famous Barry Halper auction when it brought about $1,800 or $2,000. That's not much to go on, but I decided we could probably sell the book for a profit, so I told her, "Okay, send it along." I sent her a check, and that's how I got the item.

How has the Internet affected your baseball book business?

The Internet is responsible for the biggest change in the baseball book environment by far, and what it has done is strange. The Internet has made common books more common and rare books more rare. Because of the Internet common baseball books are easier to find now, and prices for those books have been lowered. I used to get a lot of calls for the various Mickey Mantle biographies, but not anymore since people go on-line to find them. On the other hand, the Internet has raised prices on the rare baseball books because it has made everyone aware of just how rare those rare baseball books are. And, strangely enough, just as the Internet has made it harder to sell $5 books, the Internet has made it easier to sell $5,000 books, which is good for me since I make my living on rare books.

What is the current state of the baseball book business and what do you foresee as its future?

I don't see any decrease at the moment in the baseball book business. I personally have seen a decline in the sales of common books because of the Internet, especially from some of the guys who make an annual pilgrimage here to Cooperstown. They used to load up on baseball books here, but they tell me, "Now I find the books I need at home on the Internet.... It's just so easy." But this doesn't mean that there is an overall decline in demand for baseball books; it just means that there is a decline in demand for the common books from me. Because of the Internet my customers can get common books from dealers all over the country. As I said before though, the demand for rare baseball books is stronger than ever, and that's really my bread and butter.

As for the future, it's hard to say. As long as I have been in the business some people have predicted a very dismal future for books. They have predicted that books would be made obsolete by everything from microfiche to electronic formats, and so far they have been wrong. In my opinion, no matter what else they invent, enough people will continue to want the real thing to keep books around and the book business going. I also think baseball book collectors are here to stay and that baseball books will continue to sell.

BIBLIOGRAPHY

Adomites, Paul D., compiler. "The Essential Baseball Library." *The SABR Review of Books* (Vol. 2, No. 1, 1987): 9–19.

Adomites, Paul D. "The Ultimate Baseball Library." In *Total Baseball*, edited by John Thorn and Pete Palmer. New York: Warner Books, 1989.

Bjarkman, Peter J. *Baseball & the Game of Life: Stories for the Thinking Fan*. Otisville, New York: Birch Book Press, 1990.

Block, David. *Baseball Before We Knew It: A Search for the Roots of the Game*. Lincoln and London: University of Nebraska Press, 2005.

Dirda, Michael. *Caring for Your Books*. New York: Book-of-the-Month Club, 1990.

Donaldson, Gerald. *Books: Their History, Art, Power, Glory, Infamy and Suffering According to Their Creators, Friends and Enemies*. New York: Van Nostrand Reinhold Company, 1981.

Ellis, Estelle, with Wilton Wiggins and Douglas Lee. *The Booklover's Repair Manual*. New York: Knopf, 2000.

Ellis, Ian C. *Book Finds: How to Find, Buy, and Sell Used and Rare Books*. New York: Perigee Books, 1996.

Grobani, Anton. *Guide to Baseball Literature*. Detroit: Gale Research Company, 1975.

James, Bill. *The Bill James Historical Baseball Abstract*. New York: Villard Books, 1988.

Bibliography

Johnson, Barbara. *Book Scouting: How to Turn Your Love for Books into Profit.* Englewood Cliffs, New Jersey: Prentice-Hall, Inc., 1981.

Kahn, Roger. *Memories of Summer: When Baseball Was an Art, and Writing about It a Game.* New York: Hyperion, 1997.

Kaplan, George R. "The Absolutely Indispensible Irreducible 25-Book Baseball Library." *The Minneapolis Review of Baseball: A Journal of Writing about Baseball* (Vol. 4, Winter 1984): 23–31.

Lorimer, Lawrence. *The National Baseball Hall of Fame and Museum Baseball Desk Reference.* London, New York, Delhi, Munich and Melbourne: Dorling Kindersly, 2002.

MacCambridge, Michael, editor. *ESPN SportsCentury.* New York: Hyperion, 1999.

McCallum, Jack. "Jock Lit." *Sports Illustrated* (Vol. 67, No. 13, September 21, 1987): 80–92.

McCue, Andy. *Baseball by the Books: A History and Complete Bibliography of Baseball Fiction.* Dubuque, Iowa: Wm. C. Brown Publishers, 1991.

McEntegart, Pete, et al. "The Top 100 Sports Books of All Time." *Sports Illustrated* (Vol. 97, No. 24, December 16, 2002): 128–48.

Muir, P. H. *Book Collecting as a Hobby.* London and Chesham: Gramol Publications Ltd., 1945.

Petroski, Henry. *The Book on the Shelf.* New York: Knopf, 1999.

Rabinowitz, Harold, and Rob Kaplan. *A Passion for Books: A Book Lover's Treasury of Stories, Essays, Humor, Lore and Lists on Collecting, Reading, Borrowing, Lending, Caring for, and Appreciating Books.* New York: Times Books, 1999.

Shannon, Mike. *Baseball: The Writers' Game.* South Bend, Indiana: Diamond Communications, 1992.

Shannon, Mike. *Diamond Classics: Essays on 100 of the Best Baseball Books Ever Published.* Jefferson, N.C.: McFarland, 1988.

Smith, Jr. Myron J. *Baseball: A Comprehensive Bibliography.* Jefferson, N.C.: McFarland, 1986.

Thorn, John, and Bob Carroll, editors. *The Whole Baseball Catalog.* New York: Simon and Schuster, 1990.

INDEX

A.G. Spalding and the Rise of Baseball 105
Aaron to Zuverink 105
Aaron, Hank 26, 105, 108, 138
Aaron 105
Aaron, r.f. 105
"The Absolutely Indispensible Irreducible 25-Book Baseball Library" 49
Ace: Phil Marchildon, Canada's Pitching Sensation and Wartime Hero 105
Adair, Robert Kemp 156
Addeo, Ed 145
Addie Joss: King of Pitchers 105, 198
Adelman, Bob 154
Adelson, Bruce 120
Adios to Ghosts 17, 105, 188
Adler, Bill 145
Adomites, Paul 51, 53
Aethlon: The Journal of Sport Literature 64
After the Miracle: The Amazin' Mets Twenty Years Later 105
Ahrens, Art 133, 151
Al Kaline and the Detroit Tigers 105
The Al Kaline Story 105
Alexander, Charles 23, 119, 142, 154, 161, 171, 192, 203
All About Baseball Books 63
All G.O.D.'s Children 27
All My Octobers 190
All Time All Stars of Black Baseball 105
All Time Rosters of Major League Baseball Clubs 105

Allen, Dick 124, 182
Allen, Ethan 146
Allen, John 79, 80–81
Allen, Lee 19, 106, 107, 123, 127, 133, 138, 143, 151, 154, 176, 196
Allen, Maury 105, 110, 115, 118, 125, 141, 148, 153, 159, 161, 167, 174, 178
Allen, Mel 140, 178
Allison, Bob 18
All-Star Baseball Since 1933 105
The All-Star Game 105
Alomar, Roberto 163
Alou, Felipe 149
Alston and the Dodgers 105
Alston, Walter 105, 177
Alvarez, Mark 12
Always on the Offense 106
Amazin': The Miraculous History of New York's Most Beloved Baseball Team 28
The Amazing Mets 106
Amazing: The Miracle of the Mets 106
America through Baseball 106
America's Dizzy Dean 106
America's National Game 106
American Baseball 106
The American Baseball Review 63
American Baseball: From the Commissioners to Continental Expansion 22
American Baseball: From Gentleman's Sport to the Commissioner's System 22
American Baseball: From Postwar Expansion to the Electronic Age 22
The American Boys Book 9
The American Diamond 106

Index

The American Dream and the National Game 64, 106
The American League: An Illustrated History 106
The American League Story 106
Anderson, Dave 177
Anderson, Sparky 117, 146, 165
Anderson, Wayne J. 135
Anderson, William M. 126
Andreano, Ralph 152
Andy Pafko: The Solid Man 106
Angell, Roger 26. 51, 130, 144, 163, 167
The Angels 106
Angle, Paul 156
The Annotated Casey at the Bat 106, 180
Anson, Adrian "Cap" 13, 108
The Answer Is Baseball 106
Appel, Marty 28, 31, 51, 63, 114, 153, 164, 170, 176, 178, 202
Archibald, Joe 117, 160
Ardizonne, Tony 136
Arete 64
The Armchair Book of Baseball 5, 21, 52, 106
The Armchair Book of Baseball, II 106
Arnow, Jan 145
Around the World with the Baseball Bugs 16, 106
The Art of Baseball 36, 107
The Art of the Bookplate 183
The Art of Pitching and Fielding 107
The Artful Dodger (Lasorda & Fisher) 107
The Artful Dodgers (Meany) 107
Ashhenback, Edward 16
Asinof, Eliot 23, 65, 128, 146
Astor, Gerald 112
At the Crack of the Bat 107
At Fenway: Dispatches from Red Sox Nation 107
Athletic Sports in America, England and Australia 13, 107
Athlon Sports Baseball 181
Atlantics 10
Axelson, G.W. 14, 100, 124

The Babe and I 107
Babe: The Legend Comes to Life 26, 51, 55, 56, 65, 107, 195

The Babe in Red Stockings 107
Babe Ruth (Meany) 107
Babe Ruth (Weldon) 18, 107
Babe Ruth and the American Dream 107
Babe Ruth: Baseball Boy 107
Babe Ruth Caught in a Snowstorm 27
Babe Ruth: His Life and Legend 26, 107
Babe Ruth: His Story in Baseball 107
Babe Ruth: The Idol of the American Boy 107
Babe Ruth: Idol of American Boyhood 16
The Babe: A Life in Pictures 37–38, 107
The Babe Ruth Story 18, 107, 181
Babe Ruth's America 107
Babe Ruth's Baseball Advice 108
Babe Ruth's Big Book of Baseball 108
Babe Ruth's Own Book of Baseball 65, 108
Backstage at the Mets 108
The Bad Guys Won 108
Bad Henry 108
Bailey, Bob 137
Bak, Richard 124, 145, 157, 171
Baker, Frank 32
Baker, Kevin 196
Baldwin, Stan 108
Ball Four 27–28, 50, 51, 55, 56, 108
A Ball Player's Career 13
Ball, Bat and Bishop 8, 19, 108
Ballads of Baseball 108
Balldom: The Britannica of Baseball 108
Ballpark Figures: The Blue Jays and the Business of Baseball 108
Ballpark: Camden Yards and the Building of an American Dream 108
The Ballparks 27, 36, 68–69, 108
Ballparks of North America 39, 108
A Ballplayer's Career 108
The Ballplayers 40, 108
Ballplayers Are Human Too 108
Balls 108
Baltimore Orioles 17, 18
The Baltimore Orioles 108
The Baltimore Orioles: 40 Years of Magic from 33rd Street to Camden Yards 108
Ban Johnson 108
Banana Bats and Dingdong Balls: A Century of Baseball Inventions 36, 109

Index

Bang the Drum Slowly 20, 51, 54, 56, 109
Bankes, James 157
Banks, Ernie 148
Barbarians at the Gate 35
Barber, Red 119, 152, 160
Barnell, Hal
Barney, Rex 160
Barrow, Edward Grant 149
Barry Bonds: Baseball's Superman 109
Bartell, Dick 161
Bartlett, Arthur 110
Base Ball A.B.C. 109
Base Ball: How to Become a Player 12, 65, 109
Base Ball in Cincinnati 109
Base Ball Players' Pocket Companion 10
Baseball (Clark) 109
Baseball (Crane) 12, 109
Baseball (Iooss & Angell) 37, 109
Baseball (Knowles & Morton) 12, 109
Baseball (Smith) 19
The Baseball Abstract 30
A Baseball Album 110
Baseball America 63, 110, 180, 197
Baseball and the American Dream 110
Baseball: America's Diamond Mind 1919–1941 109
Baseball: America's National Game 14–15, 73
Baseball Anecdotes 111
Baseball as I Have Known It 111
Baseball as Viewed by a Muffin 111
Baseball Ballads 16, 111
Baseball the Beautiful: Decoding the Diamond 113
Baseball Before We Knew It 6–9, 111, 203
Baseball Between the Lines 24, 111
Baseball Between the Wars 111
The Baseball Bible 111
Baseball and Billions: A Probing Look Inside the Business of Our National Pastime 35, 110
The Baseball Business 111
Baseball by the Books 6, 40, 66–67, 111, 182
Baseball by the Numbers: A Guide to the Uniform Numbers of Major League Teams 40
Baseball Cartes: The First Baseball Cards 111
A Baseball Century: The First 100 Years of the National League 36
The Baseball Chronology 40
Baseball and the Cold War 110
Baseball Complete 111
Baseball: A Comprehensive Bibliography 6, 40, 109, 182
Baseball Confidential 111
The Baseball Cyclopedia 16, 111
Baseball: Diamond in the Rough 109
Baseball: The Early Years 22
Baseball (1888) from the Newspaper Accounts 111
Baseball, 1845–1871 13–14, 111
Baseball (1845–1881) from the Newspaper Accounts 111
The Baseball Encyclopedia 19, 38–39, 51, 56, 111, 181, 199
Baseball Extra 112
Baseball: The Fan's Game 16, 109
Baseball Fanthology 17, 112
Baseball Fever: Early Baseball in Michigan 203
Baseball for the Love of It 112
Baseball: From Backyard to Big League 109
Baseball & the Game of Life 53
Baseball Giant Killers: The Spudders of the '20s 112, 181
Baseball: The Golden Age 22
Baseball Graphics 112
Baseball Grins 112
Baseball: A Historical Narrative of the Game 109
Baseball: A History of America's Game 109
The Baseball Hall of Fame 50th Anniversary Book 112
Baseball History in Limerick, Verse & Sketch 112
Baseball I Gave You All the Best Years of My Life 20–21, 112, 181
Baseball I Love You 112
Baseball: An Illustrated History (Ward & Burns) 37, 109
Baseball Immortals 112
Baseball in America: From Sandlots to Stadiums, A Portrait of Our National

215

Index

Pastime by 50 of Today's Leading Photographers 112
Baseball in America: An Illustrated History of Our National Pastime 112
Baseball in the Big Leagues 112
Baseball in Cincinnati (Ellard) 14
Baseball in the '50s 112
Baseball in '41 112
Baseball in the Movies (Erickson) 36, 112
Baseball in Old Chicago 112
Baseball in the '30s 112
Baseball: Individual Play and Team Strategy 110
Baseball: An Informal History 8, 110
Baseball Is a Funny Game 22, 113
Baseball Is Their Business 113
Baseball Jokes, Stories and Poems 113
Baseball Lingo 113
Baseball Lives 113
Baseball: The Lives behind the Seams 110
Baseball Magazine 16
Baseball Memorabilia 113
Baseball and Mr. Spalding 110
Baseball: The National Game of the Americans 13, 110
Baseball Nicknames (Skipper) 40
Baseball on the Border: A Tale of Two Laredos 113
Baseball Palace of the World 113
Baseball: The People's Game 23, 194–95, 201
Baseball: The Perfect Game 110
Baseball Personalities 113
The Baseball Player: An Economic Study 113
Baseball Player's Pocket Companion 113
Baseball Players and Their Times: Oral Histories of the Game, 1920–1940 113
Baseball: The Presidents' Game 110
Baseball Prospectus 31
The Baseball Reader: Favorites from the Fireside Books of Baseball 113
Baseball Records Registry 113
Baseball Research Journal 197
The Baseball Story 113
The Baseball Timeline 40, 113
The Baseball Trade Register 113
Baseball Treasures: Memorabilia from the National Pastime 113

Baseball: A Treasury of Art and Literature 37, 110
Baseball Uniforms of the 20th Century 36, 39, 113
Baseball: Vol. 1, The Early Years 110
Baseball: Vol. 2, The Golden Age 110
Baseball: Vol. 3, The People's Game 110
Baseball Weekly 63, 180
Baseball When the Grass Was Real 24, 114
A Baseball Winter: The Off-Season Life of the Summer Game 114
Baseball: The Writers' Game 65, 110
Baseball's All-Star Game: A Game-by-Game Guide 114
Baseball's Back in Town 114
Baseball's Benchmark Boxscores 114
Baseball's Best 114
Baseball's Best: The Hall of Fame Gallery 114
Baseball's Best Managers 114
Baseball's Famous First Basemen 114
Baseball's 50 Greatest Games 114
Baseball's Golden Age: The Photographs of Charles M. Conlon 37, 114
Baseball's Great Experiment 23, 29, 56, 57, 114
Baseball's Great Tragedy 42, 114
Baseball's Greatest Catchers 114
Baseball's Greatest Drama 114
Baseball's Greatest Hitters 114
Baseball's Greatest Lineup 114
Baseball's Greatest Managers (Frommer) 114
Baseball's Greatest Managers (Pope) 114
Baseball's Greatest Pitchers (Meany) 115
Baseball's Greatest Pitchers (Shapiro) 114
Baseball's Greatest Rivalry 115
Baseball's Greatest Sluggers 115
Baseball's Greatest Teams 115
Baseball's Hall of Fame 115
Baseball's Last Dynasty: Charlie Finley's Oakland A's 203
Baseball's Most Colorful Managers 115
Baseball's Most Valuable Players 115
Baseball's Natural: The Story of Eddie Waitkus 115
Baseball's 100: A Personal Ranking 115
Baseball's Pennant Races: A Graphic View 115

Baseball's Pivotal Era 1945–1951 115, 203
Baseball's Radical for All Seasons; A Biography of John Montgomery Ward 115
Baseball's Strangest Moments 193
Baseball's Ten Greatest Games 115
Baseball's 10 Greatest Teams 115
Baseball's 25 Greatest Pennant Races 115
Baseball's Unforgettable Games 115
Baseballogy 16, 114, 193
Basepaths (Klinkowitz) 33
Basepaths: The Best of the Minneapolis Review of Baseball 115
Basepaths: From the Minor Leagues to the Majors and Beyond 115
Bashe, Philip 127
Baskin, John 71, 100, 123
Bat Boy of the Giants 116
Batboy of the Braves 116
Bats 116
Batting (Lane) 65, 116
The Battle of Baseball 16, 116
Bauer, Fred 158
Bauer, Paul 121
Baumgartner, Stan 17, 156
Bavasi, Buzzie 153
Baylor, Don 128
Beadle's Dime Baseball Player 10, 188
Bealle, Morris 173
Beane, Billy 43
Beard, Gordon 117
Beating the Bushes 116
Beckham, Barry 162
Bee, Clair 56, 193
The Beer and Whiskey League 116
Behind the Mask (Freehan) 116
Behind the Mask (Pallone) 116
Belinsky, Bo 182
Bell, George 135
Bell, John 164
Bell, Joseph 176
Bench, Johnny 121, 131
Benson, Michael 39, 108
Berg, Ethel 149
Berkow, Ira 121, 159
Bernotas, Bob 152
Bernstein, Ralph 166
Berra, Yogi 178
Berry, Henry 118

The Best in Baseball (Offit) 116
The Best of Baseball (Shoemaker) 116
The Best Seat in Baseball, But You Have to Stand 65, 116
The Best Team Money Could Buy: The Turmoil and Triumph of the 1977 New York Yankees 116
Between the Lines 116
Betzold, Mike 158
Beverage, Dick 51
Beverage, Richard 106, 137
Beyond the Shadows of the Senators: The Untold Story of the Homestead Grays 116
Beyond the Sixth Game 116
The Big Baseball Book for Boys 116
Big League Batting Secrets 116
Big Red Dynasty 41, 116
The Big Red Machine 116
Big Sticks: The Batting Revolution of the Twenties 32, 116
Big-Time Baseball 21, 116
The Bill James Baseball Abstract 30–31, 54, 117, 179, 198
The Bill James Guide to Baseball Managers 31
The Bill James Historical Baseball Abstract 30, 49–50, 56, 117, 201
Bill Stern's Favorite Baseball Stories 117, 194
Bill Veeck: A Baseball Legend 117
Billy 117
The Billy Evans Course in Umpiring 17
Billy Martin 117
The Billy Martin Story 117
Billy Sunday: The Man and His Message 117
Billyball 117
Bilovsky, Frank 40
Binette, Wilfred 143
The Bingo Long Traveling All-Stars and Motor Kings 27, 55, 56, 117
The Biographical Encyclopedia of the Negro Baseball Leagues 40, 117
Bird, John 171
Bird, Tom 136, 143, 175
Birds on the Wing 117
Bisher, Furman 105, 148, 166
Bishop, Michael 33, 119
Bissinger, Buzz 170

217

Index

Bjarkman, Peter C. 36, 53, 126, 128, 164
Black Baseball's National Showcase: The East-West All-Star Game, 1933–1953 117
Black Diamonds 117
Black Writers/Black Baseball (Reisler) 36, 117
Blackball Stars 117, 201
Blackwell, Ewell 18
Blackwood, W. R. 164
Bleachers: A Summer in Wrigley Field 32, 117
Bleep! 117
Bless You Boys 117
Block, David 6–9, 111, 203
Block, Lawrence 33
Bloom, Barry 117
The Blooper Man 117
Blue Ruin: A Novel of the 1919 World Series 33, 117
Blue, Vida 172
Blumkin, Alan 51
Bo: Pitching and Wooing 118, 182
The Bob Allison Story 118
Bob Feller: Hall of Fame Strikeout Star 118
Bob Gibson: Pitching Ace 118
Bob Lemon: The Workhorse 118
Bob Turley: Fastball Pitcher 118
Bobby Bonds: Rising Superstar 118
The Bobby Richardson Story 118
Bobby Shantz 118
Bodley, Hal 168
Boggess, Dusty 143
Boland, Kevin 170
Bonds, Bobby 190
Bonner, M.G. 116
The Book of American Pastimes 10, 118
The Book of Baseball 14, 118
The Book of Major League Baseball Clubs 118
The Book of Sports 8
The Book on the Bookshelf 87
The Booklover's Repair Manual 85
Books, Times 135
Boone, Robert 135
Born to Play Ball 27, 118
Borst, Bill 51, 63
Bosco, Joseph 119
The Boston Braves 118
Boston Red Sox 17
Boston Red Sox (Berry) 118
The Boston Red Sox (Lieb) 118
The Boston Red Sox (Meany) 118
The Boston Red Sox: An Illustrated History 118
The Boston Red Sox: An Illustrated Tribute 118
The Boston Red Sox: Memories and Memorabilia of New England's Team 37, 118
The Boston Red Sox of 1955 119
Boston Red Sox: 75th Anniversary History 1901–75 118
Boswell, John 130
Boswell, Thomas 32, 38, 136, 138, 174
Bottom of the Ninth 38
Boudreau, Lou 19, 124, 157
Bouton, Bobbie 137
Bouton, Jim 27, 28, 108, 131, 139, 203
Bowa, Larry 117
Bowman, John 126
Boyd, Brendan 33, 117, 134
Boyle, Timm 114
The Boy's Book of Sport 8
The Boy's Own Book 8
The Boys of Spring: Timeless Portraits from the Grapefruit League, 1947–2005 37, 119
The Boys of Summer 25–26, 28, 50, 51, 55, 56, 119, 180, 183
The Boys Who Would Be Cubs 119
Braathen, Sverre O. 16, 171
Brace, George 37
Bragan, Bobby 178
Branch Rickey 119
Branch Rickey: American in Action 119
Brandt, Bill 127
Brandt, Keith 155
Brashler, William 27, 117, 121, 142
The Braves First Fifteen Years in Atlanta 119
The Braves The Pick and the Shovel 119
Bready, James 137
Breaking the Slump: Baseball in the Depression Era 119, 203
Breakout: From Prison to the Big Leagues 119
Breakthrough to the Big League 119

Index

Breslin, Jimmy 65, 120
Brett, George 132
Brickhouse, Jack 169
A Brief History of Baseball 14, 119
Brittle Innings 33, 119
The Broadcasters 119
Brock, Darryl 33, 135, 139, 203
Brock, Jim 126
Brock, Lou 166
Brody, Arthur 183
Broeg, Bob 156, 159, 165, 167
The Bronx Bombers: Memories and Memorabilia of the New York Yankees 37, 119
The Bronx Zoo 28, 56, 68, 119
Brooklyn Dodgers 21, 25
The Brooklyn Dodgers 119
The Brooklyn Dodgers: An Illustrated Tribute 119
Brooklyn's Babe: The Life and Legend of Babe Herman 120
The Brooks Robinson Story 120
Brooks, Ken 144
Brooks, Noah 12, 129, 154
Broomer, Stuart 155
Brosnan, Jim 21, 22, 134, 144, 145, 155, 161, 168, 193
The Brothers K 33, 120
Broun, Heywood 167
Brown, Elijah P. 14, 158
Brown, Heywood 19
Brown, Warren 17, 196, 122
Browne, Lois 133
Browning, Reed 23, 125, 202
Bruce, Janet 143
Brunt, Stephen 163
Brushing Back Jim Crow 120
Bryan, Mike 113, 139
Bryant, Howard 42, 142, 164, 202
Buchanan, Lamont 176
Buck Leonard: The Black Lou Gehrig 120
Bud Harrelson 120
Budreck, Frank 134
Buege, Bob 148
Bukowski, Douglas 113
Bullet Bob Comes to Louisville 120
Bullet Joe and the Monarchs 120
Bums: An Oral History of the Brooklyn Dodgers 28, 120, 201

Bunning, Jim 166
Burchard, Marshall 165
Burdick, Si 105
The Burglar Who Traded Ted Williams 33
Burkholder, Ed 112
Burnett, William R. 160
Burns, Ken 37, 109
Burtt, Richard L. 157
Buser, Henry 138
Bush League: A History of Minor League Baseball 25, 120
Bushville: Life and Time in Amateur Baseball 120
The Business of Baseball (Miller) 35
The Business of Major League Baseball 35, 120
Busting 'Em 120
Butchered Baseball 120
Butler, Hal 105, 118, 135, 166, 175
Butterfield, Roger 205
By-Laws and Rules (of the New York Knickerbockers) 9
By-Laws and Rules of the Eagle Club (1852) 9

Cable, Greg 121
Cahan, Richard 132
Cairns, Bob 155
The California Angels: The Complete History 120
Calvin: Baseball's Last Dinosaur 120
Cameron, Steve 132
Campanella, Roy 140
Campen, S. Van 111
Can't Anybody Here Play This Game? 56, 65, 120
Canale, Larry 147
Candelaria, Cordelia 34, 65, 163
Caray, Harry 137
Card Sharks 120
Cardinal Classics 120
Carew 121
Carew, Rod 121
Carlson, Chuck 158
Carlson, Jack 51
Carmichael, John P. 17, 21, 149
Carney, Gene 161
Carothers, Jim 50
Carrieri, Joe 176

Index

Carroll, Bob 40, 54, 174
Carter, Gary 128, 132
Carter, Richard 21, 173
Carver, Robin 8
"Casey and the Bat" 191
Casey & Mr. McGraw 121
Casey at the Bat (Stengel) 121
"Casey at the Bat" 13, 16
Casey at the Bat: A Centennial Edition 121
Casey Award 23, 26, 29, 30, 31, 32, 57–58, 104, 183, 201–202, 205
Casey, Ethan 158
Casey: The Life and Legend of Charles Dillon Stengel 121
Casey on the Loose: What Really Might Have Happened 121
Casey Stengel (Graham) 121
Casey Stengel (MacLean) 121
Casey Stengel: Baseball's Greatest Manager 121
Casey Stengel's Secret 121
Cash, Norm 18
Castro, Tony 147
Cataneo, David 155, 170
Catch: A Major League Life 121
Catch You Later 121
Catcher in the Rye 121
The Catcher Was a Lady: The Clem Dreisewerd Story 121
The Catcher Was a Spy 121
Catching 121
Catching Dreams 121
Catfish 121
Catfish Hunter 122
Catfish: The Three Million Dollar Pitcher 122
Caught Short 122
Cauz, Louis 114
The Celebrant 29, 32, 42, 52, 56, 57, 65, 122, 201
Celizic, Mike 153
Center Field Grasses: Poems from Baseball 33, 122
Cepeda, Orlando 136, 150
Chadwick, Bruce 37, 118, 119, 122, 123, 127, 133, 174, 198
Chadwick, Henry 9, 10–11, 12, 13, 66, 107, 132
Chadwin, Dean 169

Chalberg, Chuck 63
Champagne and Baloney 122
Champions of the Bat 122
Chandler, Happy 136
Chapman, Ray 34
Charboneau, Joe 167
Charley Hustle 122
Charlie O. and the Angry A's 122
Charlie O: Charles Oscar Finley Vs. the Baseball Establishment 122
Charlton, James 40
Charyn, Jerome 27
Chase, Hal 32
Chasing October: The Dodgers-Giants Pennant Race of 1962 122
A Checklist of Books on Cincinnati Baseball 182
Cheering for the Home Team: The Story of Baseball in Canada 122
The Chicago Cubs (Brown) 122
Chicago Cubs (Enright) 122
The Chicago Cubs: An Illustrated History 122
The Chicago Cubs: Memories and Memorabilia of the Wrigley Wonders 122
Chicago White Sox 14, 23
The Chicago White Sox 122
Children's Amusements 7, 8
Chouinard, E. James 119
Chris Von der Ahe and the St. Louis Browns 122
Chrisman, David F. 137
Christy Mathewson 122
The Chrysanthemum and the Bat 25, 122, 185
Church, Seymour 14, 111
Cincinnati and the Big Red Machine 123
The Cincinnati Game 32, 70–71, 100, 123
Cincinnati Red Stalkings (Soos) 33
Cincinnati Red Stockings 11, 12
Cincinnati Reds 14, 24
Cincinnati Reds Horoscope 123
The Cincinnati Reds: An Illustrated History 123
The Cincinnati Reds: An Informal History 123
The Cincinnati Reds: Memories and Memorabilia of the Big Red Machine 123

Index

The Cincinnati Reds: A Pictorial History of Professional Baseball's Oldest Team 123
Cincinnati Reds Scrapbook 123
Cincinnati Seasons 123
The Cinema of Baseball 123
Circling the Bases 123
Clark, Ellery H., Jr. 118, 159
Clark, Tom 109, 122, 129, 152, 154, 190
Clarkson, Rich 124
Classic Baseball Cards 37
Classic Baseball: The Photography of Walter Iooss Jr. 37
Claudy, C.H. 16, 116
Clemens, Roger 161
Clemente! 123
Cleon 123
The Cleveland Indian 123
The Cleveland Indians 123
The Cleveland Indians Flagpole Sitter 123
Cleveland, Charles 134
A Clever Base-Ballist: The Life and Times of John Montgomery Ward 123
Clough, S. DeWitt 16, 144
Clout! The Top Home Runs in Baseball History 123
Clowning Through Baseball 19, 123
Cobb 123
Cobb, Ty 2–3, 24, 120, 150, 189
Cobb Would Have Caught It 124
Cobbledick, Gordon 128
Coberly, Rich 152
Cochrane, Mickey 16, 109
Coffin, Tristram Potter 139, 153
Cohen, Joel H. 140, 141, 146, 166
Cohen, Marvin 113
Cohen, Richard M. 38–39, 176
Cohen, Ron 193
Cohen, Stanley 146
Coleman, Ken 139
The College World Series: A Baseball History 1947–2003 124
Collett, Ritter 123, 147
Colletti, Ned 178
Colliers Magazine 15
Collins, J.F. 132
Collins, Jim 143
Collision at Home Plate: The Lives of Pete Rose and Bart Giamatti 124, 179

Colorado Rockies: The Inagural Season 124
Comeback (Dravecky) 189
The Comeback (Duren) 124, 193
Coming Apart at the Seams 35, 124
Coming Back with the Spitball 124
Comiskey, Charles 13
Commy 14, 100, 124
The Complete Armchair Book of Baseball 56
The Complete Book of Baseball's Negro Leagues 40
Condon, Dave 133
Congdon-Martin, Douglas 113
Conigliaro, Tony 163
Conlan, Jocko 141
Conlon, Charles 37
Conner, Floyd 125
Connie Mack 124
Connie Mack's Baseball Book 124
Connor, Anthony J. 112
Considine, Bob 18, 107, 181
Constitution of Olympic Ball Club of Philadelphia (1838) 9
Cook, Earnshaw 30, 155
Cook, Ira 123
Cooke, Edmund Vance 16, 114, 193
Coombs, John 110
Coomer, Joe 32–33
Cooperstown Verses: Poems about Each Hall of Famer 33, 124
Cooperstown: Where Legends Live Forever 124
Coover, Robert 24, 172
Copley, Robert 168
Costa, Richard Hauer 162
Couch, J. Hudson 119
Country Hardball 124
Couzens, Gerald Secor 110
Covering All the Bases 124
Covering the Outfield 124
Cox, William 147
Coyle, Daniel 135
Craft, David 159
Craig, John 27
Craig, Roger 140
Cramer, Richard Ben 37, 42, 62, 142, 195
Crane, Newton 12, 109

Index

Crash: The Life and Times of Dick Allen 124, 181–82
Crawford, Sam 24
Creamer, Richard Ben 168
Creamer, Robert 26, 107, 112, 141, 158, 160, 163, 166
Crepeau, Richard 109
Crissey, Harrington 168
Cromartie, Warren 164
The Crooked Pitch: The Curveball in American Baseball History 124
Crosley Field: An Illustrated History of a Classic Ballpark 41, 125
The Cubs of '69 125
Cubs Vineline 63
Cult Baseball Players 125
The Cultural Encyclopedia of Baseball 40
Cummings, Parke 127
The Curious Case of Sidd Finch 32, 125
Curran, William 32, 116, 148, 167
The Curse of the Bambino 32, 125
The Curse of Rocky Colavito 125
The Cutoff 125
Cutting the Corners 125
Cy Young: A Baseball Life 23, 125, 202
Cy Young: Baseball's Legendary Giant 125

Daguerreotypes of Great Stars of Baseball 17
Dahlen, Bill 32
Daley, Arthur 143, 170
Damn Yankee 125
Damn Yankees (the musical) 20
Damon, Johnny 28
Dandy, Day and the Devil 125
Daniel, Dan 16, 107, 158
Daniels, Jim 184
Daniels, Jon 51
Daniels, Lee 38, 141
Dark, Alvin 173
Dascenzo, Frank 139
Dave Moore Award 29, 57, 58–59, 183, 203–204
Dave Winfield: The 23 Million Dollar Man 125
Davenport, John 112, 115
Davids, L. Robert 29, 140
Davidson, Donald 122
Davies, Valentine 19

Davis, Mac 145
Dawidoff, Nicholas 121
Dawson, Andre 136
Day by Day in Cincinnati Reds History 125
Day by Day in Cleveland Indians History 125
A Day in the Bleachers 125
A Day in the Season of the Los Angeles Dodgers 125
Day with the Giants 125
Day, Laraine 125
The Days of Mr. McGraw 125
Dead Pull Hitter 125
Dean, Jerome H. Dizzy 127, 187
Debono, Paul 140
The Decline and Fall of the New York Yankees 126
Deerfield, Williams 164
Deford, Frank 121
DeGregorio, George 142
Delaney, Ed 118
The Denver Bears 126
Destiny's Darlings: A World Champion Little League Team Twenty Years Later 27, 126
Detroit Tigers 17
Detroit Tigers (Falls) 126
The Detroit Tigers (Lieb) 126
The Detroit Tigers: Club and Community, 1945–95 202
The Detroit Tigers: An Illustrated History 126
The Detroit Tigers: A Pictorial Celebration of the Greatest Players and Moments in Tigers' History 126
Deutsch, Jordan A. 163
DeValeria, Dennis 137, 188
DeValeria, Jeanne Burke 137, 188
Devaney, John 134, 176
Deveaux, Tom 173
The Devils' Coach 126
Dewitt's Baseball Guide 188
Dews, Bobby 133
Dexter, Charles 108, 178
The Diamond Appraised 30, 126
Diamond Classics: Essays on 100 of the Best Baseball Books Ever Published 52–53, 104, 126
Diamond Greats 126

Diamonds Are Forever: Artists and Writers on Baseball 126, 201
Diamonds Around the Globe: The Encyclopedia of International Baseball 126
Diamonds: The Evolution of the Ballpark 126, 201
Diamonds in the Rough: The Legend and Legacy of Tony Lucadello, One of Baseball's Greatest Scouts 126
Diamonds in the Rough: Life in Baseball's Minor Leagues 126, 193
Diamonds in the Rough: The Untold History of Baseball 126
Diary of a Yankee Hater 126
Dickerson, Gary E. 123
Dickey, Glenn 136, 137
The Dickson Baseball Dictionary 40, 127
Dickson, Paul 36, 40, 110, 127, 142
DiClerico, James 141
Dictionary of Baseball 127
Diles, Dave 152
DiMaggio, Dom 159
DiMaggio, Joe 19, 42, 43, 146
The DiMaggio Albums 127, 199
DiMaggio: An Illustrated Life 127
Dinhofer, Shelly M. 36, 107
Dittmar, Joseph J. 113, 114
The Dixon Cornbelt League 33, 127
Dixon, Phil 25, 151, 201
Diz 127
The Dizziest Season 127
Dizzy Baseball: A Gay and Amusing Glossary of Baseball Terms Used by Radio Broadcasters 127
Dizzy Dean: His Story in Baseball 127
The Dizzy Dean Story 127
Do You Know Your Baseball? (Brandt) 127
Do You Know Your Baseball? (Gittlitz) 127
Dock Ellis in the Country of Baseball 27, 127
Dodger Classics 127
Dodger Daze and Knights 127
Dodger Dogs to Fenway Franks 127
The Dodgers (Durant) 127
The Dodgers (Holmes) 127
The Dodgers Bibliography: From Brooklyn to Los Angeles 182
The Dodgers and Me 19, 127

The Dodgers: Memories and Memorabilia from Brooklyn to L.A. 127
The Dodgers Move West 127
Dog Days: The New York Yankees' Fall from Grace and Return to Glory, 1964–1976 127
Dollar Sign on the Muscle 34, 56, 128
Dolson, Frank 116, 141
Don Baylor 128
The Don Drysdale Story 128
Don't Kill the Umpire 128
Don't Knock the Rock 128
Don't Let Baseball Die 128
Double Play (Parker) 33
Double X: Jimmie Foxx: Baseball's Forgotten Slugger 128
Doubleday, Abner 8, 19
Douglas, Byrd 17, 162
Dowd, John 179
Doyle, Ed "Dutch" 131, 154
Dravecky, Dave 124, 189
A Dream Season 128
Dreaming of Heroes: American Sports Fiction, 1868–1980 64
The Dreamlife of Johnny Baseball 128
Dreisewerd, Edna 121
Drucker, Malka 133, 170
Drury, Robert 124, 193
Drysdale, Don 153
Duckett, Alfred 22, 119, 139
The Duke of Flatbush 128
The Duke of Havana 128
The Duke Snider Story 128
Duncan, David James 33, 120
Durant, John 17, 166, 177
Duren, Ryne 124, 193
Durocher, Leo 19, 22, 127
Durso, Joseph 106, 110, 121, 125, 150, 163, 177
Dyja, Thomas 33, 157, 202
Dykes, Jimmie 178
Dykstra, Lenny 150
Dynasty: The New York Yankees, 1949–1964 28, 128

Early Baseball and the Rise of the National League 32, 203
The Eastern Shore Baseball League 128
Echevarria, Roberto Gonzalez 59, 158, 203

Index

Eckfords 10
Eckhouse, Morris 125
The Eddie Mathews Story 128
Edgar Award 33
The Education of a Baseball Player 128
Edwards, Bob 131
Effa Manley and the Newark Eagles 128
Eig, Jonathan 43, 146, 202
Eight Men Out 23, 52, 56, 128
Einstein, Charles 20, 27, 113, 118, 130, 150, 154, 156, 163, 169, 175, 181, 194, 199
El Beisbol 65, 128
El Tiante 128
Elfers, James E. 171
Elias Baseball Analyst 31
Ellard, Harry 14, 109
Elliott, Bob 135
Ellis, Dock 127
Ellis, Estelle 85
Ellis, William T. 117
Elysian Fields Quarterly 58–59, 63
Encyclopedia of Major League Baseball Team Histories: American League 128
The Encyclopedia of Minor League Baseball 40, 129
The End of Baseball as We Knew It: The Players Union, 1960–81 203
Endless Summers: The Fall and Rise of the Cleveland Indians 129
Engel, Joel 42, 153
England and Australia 107
Enright, Jim 122, 148, 171
Enss, Chris 41
Epstein, Ben 147, 178
The Era 1947–1957 129
Erardi, John 116, 125, 155
Erickson, Hal 36, 112
Eskenazi, Gerald 117, 144, 177
ESPN SportsCentury 55
"The Essential Baseball Library" 50–51
Etkin, Jack 140
Evans, David 160
Evans, William G. (Billy) 138, 172
Even the Browns 129
Everett, William 12
Evers, Crabbe 33
Evers, John J. 112, 171
Evers, Johnny 16
Every Diamond Doesn't Sparkle 129

Everything Baseball 40, 129
Ewald, Dan 117, 165
Ewell Blackwell 129
Excelsiors 10
Explosion: Mickey Mantle's Legendary Home Runs 129
The Explosive Sixties: Baseball's Decade of Expansion 198
The Expos Inside Out 129
Extra Innings (Minoso) 129
Extra Innings (Robinson & Stainback) 129
Extra Innings: A Season in the Senior League 129

The Face of Baseball 37, 129
Fainaru, Steve 128
The Fairport Nine 12, 129
Falkner, David 32, 65, 134, 142, 143, 144, 152, 162, 164
The Fall of the Roman Umpire 34, 129
Falls, Joe 126
A False Spring 26–27, 52, 56, 129
Famous Baseball Stars 129
Fan Poems 129
Farrell, James T. 149
Fathers Playing Catch with Sons 129, 185
Fatsis, Stefan 175
Fear Strikes Out 129
Feeding the Green Monster 42
Fehler, Gene 33, 122
Feinstein, John 35
Feldman, Jay 51
Felker, Clay 121
Feller, Bob 19, 152, 167
Fenway 130
Fenway: A Biography in Words and Pictures 130
Fenway: An Unexpurgated History of the Boston Red Sox 28
Fenway Park: Legendary Home of the Boston Red Sox 194
Fenway Park: A Stadium Pop-Up Book 130
Fenway Voices 130
Ferguson Jenkins: The Quiet Winner 130
Fernandez, Fernando 129
Fetter, Henry D. 167
Fidrych, Mark 152, 190

Index

Fielder's Choice: An Anthology of Baseball Fiction 21, 130
The Fielders: The Game's Greatest Gloves 198
Fields, Wilmer 150
Figueroa, Ed 177
Filichia, Peter 39, 158
Fimrite, Ron 176
The Final Season: Fathers, Sons, and One Last Season in a Classic American Ballpark 130, 202, 203
Finch, Frank 145
Finch, Robert L. 166
Fiorito, Len 105
Fireballers: Baseball's Fastest Pitchers 130
The Fireside Book of Baseball 20, 130, 181, 199
The First Boys of Summer 41
The First One Hundred Years of Baseball 130
Fisher, David 34, 107, 129, 130, 160, 167, 172
Fisk of Fenway Park 130
Fitzgerald, Ed 118, 157, 178
Fitzgerald, Joe 128
Five O'Clock Comes Early 130
Five O'Clock Lightning 130
Five Seasons 130
Five Straight Errors on Ladies' Day 130
A Flag for San Francisco 130
A Flatland Fable 32
Fleet Walker's Divided Heart 58, 130, 202
Fleitz, David L. 145
Fleming, G. H. 127, 149, 172
Flood, Curt 21, 173
Ford, Whitey 164, 174
The Forever Boys 131
The Forgotten Championships: Postseason Baseball, 1882–1981 131
Forgotten Fields 131
Forker, Dom 147, 167
Fornoff, Susan 143
Forty Years a Fan 131
Foster, George 133
Foster, John 17, 150
Foster, Mark 126
Foul Ball! Five Years in the American League 131

Foul Ball: My Life and Hard Times Trying to Save an Old Ballpark 28, 131, 203
Fowler, Bob 170
Fox, Larry 144
Fox, William Price 162
Frank: The First Year 131
Frank Frisch: The Fordham Flash 131
Frank Robinson: The Making of a Manager 131
Frankenberg, Theodore 14, 189
Franklin, Robert 52
Fred Lynn: Young Star 131
Freehan, Bill 116
Freeman, Don 138
Frick, Ford C. 132
Fridays with Red 131
Frisch, Frank 131
From Behind the Plate 131
From Cobb to Catfish 131
From Ghetto to Glory 21, 131
From Sandlot to Big League 131
From Scratch 131
Frommer, Harvey 114, 115, 151, 158, 160, 163, 170
Full Count: Inside Cuban Baseball 131
Fullerton, Hugh S. 16, 112, 171
Fun and Frolic with an Indian Ball Team 13, 131
The Further Adventures of Slugger McBatt 33, 131

G. I. Had Fun 131
The Gabby Hartnett Story 42, 132
Gagnon, Cappy 41, 51
Gallagher, Mark 40, 51, 129
Gallico, Paul 18, 145
The Game for All America 132
The Game and the Glory 36, 132
The Game Is Never Over: An Appreciative History of the Chicago Cubs 132
The Game of Baseball (Chadwick) 11, 65–66, 132
The Game of Baseball (Hodges & Slocum) 132
A Game of Inches 202
The Game That Was: The George Brace Baseball Photography Collection 37, 132
The Gamer 132

Games, Asterisks, and People 132
Gammon, Wirt 178
Gammons, Peter 35, 116, 124, 161
Garagiola, Joe 22, 51, 113, 140
Gardner, Martin 106, 136, 180
Gardner, Steve 140
Garner, Wendell R. 30, 155
Garreau, Garth 116
Garrity, John 132
The Garry: A Book of Humorous Cartoons: Pickings from the Diamond 14, 132
Garvey (Garvey & Rozin) 132, 181
Garvey, Steve 132, 181
The Gashouse Gang (Hood) 132
The Gashouse Gang (Stockton) 132
Gat, Dimitri V. 27, 164
Gateway to the Majors: Williamsport and Minor League Baseball 132
Gehrig, Eleanor 150
Gehrig, Lou 18
Gelman, Steve 134
General Baseball Doubleday 132
George Brett: From Here to Cooperstown 132
George Brett: Last of a Breed 132
The George Brett Story 132
The George Foster Story 133
George Wright's Book for 1875 208
George Wright's Record Book of the Boston Club 133
The Georgia-Florida League 1935–1958 133
Gergen, Joe 143
Gerlach, Larry 56, 147
Germano, Eddie 159
Gershman, Michael 126, 201
Get That Nigger Off the Field 133
Giamatti, A. Bartlett 167
The Giants and the Dodgers 133
The Giants: Memories and Memorabilia from a Century of Baseball 133
The Giants of the Polo Grounds 133
The Giants of San Francisco 133
"The Giants Win the Pennant! The Giants Win the Pennant!" 133
Gibeau, Blair 191
Gibson, Bob 21, 131, 166
Gibson, Charline 174
Gibson, Kirk 38

Gies, Joseph 166
Gietschier, Steven P. 63
Gifford, Barry 151
Giglio, James N. 149
The Gil Hodges Story 133
Gilbert, Bill 128, 152, 159, 169
Gildner, Gary 173
Gilfond, Henry 122, 165
Gilmartin, Joe 126
The Ginger Kid: The Buck Weaver Story 133
The Girl Who Loved Tom Gordon 33
The Girls of Summer 133
Gittlitz, Hy 127, 128
Glory Days with the Dodgers 133
Glory Fades Away: The Nineteenth Century World Series Rediscovered 133
The Glory of Their Times 24, 51, 56, 133, 192
Glove Affairs 133
Gluck, Herb 147
Godine, David R. 121
The Go-Go Chicago White Sox 133
Gold, Eddie 133, 151
Goldblatt, Burt 114, 176
The Golden Era Cubs 1876–1940 133
Goldstein, Richard 165
Goldstein, Tom 63
Goldstein, Warren 157
Golenbock, Peter 27, 108, 116, 119, 120, 128, 130, 131, 135, 153, 165, 175, 176, 201
Good Enough to Dream 26, 133, 201
Good Examples for Boys 8
Goodbye Old Friend: A Pictorial Essay on the Final Season at Old Comiskey Park 134
Gooden, Dwight 161
Goodman, Irv 165
Goodman, Murray 131
Gordon, Alison 33, 125, 131
Gordon, Peter H. 126, 201
Gorman, Bob 128
Gorman, Tom 169
Gothams 10
Government and the Sports Business 49
Grabowski, Richard Henry 177
Grace, Kevin 182
Graham, Frank 17, 18, 19, 112, 119, 121, 145, 147, 151, 196

Index

Graham, John Alexander 27
Grand Junction's Juco World Series (Schrag) 41
Gray, Pete 32
Grayson, Harry 169
The Great American Baseball Card Flipping Trading and Bubble Gum Book 134
The Great American Baseball Scrapbook 134
The Great American Novel 26, 56, 134
Great Baseball Managers 134
The Great Baseball Mystery: The 1919 World Series 134
Great Baseball Pitchers 134
The Great Encyclopedia of 19th Century Major League Baseball 40, 134
Great Infielders of the Major Leagues 134
Great Negro Baseball Stars 134
Great Rookies of the Major Leagues 134, 193
Great Time Coming 134
The Greatest American Leaguers 134
The Greatest Ballpark Ever 204
The Greatest Cardinals of Them All 134
The Greatest Dodgers of Them All 134
The Greatest Game Ever Played 134
The Greatest Giants of Them All 134
The Greatest of All: The 1927 NY Yankees 134
The Greatest Summer: The Remarkable Story of Jim Bouton's Comeback to Major League Baseball 134
Greatest World Series Thrillers 135
The Greatest Yankees of Them All 135
Green, Guy 13, 131
Green, Jerry 177
Green, Paul 131
Green Cathedrals 39, 135
Green Cathedrals: The Ultimate Celebration of All 271 Major League and Negro League Ballparks Past and Present 135
Green Fields and White Lines: Baseball Poems 135
Greenberg, Eric Rolfe 29, 122, 201
Greenberg, Hank 135
Greene, Wayne 13, 79–81- 184, 190
Gregg, Eric 176

Gregorich, Barbara 36, 175
Gregory, Paul 113
Gregory, Robert 127
Grey, Zane 54
Griffey, Ken, Jr. 143
Griffith, Peggy 19
Grimm, Charlie 112
Groat, Dick 139, 176
Grobani, Anton 6–9, 12, 13, 39, 66, 104, 135, 180, 182
Gropman, Donald 162
Gross, Milton 177
Grossinger, Richard 21, 112, 128, 140, 169, 181
Grunska, Gerald 135
Gruver, Edward 143
Guide to Baseball Literature 6, 39, 104, 135, 180, 182
Guidry 135
Guidry, Ron 135
Guinn, Jeff 178
Gunther, Marc 115
Gutkind, Lee 65, 116
Gutman, Bill 133, 176
Gutman, Dan 36, 109, 129

Haag, Irv 117
Hack 135
Hageman, William 137, 189
Hagen, Paul 138
Hal Chase: The Defiant Life and Turbulent Times of Baseball's Biggest Crook 135
Halberstam, David 34, 42, 153, 167, 168
Hall of Fame Cartoons of Major League Ball Parks 135
Hall, Donald 27, 127, 129, 149, 157, 185
Hall, Susan 154
Halper, Barry 11
The Hank Aaron Story 135
Hank Greenberg: The Story of My Life 135
Hank Sauer 135
Hanneman, David V. 126
Hano, Arnold 125, 134, 161, 162, 175
Hardball 135
Hardball: The Education of a Baseball Commissioner 135

227

Index

Hardball: A Season in the Projects 135
Hardwick, Leon 151
Hargrove, Sharon 162
Harkness, Linda 40
Harmon Killebrew: Baseball's Superstar 135
The Harmon Killebrew Story 135
Harper, John 168, 176
Harrelson, Ken 136
Harrigan, Patrick 202
Harris, Fred C. 134
Harris, Mark 19, 109, 165
Harris, Stanley "Bucky" 16, 157
Harrison, Robert L. 135
Harry Hooper 135
Harshman, Dorothy 177
Hart, Harold H. 21, 116
Harwell, Ernie 171
Havana Heat 33, 135, 203
Hawk (Dawson) 136
Hawk (Harrelson) 136
Hawkins, Jim 119
Hays, Hobe 167
The Head Game 136
The Heart of the Game 136
Heart of the Order (Ardizzone) 136
The Heart of the Order (Boswell) 32, 136
Hefley, James 155
Heiman, Lee 133
Heimerdinger, Debra 172
Heitz, Thomas R. 58
Helm, Ernie 143
Helyar, John 35, 145, 201
Hemphill, Paul 27, 65, 136
Henderson, Rickey 153
Henderson, Robert W. 8, 19, 108
Hendricks, Randall A. 140
Henning, Lynn 38
Henrich, Tommy 130
Henry Aaron: A Quiet Superstar 136
Hernandez, Keith 139
Heroes Behind the Mask 136
Heroes of Baseball 136
Heroes of the Bullpen 136
Heroes of the Major Leagues 136
Heroes, Plain Folks, and Skunks 136
Herrman, Garry 14
Hershiser, Orel 154
Herskowitz, Mickey 121, 152, 190
Hertzel, Bob 116, 122
Herzog, Whitey 174, 178
Hetrick, J. Thomas 122, 148
Heward, Bill 27, 164
Heyen, William 184
The Hidden Game of Baseball 30, 136, 198
Higbe, Kirby 136
Higdon, Hal 138
Higgins, George V. 158
Higgs, Robert J. 65
High and Inside: A Chronicle of 1987's Daze of Autumn from the Metrodome to Kent Hrbek's Duck Blind 136
High & Inside: Orlando Cepeda's Story 136
The High Hard One 136
High Inside: Memoirs of a Baseball Wife 136
Hill, Art 128, 138
Hirshberg, Al 18, 105, 108, 114, 119, 128, 130, 134, 136, 141, 159, 173, 177
Hirshberg, Dan 155
The History of American League Baseball Since 1901 136
History of Baseball in California and the Pacific Coast Leagues 1847-1938 17, 136
A History of the Boston Baseball Club 11, 137
The History of the International League 1919-1960 Part 1 137
History of the Junior World Series 137
History of the National Association of Professional Baseball Leagues 17
The History of National League Baseball Since 1876 136
The History of the Piedmont League (1920-1955) 137
History of the Texas League 17
History of the Virginia League 137
The History of the World Series Since 1903 137
History of the World's Tour 14, 137
Hitter: The Life and Turmoils of Ted Williams 137
Hitting Into the Wind 33
Hittner, Arthur D. 32, 137, 188, 202
Hoard, Greg 141
Hobson, Charles 144

Index

Hodges, Gil 132
Hodges, Russ 111, 149
Hoffman, John 106, 135
Hoie, Bob 51
Hollander, Zander 113, 137, 176
Holloman, Nan 169
The Hollywood Stars 137
Holmes, Tommy 127
Holmes, Tot 120
Holt, Henry 154
Holtzman, Jerome 21, 24, 130, 152, 169
Holway, John 24, 25, 40, 117, 120, 141, 142, 143, 156, 172, 201
Holy Cow! 137
Holzman, Robert S. 132
Home Games 137
The Home Run Heard 'Round the World 137
The Home Run Story 137
The Home Team: 100 Years of Baseball in Baltimore 137
Honig, Donald 24, 27, 37, 105, 106, 110, 111, 112, 114, 115, 118, 119, 122, 123, 139, 145, 146, 150, 151, 153, 154, 156, 158, 162, 163, 172, 176
Honus: The Life and Times of a Baseball Hero 137, 189
Honus Wagner: A Biography 137, 188
Honus Wagner: The Life of Baseball's "Flying Dutchman" 32, 137, 188, 202
Hood, Robert E. 132
Hoopes, Spencer 173
Hoopla 29, 57, 138
Hope, Bob 173
Hoppel, Joe 163
Hopper, James 124
Hornsby, Rogers 149, 150
Horrigan, Kevin 174
The Horse That Played Center Field 138
Horton, Tom 178
Horton, Willie 18
The Hot Stove League 138
Hough, John, Jr. 128, 157
Houk, Ralph 108, 163
House, Tom 30, 126, 141
How Life Imitates the World Series 32, 65, 138
How to Get to First Base 138
How to Hit 138, 189

How to Pitch Real Curves 138
How to Play Baseball (Mack) 138
How to Play Baseball (Ruth) 138
How to Steal a Pennant 138
How to Talk Baseball 138
How to Umpire 138
Howard, Elston 121
Howe, Steve 116
Hoyt, Waite 32
Hubler, Richard 145
Humber, William 122, 144
Hummers, Knucklers, and Slow Curves 33
The Humming Bird 138
Humor Among the Minors 16
Hunsinger, Louis E., Jr. 132
Hunter, Jim 121
The Hurlers: Pitching Power and Precision 198
Hustle: The Myth, Life, and Lies of Pete Rose 138
The Hustler's Handbook 138
Hygiene for Baseball Players 138
Hynd, Noel 133, 146

I Ain't an Athlete, Lady 138
I Don't Care If I Never Come Back 138
I Had a Hammer 138
I Hit and Ran 139
I Love This Game! 139
I Managed Good, But Boy Did They Play Bad 139
I Never Had It Made 21–22, 139
I Was Right on Time 139
I'd Rather Be a Yankee 139
If at First 139
If I Never Get Back 33, 139
If They Don't Win It's a Shame 139
The Illustrated Book of Baseball Folklore 139
I'm Glad You Didn't Take It Personally 139
The Image of Their Greatness 27, 139
Imagining Baseball: America's Pastime and Popular Culture 34, 139
The Imperfect Diamond 139
The Impossible Dream 139
The Impossible Dream Remembered: The 1967 Red Sox 139
The Impossible Takes a Little Longer:

229

Index

The Texas Rangers from Pretenders to Contenders 139
In Memoriam: Aaron Burt Champion 12
The Incredible Giants 139
The Indianapolis ABCs 140
Innings Ago: Recollections by Kansas City Ballplayers of Their Days in the Game 140
Inside Big League Baseball 140
Inside Corner: Talks with Tom Seaver 140
Inside Pitch 140
Inside Pitching 140
Inside the Strike Zone 140
Inside the Yankees 140
Insider's Baseball 29, 57, 140
Into the Temple of Baseball 140
Invisible Men 29, 52, 140
Iooss, Jr. Walter 37, 109
The Iowa Baseball Confederacy 32, 140
Iron Horse 140
Iron Man: The Cal Ripken Story 140
Irvin, Monte 151
Irving, Elliott 160
It Beats Working 54
It Happens Every Spring 19–20
It Looked Like Forever 20
It Pays to Steal 140
It Takes Heart 140
It's Anybody's Ball Game 140
It's Gone ... No, Wait a Minute 140
It's Good to Be Alive 140
It's What You Learn After You Know It All That Counts 140
Izenberg, Jerry 134

The Jackie Jensen Story 141
Jackie Robinson 141
Jackie Robinson: A Biography 141
Jackie Robinson: An Intimate Portrait 38, 141
Jackie Robinson: A Life Remembered 141
Jackie Robinson: My Own Story 19, 141
Jackie Robinson of the Brooklyn Dodgers 141
The Jackie Robinson Story 141
Jackson, "Shoeless" Joe 14
Jackson, Reggie 159
Jackson, Robert 130, 169
Jacob, Mark 132
Jacob, Morse 165
Jacobson, Steve 116, 157
Jamail, Milton H. 131
James, Bill 30, 38, 51, 117, 158, 169, 179, 201
Japan Is Big League in Thrills 141
Japanese Baseball: A Fan's Guide 141
Japanese Baseball: A Statistical Handbook 40
Jenkins, Ferguson 140, 144
Jenkins, Jerry 108, 154
Jennison, Christopher 172, 177
Jensen, Jackie 18, 190
The Jersey Game 141
Jewish Baseball Stars 141
Jim Bunning: Baseball and Beyond 141
Jim Konstanty 141
Jim Palmer: Great Comeback Competitor 141
"Jock Lit" 51–52
The Jock's Itch 141
Jocko 141
Joe DiMaggio (DeGregorio) 142
Joe DiMaggio (Schoor) 141
Joe DiMaggio: Baseball's Yankee Clipper 142
Joe DiMaggio: A Bio-Bibliography 142
Joe DiMaggio: The Golden Year 1941 142
Joe DiMaggio: The Hero's Life 42, 56, 62, 142
Joe DiMaggio: Yankee Clipper 142
Joe & Marilyn: A Memory of Love 141
Joe Morgan: A Baseball Life 142
Joe: Rounding Third and Heading for Home 141
The Joe Williams Baseball Reader 142
Joe, You Coulda Made Us Proud 142
John McGraw 142
John, Sally 170
John, Tommy 167, 170
Johnny Bench: Catching and Power Hitting 142
Johnny Bench: King of the Catchers 142
Johnson, Daniel E. 40
Johnson, Davey 116
Johnson, Dick 37, 127, 168
Johnson, Don 33
Johnson, Harold "Speed" 16–17, 174
Johnson, Harry "Steamboat" 16, 165

Index

Johnson, Lloyd 40, 51, 54, 58, 129
Johnson, Owen 138
Johnson, Richard A. 159, 177
Johnson, Walter 187
Johnstone, Jay 34, 155, 165, 169
Jones, Cleon 123
Jones, Martin J. 174
Jordan, David M. 170
Jordan, Pat 26, 129, 152, 167
Josh Gibson 142
Josh and Satch 142
Joswick, Tom 51
The Journal of Sport History 56
Joy in Mudville 142
The Joy of Keeping Score 36, 142
Judge & Jury: The Life and Times of Judge Kenesaw Mountain Landis 31, 142, 202
Judge Landis and Twenty-Five Years of Baseball 19, 50, 142
Juicing the Game 142
July 2, 1903: The Mysterious Death of Hall-of-Famer Big Ed Delahanty 142
Junior: Griffey on Griffey 143

Kaese, Harold 118, 148
Kahn, James M. 149, 172
Kahn, Roger 25–26, 54, 119, 129, 133, 136, 140, 141, 147, 155, 163, 180, 201
Kalinsky, George 27, 36, 68, 108
The Kansas City Athletics 143
The Kansas City Monarchs 143
Kaplan, George R. 49
Kaplan, Jim 144, 156, 157
Karlen, Neal 164, 202
Karst, Gene 174
Kashatus, William C. 203
Kashmanian, John 113
Kaufman, Louis 149
Kaufman, Murray 138, 189
Kavanaugh, Jack 51
Keenan, James P. 183
Keene, Kerry 107
Kelley, Brent 172
Kelly, Jerry 120
Kelly, Mike "King" 11, 12, 157
Kelly, Tom 163
Ken Boyer 143
Ken Boyer: Guardian of the Hot Corner 143

Kendall, Brian 105
Kennedy, Lucy 19
Kerr, Jon 120
Kerrane, Kevin 21, 34, 112, 128, 140, 181
Keteyian, Armen 121
Kettle, Jerry 145
The Kid from Cuba: Zolio Versalles 143
The Kid from Tompkinsville 56
Kiernan, Thomas 148
Kiersh, Edward 191
Kill the Ump 143
Kiner, Ralph 143
Kiner's Korner 143
King of Swat 143
King, Joe 162
King, Stephen 33
Kings of the Diamond 143
Kings of the Home Run 143
Kings of the Mound: A Pitcher's Rating Manual 30
Kinsella, W.P. 32, 33, 127, 131, 140, 163, 170
Kirk, William F. 16, 160
Kirwin, Bill 64
Kiss It Goodbye 143
Klapisch, Bob 176
Klein, Alan 113
Klein, Dave 134
Klinkowitz, Jerry 33
Klobuchar, Jim 136
Know Your Vols 143
Knowles, Richard G. 12, 109
Knuckle Balls 143
Knuckler: The Phil Niekro Story 143
Kohout, Martin Donell 135
Konstanty, Jim 18, 190
Koppett, Leonard 49, 51, 146, 151, 169
Korr, Charles 203
Koufax (Gruver) 143
Koufax (Koufax) 143
Koufax, Sandy 143
Kowet, Don 172
The Krank: His Language and What It Means 12–13, 143
Kraus, Robert 160
Kravitz, Bob 148
Krich, John 65, 128, 172
Krueger, Joseph 114
Kruk, John 138

Index

Kubek, Tony 51, 164
Kuenn, Harvey 116
Kuenster, John 131
Kuhn, Bowie 27, 135
Kuklick, Bruce 23, 170, 201

Lady in the Locker Room 143
Lally, Dick 156, 176
Lamb, David 96, 166
Lanctot, Neil 151, 203
Lane, F.C. 65, 116
Lang, Jack 151
Lange, Fred W. 17, 136
Langford, Jim 132
Lanigan, Ernest J. 16, 111
Lansche, Jerry 131, 133, 165
Lardner, John 54
Lardner, Ring 14, 19, 20, 178
Lasorda, Tommy 107
The Last Best League 143
The Last .400 Hitter 143
The Last Hero: The Life of Mickey Mantle 143
The Last Night of the Yankee Dynasty 144
The Last Rebel Yell 144
Last to First: The Story of the Mets 144
The Last Yankee 144
Late Innings 144
Laughs from the Dugout 144
Laurel and Thorn: The Athlete in American Literature 65
Lautier, Jack 130
Lawson, Earl 123
Lawson, Thomas W. 12–13, 143
LaZebnik, Ken 115
Lazzeri, Tony 32
Leagues Apart: The Men and Times of the Negro Baseball Leagues 144, 193
Leavy, Jane 162
Lebovitz, Hal 156
Lee, Bill 176
Lee, Douglas 85
LeFlore, Ron 119
Lefty Grove: American Original 144
A Legend for the Legendary 144
A Legend in the Making: The New York Yankees in 1939 144
Legends at the Stick 144
Lehman, Stephen 63, 115

Lehmann-Haupt, C. 147
Leitner, Irving 109
Lenburg, Jeff 114
Leonard, Buck 120
Leonard, George 172
Leonardo Knows Baseball 144
Lester, Larry 25, 117
Let's Play Ball!: Inside the Perfect Game 144
Letters from a Baseball Fan to His Son 16, 144
Leuf, A. H. P. 138
Levine, Ken 140
Levine, Peter 105
Lew Burdette of the Braves 144
Lewine, Harris 27, 172
Lewis, Allen 156
Lewis, Franklin 123
Lewis, Michael 43, 149, 202
Libby, Bill 115, 120, 122, 131, 133, 152, 154, 155, 159, 165, 170, 172, 175
Liberman, Noah 133
Library Journal 64
Lieb, Fred 17, 108, 111, 113, 118, 124, 126, 156, 157, 162, 166, 196
Liebling, A.J. 56
The Life of Casey Stengel 178
The Life that Ruth Built 26, 144
Light, Jonathan Fraser 40
Lights On! The Wild Century-Long Saga of Night Baseball 36, 145
Like Nobody Else 144
Lindberg, Richard 29, 174
Lindt, Carson Van 163
Lindy's Baseball Scouting Report 181
Linn, Ed 21, 22, 137, 138, 140, 143, 152, 166, 168, 172
Linthurst, Randolph 151, 152
The Lip: A Biography of Leo Durocher 144
Lipman, David 118, 143, 146, 148, 181
Liss, Howard 147, 149, 162, 175
Little League to Big League 144
A Little Pretty Pocket-Book 7–9
The Lively Ball: Baseball in the Roaring Twenties 198
Lizotte, Ken 136
Loan, Charles Van 162
Logan, Bob 148
The Long Ball 184

Long Gone 27, 65
The Long Season 22, 51, 56, 65, 145
Longert, Scott 105, 198
Lopez, Al 32
The Lords of Baseball 27, 145
Lords of the Realm: The Real History of Baseball 35, 56, 145, 201
Lore and Legends of Baseball 145
Lorimer, Lawrence 55–56
The Los Angeles Dodgers 145
The Los Angeles Dodgers: The First Quarter Century 145
The Los Angeles Dodgers: The First Twenty Years 145
The Los Angeles Dodgers: An Illustrated History 145
Lost Ballparks 145
Lou Gehrig: An American Classic 145
Lou Gehrig: Courageous Star 145
Lou Gehrig: The Iron Horse of Baseball 145
Lou Gehrig: Pride of the Yankees 18, 145
Lou Gehrig: A Quiet Hero 18, 145
Louis Sockalexis: The First Cleveland Indian 145
Louisville Slugger: The Making of a Baseball Bat 145
Love Letters to the Mets 145
Low & Inside 145
Low & Outside 145
Low and Outside: Baseball in the Depression, 1930–1939 198
Lowell 114
Lowenfish, Lee 139
Lowry, Philip J. 39, 51, 135
Luce, Vern 51
Luciano, Ron 129, 160, 167, 172
Luciano, Ron 34
Luckiest Man: The Life and Death of Lou Gehrig 43, 146, 202
Lucky to Be a Yankee 19, 146
Luhrs, Victor 134
Lupica, Charles 123
Lupica, Mike 159
Lupien, Tony 139
Lyle, Sparky 27, 119
Lyman, Edward 17, 112
Lynch, R. G. 148
Lyttle, Richard A. 177

MacCambridge, Michael 55
Macht, Norman 160, 161
Mack, Connie 124, 131, 138, 150
Mack, Gene 135
The Mackmen 146
MacLean, Norman 121
MacPhail, Lee 150
Madden, W. C. 124
The Magic of Indians' Baseball 146
A Magic Summer: The '69 Mets 146
Maglie, Sal 32
The Magnificent Yankees 146
The Main Spark 146
Maitland, Brian 141
Major League Baseball 146
Major Leagues 146
Making the Team: The Cultural Work of Baseball Fiction 34, 65
Malamud, Bernard 19, 151
A Man and His Diamonds: A Story of Andrew "Rube" Foster ... 146
The Man in the Dugout (Honig) 146
The Man in the Dugout (Koppett) 146
Man on Spikes 23, 65, 146
The Man Who Invented Baseball 27, 146
Mandel, Mike 162
Mandell, Barry 63
Manley, Effa 151
Mann, Arthur 111, 119, 141, 159
Mann, Jack 126
Manny Sanguillen: Jolly Pirate 146
Mantle, Mickey 128, 147, 149, 158, 189, 190
Manual of Cricket and Base Ball (1858) 9, 10, 146
Maranville, Rabbit 161
Marazzi, Rich 105
Marichal, Juan 156
Maris, Roger 161
Marketing Your Dreams: Business and Life Lessons from Bill Veeck 146
Markus, Bob 136
Markusen, Bruce 203
Marquard and Seeley 146
Marsans, Armando 32
Marshall, Bob 126
Marshall, Nancy 137
Marshall, William 115, 203
Martens, Chris 149

Index

Martin, Billy 28, 117, 153
Martin, Pepper 32
Massarotti, Tony 168
Masterson, Dave 114
Mathewson, Christy 16, 29, 157, 175, 187
Matthews, Gary 169
Matty: An American Hero 146
Maybe I'll Pitch Forever 146, 181
Mayer, Ronald 63, 152
Mays, Carl 34
Mays, Mantle, Snider 146
Mays, Willie 27, 118, 150, 162, 175
McAuley, Ed 118
McCabe, Constance 114
McCaffrey, Eugene V. 157
McCaffrey, Roger A. 157
McCallum, Jack 51–52
McCallum, James 171
McCallum, John 170
McConnell, Bob 39
McCoy, Hal 160, 161
McCue, Andy 6, 40, 66–67, 111, 182
McGarigle, Bob 42, 114
McGee, Bob 204
McGill, William J. 63, 161
McGimpsey, David 34, 139
McGraw of the Giants 19, 147
McGraw, John J. 16, 150, 187
McGraw, Mrs. John 159
McGraw, Tug 163
McLain, Denny 152, 167
McNary, Kyle P. 168
McSpadden, J. W. 14, 118
McSweeny, Bill 139
Me and DiMaggio 147
Me and My Dad 147
Me and the Spitter 147
Mead, William B. 110, 129, 171
The Meaning of Nolan Ryan 147
Meany, Tom 18, 107, 114, 115, 118, 139, 142, 143, 146, 148, 149, 158, 165, 168, 177
Mehl, Ernest 143
Meissner, Bill 33
The Mel Ott Story 147
Melville, Herman 34
Melville, Tom 32, 203
Memories of Summer: When Baseball Was an Art, and Writing About It a Game 26, 54, 147
Men at Work 28, 34, 147, 207
The Men in Blue 147
The Men of Autumn: An Oral History of the 1949–53 World Champion New York Yankees 147
Men of the Machine 147
Mercantile Base Ball Club of Philadelphia 9
Merkin, Richard 193
Messenger, Christian K. 65
Metcalf, Paul 175
The Mets from Mobile: Cleon Jones and Tommie Agee 147
The Mets Will Win the Pennant 147
Michelson, Herbert 122
The Mick 147
The Mickey Mantle Album 147
Mickey Mantle: America's Prodigal Son 147
Mickey Mantle: Mr. Yankee 147
Mickey Mantle of the Yankees 147
The Mickey Mantle Story 147
Mickey Mantle: Yankee Slugger 147
Mickey Mantle: The Yankee Years: The Classic Photography of Ozzie Sweet 37, 147
The Midsummer Classic: The Complete History of Baseball's All-Star Game 40
Mighty Casey: All American 147
Mike Schmidt: Baseball's Young Lion 148
Mile High Madness: A Year with the Colorado Rockies 148
Millard, Tex 125
Miller, James E. 35, 111
Miller, Marvin 174
Miller, Richard D. 63
Millson, Larry 108
The Milwaukee Braves (Buebe) 148
The Milwaukee Braves (Kaese & Lynch) 148
Milwaukee Braves 26
Milwaukee's Miracle Braves 148
Minkoff, Randy 161
The Minneapolis Review of Baseball 33, 49, 63
Minor Miracles: The Legend & Lure of Minor League Baseball 148

Index

The Minors 148
Minoso, Minnie 129
The Miracle at Coogan's Bluff 148
Miracle in Atlanta 148
Miracle in Buffalo 148
Miracle Man 148
The Miracle New York Yankees 148
Miracle on 35th Street 148
Misfits! The Cleveland Spiders in 1899 148
Mitchell, Fred 169
Mitchell, Jerry 106, 162
Mitts: A Celebration of the Art of Fielding 32, 148
Mize, Johnny 138, 189
Modern Baseball Science 149
Modin, D. 123
Modra, Ron C. 37
Moe Berg: Athlete, Scholar, Spy 149
Molloy, Paul 155
Moneyball: The Art of Winning an Unfair Game 43, 149, 202
Monie, Willis 97, 205–09
Montville, Leigh 43, 168, 202
Moore, Dave 59
Moore, Jack B. 142
Moore, Joseph Thomas 158
Moore, Terry 124
More Strange but True Baseball Stories 149
Moreland, George L. 108, 130
Morgan, Joe 142
Morris, Jim 42, 153
Morris, John 120
Morris, Peter 202, 203
Morris, Timothy 34, 65
Morrison, Lillian 107
Morse, Jacob 10, 66
Morton, Richard 12, 109
Mosedale, John 134
Moser, Barry 121
Mostly Baseball 149
Mote, James 40, 129
Mowbray, William W. 128
Mr. Baseball: The Story of Branch Rickey 148
Mr. Cub 148
Mr. October 148
Mr. Ump 148
Mullarkey, Karen 112

Munson, Thurman 32, 170
Murder at Fenway Park 33, 149
Murderers' Row: The 1927 New York Yankees 149
Murdock, Eugene 108, 111, 113, 147
Murph 149
Murphy, Dale 149
Murphy, J.M. 150
Murphy, James M. 42, 132
The Museum of Clear Ideas 149
Musial: From Stash to Stan the Man 149
Musial, Stan 165, 173
Musick, Phil 174
Musser, Joe 170
Mutual Baseball Almanac 180
Mutuals 10
My Baseball Diary 149
My Brother Morris Berg: The Real Moe 149
My Dad, the Babe 149
My Dad's Baseball 193
My Favorite Summer 149
My 50 Years in Baseball 149
My Giants 149
My Greatest Baseball Game 149
My Greatest Day in Baseball 21, 149
My Kind of Baseball 149
My Life and Baseball 149
My Life as a Fan 150
My Life In and Out of Baseball 150
My Life in Baseball: The True Record 21, 150
My Life in the Negro Leagues 150
My Life Is Baseball 150
My Luke and I 150
My 9 Innings 150
My Own Particular Screwball 150
My 66 Years in the Big Leagues 150
My Thirty Years in Baseball 16, 150
My Turn at Bat 21, 150
My Ups and Downs in Baseball 150
My War with Baseball 150
Myers, Weldon 171

Nagle, Walter 130
Nahrstedt, Mike 167
Nails 150
Napoleon Lajoie: Modern Baseball's First Superstar 150
National Association of Professional Base-

Index

ball Leagues Silver Jubilee 1902–1926 150
The National Baseball Hall of Fame and Museum Desk Reference 55–56
The National Game (Spink) 14, 150, 194
The National League: An Illustrated History 150
The National League Story 151
The National Pastime (SABR journal) 197–98
The Natural 19–20, 51, 56, 151
Neal, Reidenbaugh, 114
Neft, David S. 38–39
Negro Baseball before Integration 151
The Negro Baseball Leagues: A Photographic History 151, 201
Negro League Baseball: The Rise and Ruin of a Black Institution 151, 203
The Neighborhood of Baseball 151
Nelson, Lindsey 108
Nemec, David 40, 116, 134
Nettles, Graig 28, 108
Neuman, Jeffrey 34–35, 114
The New Chicago White Sox 151
The New Era Cubs 1941–1985 151
The New Klondike: A Story of a Southern Baseball Training Camp 19
New Orleans Pelicans 14
The New Professionals: Baseball in the 1970s 198
New York City Baseball: The Last Golden Era 1947–1957 151
New York Giants 12, 14, 21
The New York Giants 151
New York Knickerbockers 9, 10
The New York Mets: The First Quarter Century 151
The New York Mets: Twenty-Five Years of Baseball Magic 151
The New York Mets: The Whole Story 151
New York Times 28
New York Times Book Review 64
New York Yankees 18, 24
The New York Yankees (Graham) 151
The New York Yankees (Honig) 151
The New Yorker 26
Newark Bears 151
Newark Bears: The Final Years 151

Newark Bears: The Middle Years 151
Newberry, John 7
Newcombe, Jack 130
Newhan, Ross 120
Neyer, Rob 42
Nice Guys Finish First 151
Nice Guys Finish Last 22, 50, 54, 55, 152
A Nice Tuesday 152
The Niekro Files 152
Niekro, Joe 152
Niekro, Phil 143, 152
Nine Innings 152
Nine: A Journal of Baseball History and Social Policy Perspective 64
Nine Sides of the Diamond 32, 152
The 1937 Newark Bears 152
The 1947 Trenton Giants 152
1947: When All Hell Broke Loose 152
Nineteenth Century Stars 198
No Big Deal 152, 190
No Cheering in the Press Box 56, 152
No Joy in Mudville 152
Noble, Marty 150
Nobody's Perfect 152
The No-Hit Hall of Fame 152
Nolan Ryan: The Authorized Pictorial History 38, 152
Nolan Ryan Fireballer 152
Nolan Ryan: The Road to Cooperstown 152
Noll, Roger G. 49
The North American Society for Sports History 61
Nothing to Prove: The Jim Abbott Story 152
Notre Dame Baseball Greats 41
Now I Can Die in Peace: How ESPN's Sports Guy Found Salvation ... 152
Now Pitching Bob Feller 152
Now Pitching for the Yankees 153
Now Wait a Minute Casey 153
Nowlin, Bill 37, 168
Number 1 153
The Numbers Game: Baseball's Lifelong Fascination with Statistics 153

O'Connell, T.S. 63
O'Neal, Bill 165, 169
O'Neal, Buck 139

Index

O'Neill, Paul 147
O'Rourke, Jim 32
Oakland A's 43
Obojski, Robert 25, 105, 113, 120, 160, 181, 193
October 1964 153
The October Heroes 24, 153
October's Game: The World Series 198
Off Base: Confessions of a Thief 153
Off the Record 153
The Official Encyclopedia of Baseball 19, 153
The Official History of the National League (75th Anniversary) 153
Offit, Sidney 116
Ogle, Jim 161
Oh, Sadaharu 162
Okkonen, Marc 36, 39, 113
Okrent, Daniel 27, 31, 51, 111, 152, 172
Olan, Ben 115
The Old Ball Game: Baseball in Folklore and Fiction 153
The Old Ball Game: Baseball's Beginnings 198
Old Baseball Scout and His Players 153
The Oldest Rookie 42, 153
Oliva, Tony 170
Oliver, Ted 30
Olney, Buster 144
On Days Like This: Poems 153
On the Run 153
On to Nicollet: The Glory and Fame of the Minneapolis Millers 153
Once a Bum Always a Dodger 153
Once Upon the Polo Grounds: The Mets That Were 154
One for the Record 27, 154
The 100 Greatest Baseball Players of All Time 154
The 100 Seasons of Buffalo Baseball 154
100 Years of Baseball 19, 154
100 Years of National League Baseball 154
One Last Round for the Shuder 154
One Pitch Away 154
One Strike Away: The Story of the 1986 Red Sox 32, 154
Only the Ball Was White 25, 55, 56, 154
The Only Game in Town 154, 194

The Only One: The Babe 154
Opening Day: Celebrating Cincinnati's Baseball Holiday 41
Oppenheimer, Joel 176
Orem, Preston D. 111
The Other Game 154
Our Baseball Club and How It Won the Championship 12, 154
Our Game: An American Baseball History 154
Our Lugnuts, Year One! 154
Our Tribe 154
Out of the Blue 154
Out of Left Field: Willie Stargell and the Pittsburgh Pirates 154
Out of My League 154
Out of the Red 54
Outlar, Jesse 122
Over the Edge: Baseball's Uncensored Exploits from Way Out in Left Field 34, 155
Overfield, Joseph M. 154
Overmyer, James 128
Owed 2 Base Ball in Three Cant-Oh's! 8
Owens, Tom 159

The Pacific Coast League: One Man's Memories 1938-1957 155
Pafko, Andy 18
Paige, Leroy "Satchel" 146, 156, 181
Pallone, Dave 116
Palmer, Harry Clay 107, 110, 164, 166
Palmer, Henry C. 13
Palmer, Howard 158
Palmer, Joe E. 153
Palmer, Pete 30, 38, 51, 53, 136, 171, 198
Panek, Richard 173
Pardon, John 51
Parker, Al 112, 181
Parker, Kathryn 173
Parker, Robert B. 33
Parker, Tom 175
Parrott, Harold 27, 145
Pashko, Stanley 130
Past Time: Baseball as History 203
Patten, William 14, 118
Patterson, Ted 108
Paul Molitor: Good Timing 155
Pavelec, Barry 141

Index

Paxton, Harry T. 121, 174
Peanuts and Crackerjack 155
Pearlman, Jeff 108
Pearson, F. S. 120
Peary, Danny 125, 173
The Pee Wee Reese Story 155
Peeler, Tim 33
Pen Men 155
A Pennant for the Kremlin 155
Pennant Race 22, 155
People (magazine) 64
Pepe, Phil 21, 117, 131, 164, 173, 175
Pepitone, Joe 142
Percentage Baseball and the Computer 155
Percentage Baseball 30, 155, 198
The Perfect Game: America Looks at Baseball 155
The Perfect Game: Tom Seaver and the Mets 155
Perlstein, Steve 159
Perry, Gaylord 147
Pete Rose: 4,192 155
Pete Rose: Mr. .300 155
Pete Rose: My Life in Baseball 155
Pete Rose: My Story 155
The Pete Rose Story 155
Pete Rose: They Call Him Charlie Hustle 155
Peters, Alexander 136
Peterson, Harold 27, 146
Peterson, Richard 23
Peterson, Robert 24, 154
Petroski, Henry 87
Peverelly, Charles A. 10, 118
Phelon, W. A. 108
Phelps, Frank 51, 53
Phil Regan 155
Phil Rizzuto 155
The Phil Rizzuto Story 156
Phil Rizzuto: A Yankee Tradition 155
Philadelphia A's 17
Philadelphia Phillies 17, 18, 196
The Philadelphia Phillies 156
The Philadelphia Phillies: An Illustrated History 156
The Philadelphia Phillies: A Pictorial History 156
Philip K. Wrigley 156
The Phillies Encyclopedia 40

Phillips, David R. 36, 169
The Physics of Baseball 156
Picking, Ken 152
Pictorial History of the Dodgers 156
Pictorial Negro League Legends Album 156
Picture History of the Boston Red Sox 156
Piersall, Jim 129, 171
Pietrusza, David 31, 36, 37, 142, 145, 146, 148, 202
Pig Iron Baseball 21
The Pilot Light and the Gas House Gang 156
Pinelli, Babe 148
Pine-Tarred and Feathered: A Year on the Baseball Beat 156
Pingel, D. Kent 38
Piniella, Lou 167
Pinstriped Pandemonium: A Season with the Yankees 156
Pinstriped Summers 156
Pioneers of Baseball 156
The Pirates 156
Pirone, Dorothy Ruth 149
The Pitch That Killed 34, 201, 156
The Pitcher 156
A Pitcher's Story 156
Pitchin' Man 156
Pitching in a Pinch 16, 157
The Pitching Staff 157
Pitts, Jonathan 178
Pittsburgh Baseball through the Years 157
The Pittsburgh Crawfords 157
Pittsburgh Pirates 17
The Pittsburgh Pirates 157
The Pittsburgh Pirates: An Illustrated History 157
The Pittsburgh Pirates: A Pictorial History 157
A Place for Summer: A Narrative History of Tiger Stadium 157
Plagenhoef, Vern 140
Plapinger, Bobby 39, 72–73, 79–82, 181, 183, 184, 193, 195
Plaut, David 122
Plaut, David 63
Play Ball (Kelly) 11, 12
Play Ball: The Life and Troubled Times

of *Major League Baseball* (Feinstein) 35
Play Ball: Stories of the Ball Field 157
Play for a Kingdom 33, 157, 202
Playboy 64
Player for a Moment: Notes from Fenway 157
Player-Manager 19, 157
Players League 12
Players' Choice: Major League Baseball Players Vote on the All-Time Greats 157
Playing Around: The Million Dollar Infield Goes to Florida 157
Playing the Game 16
Playing the Game: From Mine Boy to Manager 157
Playing the Field: Why Defense Is the Most Fascinating Art in Major League Baseball 157
Playing for Keeps: A History of Early Baseball 157
Playing for Time: The Death Row All Stars 41
Plimpton, George 27, 32, 125, 154, 183
Pluto, Terry 65, 114, 125, 134, 154
The Politics of Glory: How Baseball's Hall of Fame Really Works 31, 158
Polner, Murray 119
Pope, Edwin 114, 168
Porter, Darrell 164
Postema, Pam 178
Povich, Shirley 18, 173, 196
The Power Hitters 158
Powers, Jimmy 113
Powers, John 177
Prell, Ed 112
Price, George 145
Pride Against Prejudice: The Biography of Larry Doby 158
Pride of the Bimbos 27
The Pride of Havana: A History of Cuban Baseball 59, 158, 203
Prime, Jim 168
Prime, Jim 37
Primitive Baseball: The First Quarter Century 158
Professional Baseball Franchises 39, 158
The Progress of the Seasons: Forty Years of Baseball in Our Town 158

Prophet of the Sandlots 34, 158
The Psychologist at Bat 158
Publishers Weekly 34–35, 64, 197
Puck! Kirby Puckett: Baseball's Last Warrior 158
Puckett, Kirby 139
Putting It All Together 158
The Quality of Courage 158
Queen of Diamonds: The Tiger Stadium Story 158
Quigel, James P., Jr. 132
Quigley, Martin 113, 124, 170
Quisenberry, Dan 153

Rader, Benjamin G. 109
Rain Delays: An Anecdotal History of Baseball ... 158
Rains, Rob 175
Ralbovsky, Martin 27, 126
Ralph Kiner: The Heir Apparent 158
Rampersad, Arnold 141
Rankin, E. B. 149
Rappoport, Ken 126, 193
Rathgeber, Bob 123
Reach Baseball Guide 188
The Real Babe Ruth 158
The Real Baseball Story 158
The Real Billy Sunday 14, 158
Real Grass/Real Heroes 159
The Real McGraw 159
Reaves, Joseph A. 173
Rebel Baseball 159
Record of the Boston Baseball Club, 1871–74 11, 159, 208
Red: A Biography of Red Smith 159
The Red Headed Outfield and Other Baseball Stories 54
Red Schoendienst: The Man Who Fought Back 159
The Red Sox the Bean and the Cod 159
Red Sox Century 159
Red Sox Drawing Board: 25 Years of Cartoons 159
Red Sox Fever! 159
Red Sox Forever 159
Redbirds: A Century of Cardinals' Baseball 159
Redbirds Revisited 159
Reddick, David 146
Redleg Journal: Year by Year and Day by

Index

Day with the Cincinnati Reds Since 1866 41, 159
Reds in Black and White: 100 Years of Cincinnati Reds Images 41
Reed, Robert 164
Reese, Pee Wee 18
Reflections of the Game: Lives in Baseball 37
Regalado, Samuel O. 172
Regan, Jack 16, 106
Regan, Phil 155
Reggie 159
The Reggie Jackson Story 159
Reggie Jackson: The $3 Million Man 159
Reggie Jackson: The True Life Story of Baseball's Greatest Clutch Hitter 159
Reggie Jackson's Scrapbook 160
Reggie: A Season with a Superstar 159
Reichler, Joe 36, 113, 115, 132, 176
Reid, Kevin 124
Reidenbaugh, Lowell 29, 115, 124, 154, 167
Reinhardt, Bryson 130
Reiser, Pete 32
Reisler, Jim 36, 117
The Relentless Reds 160
The Relief Pitcher 160
Remembering the Soos 160
Remembering the Vees 160
Remembrance of Swings Past 34, 160
Reston, James, Jr. 124
Retort, Robert D. 156
The Return of Billy the Kid 160
Reuther, David 136
Rex Barney's Thank Youuuu 160
Rhodes, Greg 41, 116, 125, 159
Rhubarb 160
Rhubarb in the Catbird Seat 160
The Rhubarb Patch 160
Ribalow, Harold U. 141
Ribalow, Meir Z. 141
Rice, Cy 129
Rice, Grantland 16, 111
Rich, Michael 174
Richardson, Bobby 118
The Richie Ashburn Story 160
Richmond, Peter 108
Richter, Ed 172
Richter, Francis 14, 119, 160

Richter's History and Records of Baseball, the American Nation's Chief Sport 14, 160
Rickey and Robinson 160
Rickey, Branch 106
Riess, Stephen 171
Riger, Robert 106
Right Off the Bat 16, 160
Riley, James A. 105, 117, 120, 125, 151
Riley, James C. 25, 40
The Ripening of Pinstripes 160
Riper, Guernsey Van, Jr. 107
The Rise of Japanese Baseball Power 160
Ritter, Lawrence 24, 27, 37, 51, 91, 107, 133, 139, 144, 145, 154, 166, 192, 193
Rizzuto, Phil 148, 189
The Road to Cooperstown 160
The Roar of the Crowd 160
The Roaring Redhead: Larry MacPhail 160
Roberto Clemente: Batting King 161
Roberts, Robin 174
Robertson, John 162
Robinson, Brooks 158, 169
Robinson, Frank 129, 131, 150
Robinson, Frazier "Slow" 121
Robinson, Jackie 19, 21, 23, 38, 42, 119, 139, 141
Robinson, Rachel 38, 141
Robinson, Ray 115, 135, 137, 140, 146, 165, 177
Robinson, Ted 163
The Rock Springs Chronicles 161
Rock, Brad 149
Rocket Man 161
Rocks, Burton 147
Rodrigues, Tom 144
Roeder, Bill 141
Roger Maris at Bat 161
Roger Maris: Home Run Hero 161
Roger Maris: A Man for All Seasons 161
Roger Maris: A Title to Fame 161
Rogers Hornsby 161
Rogers, C. Paul, III 174
Rogers, Kim 146
Rogers, Phil 139
Rogoff, Jay 125
Rogosin, Donn 25, 29, 140

Romancing the Horsehide: Baseball Poems on Players and the Game 161
Romanowski, Rev. Jerome C. 146
Romig, Ralph 125
Ron Santo: For Love of Ivy 161
Ron Santo, 3rd Baseman 161
Rookie 161
Rookie Season: A Year with the West Michigan Whitecaps 161
The Rookies 161
Rose, Pete 122, 155, 179
Roseboro, John 133
Rosen, R. D. 33, 167
Rosenbaum, Art 133
Rosenbaum, Dave 139
Rosenberg, John 166
Rosenfeld, Harvey 140, 161
Rosenthal, Harold 113, 114, 169
Ross, Dan 23
Roswell, A. K. 157
Roswell, Gene 178
Roth, Allan 51
Roth, Bob 154
Roth, Philip 26, 134
Rowdy Richard 161
Roy Campanella 161
Roy Campanella: Man of Courage 161
The Roy Campanella Story 161
Roy, Parker, 173
The Royal Reds 161
Rozin, Skip 132, 181
Rozner, Barry 163
Rubin, Louis 51
Rubin, Robert 145, 170, 171
Ruck, Rob 162, 171
Rucker, Mark 36, 37, 56, 107, 111, 164, 198
Ruggles, William 17
Run, Rabbit, Run 161
Runner Mack 162
Ruscoe, Michael 110
Russell, Fred 172
Russell, Patrick 170
Rust, Art, Jr. 133
Rusty Staub of the Expos 162
Ruth, Babe 17, 18, 26, 37–38, 107, 108, 138, 181, 187, 189
Ruth, Claire 107, 195
Ryan, Bob 172
Ryan, Nolan 38, 148, 152, 154, 170

Ryczek, William J. 173
Ryder, Jack 16

Sabbatini, John 143
Sabin, Lou 142
SABR 12, 29–30, 39, 53, 56, 61, 66, 197, 198
SABR Presents the Home Run Record Encyclopedia 39–40
The SABR Review of Books 50–51, 56, 64
Sadaharu Oh: A Zen Way of Baseball 32, 162
Safe at Home 162
Sahadi, Lou 156, 162
The Sal Maglie Story 162
Salant, Nathan 167
Salisbury, Luke 33, 106, 123
Salvatore, Bryan Di 123
Sammis, John 142
Sampson, Arthur 168
The San Francisco Giants 162
San Francisco Giants 191
S.F. Giants: An Oral History 162
Sanchez, Ray 128
Sandberg, Ryne 163
Sandlot Peanuts 162
Sandlot Seasons 162
Sands, Jack 35, 124
Sandy Koufax 162
The Sandy Koufax Album 162
Sandy Koufax: A Lefty's Legacy 162
Sandy Koufax: Strikeout King 162
Santo, Ron 161
Satchel Paige's America 162
Sauer, Hank 18
Say Hey 162
Say It Ain't So, Joe! 162
Sayles, John 27
Sayre, Rose 21
Scarecrow, Hetrick, J. 122
Schaap, Dick 49, 155, 166, 177
Schacht, Al 19, 123, 131, 150
Schiffer, Don 149
Schlossberg, Dan 51
Schmidt, Mike 106
Schneider, Russell 124, 131
Schoor, Gene 18, 117, 118, 121, 122, 125, 141, 144, 147, 155, 156, 161, 162, 163, 165, 166, 168, 170, 175

Index

Schraf, Mark 33, 63, 86, 124
Schrag, Myles 41
Schulz, Charles M. 162
Schulze, Franz 166
Schwarz, Alan 153
The Science of Baseball 17, 162
The Science of Hitting 56, 162, 189
The Scooter 162
Score by Innings 54, 162
The Scrapbook History of Baseball 163
Screwball 163
Scully, Gerald W. 35, 120
A Season in the Sun 163
Season of Dreams: The Minnesota Twins' Drive to the 1991 World Championship 163
Season of Glory 163
Season Ticket 163
Seasons in Hell 163
The Seattle Pilots Story 163
Seaver 163
Seaver, Tom 155, 170
The Second Fireside Book of Baseball 20, 163
Second to Home 163
Second to None 163
Seeing It Through: The Story of a Comeback 163
Seeking the Perfect Game: Baseball in American Literature 34, 65, 163
Segar, Charles 153
Seidel, Michael 167, 168
Senzel, Howard 110
September Swoon: Richie Allen, the '64 Phillies, and Racial Integration 203
The Series: An Illustrated History of Baseball's Postseason Showcase 1903–1989 163
The Seventh Babe 27
Seymour, Dorothy 58
Seymour, Harold 21, 22, 23, 24, 58, 110, 194–95, 199, 201
Seymour Medal 29, 57, 58, 183, 202–03
The Shadows of Summer: Classic Baseball Photographs 1869–1947 163
Shannon, Bill 27, 36, 68, 108
Shannon, Mike 110, 126
Shantz, Bobby 166
Shapiro, Milton J. 18, 114, 122, 127, 128, 133, 135, 136, 136, 141, 144, 147, 156, 161, 162, 173, 174, 175
Shatzkin, Mike 40, 108
Shaughnessy, Dan 32, 107, 125, 130, 154
Shea, John 153
Shecter, Leonard 28, 154, 161
Sheed, Wilfred 150
Shelton, Bill 164
Shoeless Joe 32, 51, 56, 163
Shoeless Joe and Ragtime Baseball 163
Shoeless Summer 164
Shoemaker, Robert 116, 166
The Short Season: The Hard Work and High Times of Baseball in the Spring 32, 65, 164
Short Season and Other Stories 33
Shropshire, Mike 163
Shut Out: A Story of Race and Baseball in Boston 42, 164, 202
Siegel, David S. 77
Siegel, Susan 77
Sights Around the World with the Base Ball Boys 13, 164
Silverman, Al 142, 147, 148, 150
Silverton, Al 21
Simmons, Bill 152
Simon, Peter 151
Simont, Marc 138
The Sinister First Baseman & Other Observations 164
The Six Perfect Games of Baseball History and Almost the Seventh 164
A Six-Gun Salute: An Illustrated History of the Houston Colt .45s 164
Sixty-One: The Team, The Record, The Men 164
Sketchbook of the Cleveland Indians 164
Skipper, John C. 40
Slate 43
Slaughter, Enos 124
Slick 164
Slide, Kelly, Slide: The Wild Life and Times of Mike "King" Kelly, Baseball's First Superstar 31, 164, 202
Sloate, Barry 56–57
Slocum, Frank 132
Slouching Toward Fargo 164, 202
The Sluggers: Those Fabulous Long Ball Hitters 198

Index

Slugging It Out in Japan 164
Smelser, Marshall 26, 144
Smilgoff, Jim 116
Smith, Claire 128
Smith, Curt 106, 172
Smith, David W. 40
Smith, Elston 117
Smith, Fred 170
Smith, H. Allen 145, 160, 169
Smith, Ira 114, 145, 169
Smith, Ken 175
Smith, Leverett T. 51, 64, 106
Smith, Lou 129
Smith, Myron, Jr. 6, 40, 66, 109, 182
Smith, Norman Lewis 160
Smith, Ozzie 175
Smith, Red 54, 138
Smith, Robert 19, 26, 107, 109, 112, 136, 156
Smith, Wendell 19, 141
Smithsonian Baseball: Inside the World's Finest Private Collections 164
Smizik, Bob 157
Smoke: The Romance and Lore of Cuban Baseball 36, 164
Snap Me Perfect 164
Snider, Duke 128
Snodgrass, Fred 24
Snyder, Brad 116, 204
Snyder, John 125, 159
Sobol, Ken 107
Sockalexis, Louis 32
Sokolove, Michael 138, 170
Sol White's Base Ball Guide 14, 66, 164
Solomon, Burt 40, 113, 174
Some Are Called Clowns 27, 164
Some of My Best Friends Are Crazy 34, 165
Sometimes You See It Coming 196
Soos, Troy 33, 149
The Southern League 165
The Southpaw 19, 165
Sowell, Mike 34, 142, 154, 156, 201
Spalding, Albert Goodwill 13, 14–15, 73, 106
Spalding's Official Baseball Guide 188
Sparky! 165
Spartan Seasons 165
Spatz, Lyle 40
The Spectacular Career of Rev. Billy Sunday, Famous Baseball Evangelist 14, 189
Speed: Baseball in the High Gear 198
Speed Kings of the Base Paths 165
Sphere and Ash 10, 66, 165
Spindell, David M. 37, 198
Spink, Alfred H. 14, 150, 194
Spink, C. C. Johnson 168
Spink, J.G. Taylor 19, 142
The Spirit of St. Louis: A History of the St. Louis Cardinals and Browns 28, 165
Spitball: The Literary Baseball Magazine 23, 29, 33, 52, 56, 63, 183
Spoerl, Steve 41
The Sporting Life 13
The Sporting Myth and the American Experience: Studies in Contemporary Fiction 65
The Sporting News 16, 17, 63
The Sporting News Baseball Guide 188
Sports Collectors Digest 28, 63
The Sports Encyclopedia: Baseball 38–39
Sports Hero: Fred Lynn 165
Sports Hero: Joe Morgan 165
Sports Hero: Johnny Bench 165
Sports Illusions, Sports Reality 49
Sports Illustrated 30, 51–52, 56, 63
Sports Pastimes of American Boys (1884) 9
Sports Weekly 63, 180, 197
The Sportsbook File 63
Spring Training 165
St. Louis Cardinals 17
The St. Louis Cardinals 162
The St. Louis Cardinals: An Illustrated History 162
Stadler, Ken 155
Stafford, Tim 124, 189
Stahl, Will E. 16, 106
Stainback, Berry 129, 140, 142
Stambler, Irwin 122
Stan the Man Musial: Born to Be a Ballplayer 165
Stan the Man Musial: Then ... and Now 165
Stan Musial: Baseball's Durable Man 165
Stan Musial: The Man (Goodman) 165

Index

Stan Musial: The Man (Meany) 165
Stan Musial: The Man's Own Story 165
The Stan Musial Story 165
Standing the Gaff 16, 165
Stang, Mark 40
Stanton, Tom 130, 160, 202, 203
Star Pitchers of the Major Leagues 165
Stargell, Willie 175
Stark, Benton 178
Stars of the Series 166
Stealing Is My Game 166
Stein, Barney 160
Stein, Fred 172
Stein, Harry 29, 138
Stein, Irving M. 133
Steinberg, Alan 116
Steinbrenner (Schaap) 49
Steinbrenner! 166
Steinbrenner, George 24
Steinbrenner's Yankees 166
Stengel, Casey 121
Stengel: His Life and Times 166
Stern, Bill 117
Steve Garvey: Storybook Star 166
Stevens, Bob 133
Stevens, David 115
Stewart, Patrick J. 124
Stieb, Dave 170
Stockton, J. Roy 131, 132
Stokes, Geoffrey 156
Stolen Season 96, 166
Stone, Eddie 159
Stories of the Base Ball Field 13, 166
Stormin' Norm Cash 166
The Story of Baseball (Ritter) 166
The Story of Baseball (Rosenberg) 166
The Story of Baseball in Words and Pictures 166
The Story of Bobby Shantz 166
The Story of Jim Bunning 166
The Story of Minor League Baseball 166
The Story of Ty Cobb 166
The Story of the World Series 166
The Story of Yogi Berra 166
Stout, Glenn 37, 127, 159, 168, 177
Strange but True Baseball Stories 166
Stranger to the Game 166
Strawberries in the Wintertime 54
Streak: Joe DiMaggio and the Summer of '41 167

Street & Smith Baseball 181
Strege, John 153
Strike Three (Bee) 56
Strike Three, You're Dead 33, 167
Strike Two 34, 167
Strikeout 167
Strikeout: A Celebration of the Art of Pitching 167
Strikeout Story 19, 167
Strong Cigars and Lovely Women 54
Stump, Al 123, 150
Sudyk, Bob 147
Suehsdorf, A. D. 134
Suehsdorf, Adie 51
Sugar, Burt Randolph 39, 158
The Suitors of Spring 167
Sullivan, George 118, 156, 170, 177
Sullivan, James 113
Sullivan, Neil 127, 148
Sullivan, T. R. 152
Sullivan, Ted 14, 137
The Summer Game 26, 51, 55, 56, 167
The Summer of '49 34, 167
The Sun Field 19, 167
Sunday, Billy 14
The Sunlit Field 19
Super Joe: The Life and Legend of Joe Charboneau 167
Superstars of Baseball 167
Superstars, Stars, and Just Plain Heroes 167
Surface, Bill 150, 176
Sut McCaslin: A Baseball Romance 41
Sweet Lou 167
Sweet Seasons: Recollections of the 1955–64 New York Yankees 167
Sweet, Ozzie 37, 119

T. J.: My 26 Years in Baseball 167
Take Me Out to the Ballpark 29, 57, 167
Take Time for Paradise 167
Take Two and Hit to Right 167
Taking on the Yankees: Winning and Losing in the Business of Baseball 167
A Tale of Two Cities: The 2004 Yankees-Red Sox Rivalry ... 168
Tales of the Diamonds: Gems of Baseball Fiction 168

The Tall Mexican: The Life of Hank Aguirre 168
Talley, Rick 34, 125, 155, 165
Taylor Spink: The Legend and the Man 168
The Team that Wouldn't Die 168
The Teammates 168
Teammates: A Portrait in Friendship 42
Ted "Double Duty" Radcliffe 168
The Ted Simmons Story 168
Ted Sullivan's Humorous Stories of the Ball Field 14
Ted Williams 168
Ted Williams: A Baseball Life 168
Ted Williams: The Biography of an American Hero 43, 168, 202
Ted Williams: The Eternal Kid 168
Ted Williams: The Golden Year: 1957 168
Ted Williams: Hitting Unlimited 168
Ted Williams: My Life in Pictures 37
Ted Williams: A Portrait in Words and Pictures 37, 168
Ted Williams: The Seasons of the Kid 37, 168
The Ted Williams Story 168
Ted Williams: A Tribute 37, 168
Ted, Father 143
Teenagers, Graybeards and 4-Fs 168
The Temple of Baseball 169
Temporary Insanity: The Uncensored Adventures of Baseball's Craziest Player 34, 169
The Ten Best Years of Baseball 169
Terzian, James 143
The Texas League 169
Thanks for Listening 169
That Old Ball Game: Rare Photographs from Baseball's Glorious Past 36, 169
Thayer, Ernest Lawrence 121, 191
Theodore, John 115
They Also Served: Baseball and the Home Front 1941–1945 169
They Call Me Sarge 169
They Played the Game 169
The Thinking Man's Guide to Baseball 169
Third Base Is My Home 169
The Third Fireside Book of Baseball 20, 169

Thirty-One and Six 169
This Great Game 36, 169, 188
This One and That One: The True Life Story of BoBo "No-hit" Holloman 169
This Time Let's Not Eat the Bones 31, 169
Thomas, Henry W. 173, 187, 202
Thompson, Fresco 129
Thompson, S.C. 19, 105, 153
Thomson, Bob 133
Thorn, John 5, 21, 30, 36, 38, 40, 53, 54, 61, 106, 115, 132, 136, 156, 160, 171, 174, 198
Thornley, Stew 153
Thornton, Andre 171
Those Damn Yankees 169
Three Men on Third 169
3 Nights in August 170
Three and Two! 169
The Thrill of the Grass 33, 170
The Thrilling Story of Joe DiMaggio 170
Throwing Heat 170
Thurman Munson 170
Thurman Munson: Pressure Player 170
Tiant, Luis 128
A Ticket for a Seamstitch 20
The Ticket Out: Darryl Strawberry and the Boys of Crenshaw 170
Tiemann, Robert L. 120, 127, 198
A Tiger in His Time: Hal Newhouser and the Burden of Wartime Ball 170
Tiger Tales and Trivia 170
The Tiger Wore Spikes: An Informal Biography of Ty Cobb 170
Times at Bat 170
To Everything a Season: Shibe Park and Urban Philadelphia, 1909–1977 23, 170, 201
Tobin, Jack 177
Today's Game 170
Tofel, Richard J. 144
Tolleris, Ralph 21, 116
Tom Seaver of the Mets 170
Tom Seaver: Portrait of a Pitcher 170
The Tommy Davis Story 170
The Tommy John Story 170
Tomorrow I'll Be Perfect 170
Tony C: The Triumph and Tragedy of Tony Conigliaro 170
Tony Conigliaro 170

Index

Tony O! 170
"The Top 100 Sports Books of All Time" 56
Toporcer, George "Specs" 109
Topps Baseball Cards 37, 171
Torres, Angel 111
Torreson, Rodney 160
Torrez, Danielle Gagnon 136
Torry, Jack 129
Total Baseball 38–39, 53, 171
Touching All the Bases 33
Touching Base: Professional Baseball and American Culture in the Progressive Era 171
Touching Second 16, 171
The Tour to End All Tours 171
Townsend, Doris 169, 188
Trachtenberg, Leo 175
Tracy, David 158
Trade Him 171
Travers, Steven 109
Travis, Cecil 32
Treasures of the Baseball Hall of Fame 36, 171
Treat, Roger 19, 173
Trimble, Joe 155, 178
Trimble, Vance 136
Triumph Born of Tragedy 171
The Tropic of Baseball: Baseball in the Dominican Republic 171
Trouppe, Quincy 42, 171
Trujilo, Nick 147
The Truth Hurts 171
Tullius, John 139
Tuned to Baseball 171
Tunis, John R. 56
Tuohey, George V. 11, 137
Turkey Stearnes and the Detroit Stars 171
Turkin, Hy 19, 153
Turner, Dan 129
Twelve Perfect Innings 171
20 Years Too Soon 42, 171
Twin Killing: The Bill Mazeroski Story 171
Two Spectacular Seasons 171
Ty Cobb (Alexander) 23, 171
Ty Cobb (McCallum) 171
Ty Cobb: The Greatest 171
Ty Cobb: The Idol of Baseball Fandom 16, 171
Tygiel, Jules 23, 29, 51, 114, 203

Uecker, Bob 121
The Ultimate Baseball Book 27, 36–37, 172
"The Ultimate Baseball Library" 53
Umphlett, Wiley Lee 65
The Umpire Story 172
The Umpire Strikes Back 34, 172
Umpiring from the Inside 172
Under Coogan's Bluff 172
Underwood, John 21, 150, 162, 173
The Unforgettable Season 56, 172
The Universal Baseball Association, Inc., J. Henry Waugh, Prop. 24, 56, 172
Up from the Minor Leagues 172
The Used Book Lover's Guide to the Midwest 77

Valenti, Dan 123, 139, 167
Van Loan, Charles E. 54
Vass, George 144
Vecsey, George 115, 130, 142
Veeck as in Wreck 21, 28, 51, 56, 172
Veeck, Bill 21, 138, 172
The Veracruz Blues 33, 172
Verdi, Bob 137, 153
Verkler, Linda A. 95
Vida: His Own Story 172
Vida Blue: Coming Up Again 172
View from the Dugout 172
Villani, Jim 21
Vincent, David 39, 40
The Vintage & Classic Baseball Collector 56–57
Violanti, Anthony 148
Viva Baseball: Latin Major Leaguers and Their Special Hunger 172
Vlasich, James 144
Vogt, D. C. 112
Voices from the Great Black Baseball Leagues 172
Voices from the Negro Leagues 172
Voices of the Game 172
Voigt, David Q. 22, 51, 61, 106
Vols Feats 1901–1950 172

Waddell, Rube 32
Wagenheim, Kal 26, 107, 123
Wagner, Honus 112, 188
Wait 'Til Next Year: The Yankees, Dodgers, and Giants, 1947–1957 172

Wait Till I Make the Show 172
Waiting for Godot's First Pitch 33
Waiting Game: Photographs of the Oakland A's 172
Walder, Barbara 106
Walker, Eric 164
Walker, Robert 123
Wall Street Journal 64
Wallop, Douglas 8, 19–20, 110, 177
Walsh, Christy 17, 105, 114, 187–88
Walter Johnson: Baseball's Big Train 173, 202
Walter Johnson: King of the Pitchers 19, 173
Walton, Ed 161
Waner, Lloyd 32
Waner, Paul 32
Ward, Arch 151
Ward, Geoffrey C. 37, 109
Ward, John Montgomery 12, 65, 109
Warfield, Don 160
The Warren Spahn Story 173
Warren, Elizabeth V. 155
The Warsaw Sparks 173
Warsaw to Wrigley 173
Washington Senators 18, 196
Washington Senators (Bealle) 173
The Washington Senators (Povich) 173
The Washington Senators 1901–1971 173
Waterloo Diamonds 173
"The Way I See It: Short Reactions to Important Baseball Book Topics" 56
The Way It Is 21, 173
We Could Have Finished Last without You 173
We Played the Game 173
We Saw Stars 173
We Won Today: My Season with the Mets 173
Weaver, Earl 65, 140, 175
Weaver on Strategy 65
Weekly Standard 43
Weil, Danielle 110
Weiss, John 37, 129
Welch, Bob 130
Weldon, Martin 18, 107
A Well-Paid Slave: Curt Flood's Fight for Free Agency in Professional Sports 204
Werber, Bill 123
West Coast Review of Books 37

Westcott, Rich 40, 126
What a Baseball Manager Does 173
What Do You Have to Lose? 184
What's a Nice Harvard Boy Like You Doing in the Bushes? 173
What's the Matter with the Red Sox? 173
Wheeler, Lonnie 32, 70–71, 100, 117, 123, 138, 166
When the Game Was Black and White: The Illustrated History of Baseball's Negro Leagues 174
When in Doubt, Fire the Manager 173
When Johnny Came Sliding Home: The Post-Civil War Baseball Boom 173
Where Have You Gone Joe DiMaggio? 174
Where Have You Gone, Vince DiMaggio? 191
Where They Ain't 174
Whitaker, Tim 124, 182
White Rat 174
The White Sox: A Pictorial History 174
White, Sol 164
Whitehead, Charles E. 146
The Whitey Ford Story 174
Whitey and Mickey 174
Whitfield, Shelby 143
Whitford, David 129
Whitford, Mike 138
Whiting, Robert 25, 122, 164, 178
Whitt, Ernie 121
Whittingham, Richard 127, 145, 171, 174, 199
The Whiz Kids 174
The Whiz Kids and the 1950 Pennant 174
Who Was Roberto? A Biography of Roberto Clemente 174
Who's on Third: The Chicago White Sox Story 29, 57, 174
Who's Who in Major League Baseball 16–17, 174
Who's Who in Professional Baseball 174
The Whole Baseball Catalog 40, 54, 174
A Whole Different Ballgame 174
Why Time Begins on Opening Day 32, 65, 174
Wick, Paul 116
Wickham, Mike 79, 81, 184
A Wife's Guide to Baseball 174

Index

Wiggins, Wilton 85
Wild and Outside 175
Wild, High and Tight: The Life and Death of Billy Martin 175
Wilks, Ed 118
Will, George 28, 34, 147
Williams, Billy 117
Williams, Pat 146
Williams, Pete 120, 142
Williams, Ted 21, 37, 42, 43, 150, 162, 189
The Willie Horton Story 175
Willie Mays 175
The Willie Mays Album 175
Willie Mays: Coast-to-Coast Giant 27, 175
Willie Mays: Modest Champion 175
Willie Mays: My Life In and Out of Baseball 27, 175
The Willie Mays Story (Shapiro) 175
The Willie Mays Story (Smith) 175
Willie Stargell (Libby) 175
Willie Stargell (Stargell & Bird) 175
Willie's Throw 175
Willie's Time: A Memoir 27, 175
Wills, Maury 138, 140, 153
Wilson, Hack 32
Winegardner, Mark 33, 34, 158, 172
Winehouse, Irwin 128
Winfield 175
Winfield, Dave 175
Winning! 175
The Wit and Wisdom of Yogi Berra 175
Wizard 175
Wojciechowski, Gene 178
Wolf, Bob 116
Wolff, Miles 40
Wolff, Rick 173
Women at Play: The Story of Women in Baseball 36, 175
Won in the Ninth 175
The Wonder Team: The True Story of the Incomparable 1927 New York Yankees 175
Wong, Stephen 164
Wood, Bob 127
Wood, Joe 24
Woodley, Richard 161
Working at the Stadium 176
Working the Plate 176

Works of John Greenleaf Whittier 186–87
The World Champion Pittsburgh Pirates 176
The World Series 176
World Series Classics 176
The World Series: Complete Play-by-Play of Every Game, 1903-1975 ... 176
The World Series and Highlights of Baseball 176
The World Series: A History of Baseball's Fall Classic 176
The World Series: An Illustrated History 176
The World Series, 75th Anniversary Edition 176
The World Series: The Story of Baseball's Annual Championship 176
World Series Thrills 176
World Tour, National and American League Baseball Teams 14
The Worst Team Money Could Buy: The Collapse of the New York Mets 176
Wright, Branson 161
Wright, Craig R. 30, 126
Wright, George 133, 159, 207
Wright, Harry 11, 32
Wright, Jim 148
Wrigleyville: A Magical History Tour of the Chicago Cubs 28, 176
The Wrong Season 176
The Wrong Stuff 176
Wulf, Steve 111

Yankee Batboy 176
Yankee Doodles 177
Yankee Stadium 177
Yankee Stadium: Fifty Years of Drama 177
The Yankee Story 177
Yankee Stranger 177
The Yankees 177
Yankees Century: 100 Years of New York Yankees Baseball 177
The Yankees Encyclopedia 40
The Yankees: The Four Fabulous Eras of Baseball's Most Famous Team 177
Yankees: An Illustrated History 177
Yankees Magazine 63
Yastrzemski, Carl 177

Index

Yaz 177
Yaz: Baseball, the Wall and Me 177
Yaz 2: The Ultimate Collector of Carl Yastrzemski Memorabilia 177
A Year at a Time 177
A Year in the Minors 177
The Year the Mets Lost Last Place 177
Year of the Tiger 177
The Year They Called Off the World Series 178
The Year the Yankees Lost the Pennant 19–20, 177
Yesterday's Heroes 178
Yeutter, Frank 141
Yogi 178
Yogi Berra 178
Yogi Berra: The Muscle Man 178
The Yogi Berra Story 178
Yogi: It Ain't Over 178
You Can't Beat the Hours 178
You Can't Hit the Ball with the Bat on Your Shoulder 178
You Can't Steal First Base 178
You Could Look It Up 178
You Gotta Have Heart: Dallas Green's Rebuilding of the Cubs 178
You Gotta Have Wa 178
You Know Me, Al 14, 178
You're Missing a Great Game 178
You've Got to Have Balls to Make It in This League 178
Young, A.S. "Doc" 134, 147
Young, Dick 161
Your Lookouts Since 1885 178
Zang, David 58, 130, 202
Zanger, Jack 120, 143, 163
Zeigler, Tom 178
Zempel, Edward N. 95
The Zen of Base and Ball 178
Zimbalist, Andrew 35, 110
Zimmerman, Paul 145, 177
Zimmerman, Tom 125, 176
Zingg, Paul J. 135
Zinsser, William 165
Zoss, Joel 126

www.ingramcontent.com/pod-product-compliance
Ingram Content Group UK Ltd.
Pitfield, Milton Keynes, MK11 3LW, UK
UKHW041936140426
5217IPUK00014B/516